# STEP BY STEP

# STEP BY STEP

A year book of devotions for the
whole family

## John Eddison

Authentic

15  14  13  12  11  10  09    7  6  5  4  3  2  1

First published 2009 by Authentic Media Limited
52 Presley Way, Crownhill, Milton Keynes, MK8 0ES
www.authenticmedia.co.uk

**British Library Cataloguing in Publication Data**

A catalogue record for this book is available from the British Library

ISBN 978-1-85078-819-5

Cover Design by Rachel Myatt
Printed and bound in Great Britain

# Preface

For many years I have felt the need, particularly for young people, of some sort of introduction to the practice of daily Bible reading. The ideal method, of course, is to move steadily through a book of the Bible following one of the courses suggested, for example, by Scripture Union. But as an introduction this has two snags. First, there are so many versions of the Bible today that it makes it very difficult to write helpful notes. Second, the reader who misses a day or two loses the sequence and may grow discouraged and abandon the habit altogether.

It seemed to me, therefore, that there would be great value in providing a simple, systematic method of reading for one year, after which I hope the daily practice will have become an established habit and the reader will continue with an ongoing Bible reading plan. The daily readings contained in this volume vary. More often than not they are thematic – that is, they draw various verses from different parts of the Bible together to throw light on one particular subject. Sometimes there are thumbnail character sketches, and about twice a week there is a straightforward Bible passage with no cross-references. The English Standard Version has been used throughout.

The primary purpose of this book is, therefore, to cultivate and encourage the habit of daily Bible reading, but I hope that it will serve other purposes as well. The book may prove useful, for example, in school prayers or assemblies, or perhaps for group discussions and study, and for family prayers. I hope it is not too presumptuous to think that hard-pressed preachers may find ideas in this book which will act as seed-thoughts for sermons or talks.

It has long been my belief that the best commentary on Scripture is Scripture itself, and often by 'comparing spiritual things with spiritual' we arrive at a deeper level of understanding. I would therefore advise readers to try to work out the meaning of the text for themselves and to discover the connection between the different passages and verses before reading the comment. The next step is then to return to the text and study it again, perhaps with a clearer understanding than before, thus allowing Scripture itself to have the last word.

## From everlasting to everlasting you are God.
## (Psalm 90:2)

"I am the Alpha and the Omega," says the Lord God, "who is and who was and who is to come, the Almighty" (Revelation 1:8). Jesus said . . . "Truly, truly, I say to you, before Abraham was, I am" (John 8:58). Jesus Christ is the same yesterday and today and forever (Hebrews 13:8). "Just as I was with Moses, so I will be with you. I will not leave you or forsake you" (Joshua 1:5). "For the mountains may depart and the hills be removed, but my steadfast love shall not depart from you" (Isaiah 54:10). This is God, our God for ever and ever. He will guide us forever (Psalm 48:14). The Lord will keep your going out and your coming in from this time forth and for evermore (Psalm 121:8).

*What changes do you think this coming year will bring? At the end of it you may find yourself in a new job, or living in a new home, or at a new school or college. What pleasures and disappointments, what success and failure, await you? It is perhaps better not to know? Sometimes we say that ignorance is bliss. But we know that God will go with us as our guardian and guide. We often think of mountains or hills when we try to describe something steady and constant. They never seem to change. But even if the whole world around us changes, God never does. He is changeless, and when He wanted to teach His people this fact He called Himself the great 'I AM' – the ever-present one. So as you begin a new year remember that He is with you. God forgives past failures and asks us to trust Him when we have fears about the future.*

Go before me, O Lord, into this unknown year. When I am weak, strengthen me, when I am confused, guide me, and when I am tempted to stray, lead me into the paths of righteousness for Your name's sake. Amen.

### "Be strong and very courageous," (Joshua 1:7)

So the Lord said to Moses, "Take Joshua the son of Nun, a man in whom is the Spirit, and lay your hand on him . . . that all the congregation of the people of Israel may obey" (Numbers 27:18, 20). After the death of Moses . . . the Lord said to Joshua . . . "Do not be frightened, and do not be dismayed, for the Lord your God is with you wherever you go" (Joshua 1:1, 9). When Joshua was by Jericho, he lifted up his eyes and looked, and behold, a man was standing before him with his drawn sword in his hand. And Joshua went to him and said to him, "Are you for us, or for our adversaries?" And he said, "No; but I am the commander of the army of the Lord. Now I have come." And Joshua fell on his face to the earth and worshiped and said to him, "What does my lord say to his servant?" (Joshua 5:13–14)

*Moses was a great leader, and it must have been hard for Joshua to take over from him. Joshua probably felt scared and inadequate for the task ahead. Maybe you'll have an experience like that this year, suddenly finding yourself with new responsibilities and wondering whether you can cope. Joshua had to learn two lessons. First,* confidence in God. *He learned that it was not his strength that counted, but God's, and this made him bold and courageous. Secondly,* obedience to God. *At Jericho he learned that the important question was not whether God was on his side, but whether he was on God's side. Was he willing to do everything God asked? Every leader, and every Christian, has to learn these two vital lessons – confidence in God and obedience to Him.*

**Lord, if You call me this year to take on some important task for which I don't feel prepared, as You called Joshua, help me, like him, to put myself into Your hands. Please give me courage and keep me humble. Amen.**

## I am the good shepherd. (John 10:14)

The Lord is my shepherd; I shall not want. He makes me lie down in green pastures. He leads me beside still waters. He restores my soul. He leads me in paths of righteousness for his name's sake. Even though I walk through the valley of the shadow of death, I will fear no evil, for you are with me; your rod and your staff, they comfort me. You prepare a table before me in the presence of my enemies; you anoint my head with oil; my cup overflows. Surely goodness and mercy shall follow me all the days of my life, and I shall dwell in the house of the Lord forever (Psalm 23).

*Some people think that this psalm describes a day in the life of a sheep. Notice some of the different experiences, and see how they apply to our daily lives. First, there are* pastures. *These suggest the easy, pleasant times in life when everything seems to be running smoothly and work, sport, leisure activities and friends are all bringing happiness and satisfaction. We need to thank God for such times. Then there are* paths. *These refer to the choices we have to make – sometimes trivial, sometimes important. It's not always easy to find and then to follow the right path, and we need to ask the Shepherd to lead us. Finally, there are the* valleys – *those times in life when things go wrong and we face disappointment, failure and sometimes bereavement. It is in the valleys especially that we need to remember God's presence with us and His power to encourage.*

**Help me, O Lord, always to thank You when things are going well, and to trust You in times of difficulty or doubt. Amen.**

**Let the word of Christ dwell in you richly.
(Colossians 3:16)**

"This Book of the Law shall not depart from your mouth, but you shall meditate on it day and night, so that you may be careful to do according to all that is written in it. For then you will make your way prosperous, and then you will have good success" (Joshua 1:8). Your words were found, and I ate them, and your words became to me a joy and the delight of my heart (Jeremiah 15:16). More to be desired are they than gold, even much fine gold; sweeter also than honey and drippings of the honeycomb (Psalm 19:10). Man does not live by bread alone, but man lives by every word that comes from the mouth of the Lord (Deuteronomy 8:3). Like newborn infants, long for the pure spiritual milk, that by it you may grow up to salvation (1 Peter 2:2).

*Now and then we hear of someone going on a hunger strike, depriving him or herself of food in order to force the authorities to pay attention to some protest. The person gets weaker and weaker and finally dies. Likewise, there are people who never grow to be strong Christians, who never overcome their temptations and who never have much influence for good because they don't take time to nourish themselves spiritually. They don't read the Bible, much less think over what they find there, meditate upon it or 'chew it over' in their minds. That is one reason why I've written this book – to help readers in a simple way to feed on Christ in their hearts by faith. All good food, like milk and honey, bread and meat, does two things – it strengthens and it satisfies. If you start to read the Bible and let it speak to you each day, God will use this nourishment to strengthen and equip you.*

**Help me, O Lord, to read, learn and digest the teachings of Your word, and use this time to strengthen my Christian faith. Amen.**

## The Lord knows the thoughts of man. (Psalm 94:11)

Finally, brothers, whatever is true, whatever is honourable, whatever is just, whatever is pure, whatever is lovely, whatever is commendable, if there is any excellence, if there is anything worthy of praise, think about these things (Philippians 4:8). Search me, O God, and know my heart! Try me and know my thoughts! And see if there be any grievous way in me, and lead me in the way everlasting (Psalm 139:23–24). Let the wicked forsake his way, and the unrighteous man his thoughts (Isaiah 55:7). Let the words of my mouth and the meditation of my heart be acceptable in your sight, O Lord, my rock and my redeemer (Psalm 19:14).

*Someone has said, 'You are not what you think you are; but what you think, you are.' Thoughts are the seeds from which words, and then actions, grow – and Christians have to learn how to train and control their thinking. Have you noticed that the ordinary housefly often alights upon dirty and unpleasant things? But the bee and the butterfly are different. You will find them on flowers and other plants in the garden which are lovely and pure. We need to think about where we go and what we think about. We may not be able to concentrate on any one thing for very long, but we can make sure that we feed our minds with what is good and refuse the evil things. Think, for example, about the magazines and books you read, or the films or television programmes you watch. Are you more like the housefly or the butterfly?*

**Thank You, Lord, that You created a world full of things that are lovely and pure and true. Help me to choose to think about these things, and not to allow my mind to feed upon what is unworthy and unclean. Amen.**

## The glory of the Lord shall be revealed.
## (Isaiah 40:5)

Now after Jesus was born in Bethlehem . . . wise men from the east came . . . saying, "Where is he who has been born king of the Jews? For we saw his star when it rose and have come to worship him." . . . And behold, the star . . . went before them until it came to rest over the place where the child was . . . And going into the house they saw the child with Mary his mother, and they fell down and worshiped him. Then, opening their treasures, they offered him gifts, gold and frankincense and myrrh (Matthew 2:1–11). The people who walked in darkness have seen a great light (Isaiah 9:2). And nations shall come to your light, and kings to the brightness of your rising (Isaiah 60:3). "A light for revelation to the Gentiles, and for glory to your people Israel" (Luke 2:32).

*During World War I it was the custom in some American towns to put silver stars in the windows of the homes of men who had gone to fight for their country. The star of Bethlehem, the first 'traffic sign' in history, told those who saw it that God's Son had left His home of light and glory to come to rescue humankind. 'The Father has sent his Son,' it said, 'to be the Saviour of the world' (1 John 4:14). But notice that He came to the world, and not just to Israel – that is the point of this revelation to the wise men from the east. Jesus came to be so much more than the national Messiah the Jews were expecting. He came to be the Saviour of the world and King of kings. The gifts these men offered may have had special meanings: gold was a symbol of the king's sovereignty; frankincense for a God of worship; and myrrh the sacrifice of the Saviour.*

Lord, I thank You that Your love embraces everyone in the world – regardless of who we are or what stage we are at – and that You love me, too. Amen.

## Remember also your Creator in the days of your youth. (Ecclesiastes 12:1)

In the beginning, God created the heavens and the earth (Genesis 1:1). And God saw everything that he had made, and behold, it was very good (Genesis 1:31). By the word of the Lord the heavens were made, and by the breath of his mouth all their host (Psalm 33:6). It is he who made the earth by his power, who established the world by his wisdom (Jeremiah 51:15). The Lord by wisdom founded the earth; by understanding he established the heavens (Proverbs 3:19). The heavens declare the glory of God, and the sky above proclaims his handiwork (Psalm 19:1). For his invisible attributes, namely, his eternal power and divine nature, have been clearly perceived, ever since the creation of the world, in the things that have been made (Romans 1:20). "Worthy are you, our Lord and God, to receive glory and honour and power, for you created all things, and by your will they existed and were created" (Revelation 4:11).

*Just as a watch bears every mark of intelligent design, so the only sensible explanation for this universe in which we live is that a living, personal Creator brought it into existence. The only alternative is to say that it all happened by chance, but that makes about as much sense as believing that an explosion in a printer's shop produced the complete works of William Shakespeare. Just how God made the world, or how long it took, we cannot say. But as we look at its beauty and order two things strike us – His eternal power and His wisdom. Perhaps we see His power best through a telescope, when we explore the infinite majesty of the heavens. The microscope, on the other hand, shows us the wisdom with which God designed even the tiniest particles of matter.*

**Lord, thank You for this marvellous world in which I live. I pray that I'll never stop wondering at its beauty and worshiping You, its Maker. Amen.**

## The glorious gospel of the blessed God.
## (1 Timothy 1:11)

And in the same region there were shepherds out in the field, keeping watch over their flock by night. And an angel of the Lord appeared to them, and the glory of the Lord shone around them, and they were filled with fear. And the angel said to them, "Fear not, for behold, I bring you good news of a great joy . . . For unto you is born this day in the city of David a Saviour, who is Christ the Lord" (Luke 2:8–11). I am not ashamed of the gospel, for it is the power of God for salvation to everyone who believes (Romans 1:16). In him you also, when you heard the word of truth, the gospel of your salvation, and believed in him, were sealed with the promised Holy Spirit (Ephesians 1:13). The gospel of the grace of God (Acts 20:24). "How beautiful are the feet of those who preach the good news!" (Romans 10:15).

*The word 'gospel' means 'good news', or 'good story'. ('Godspel' – the word 'spiel' meaning 'tale', or 'yarn', is still sometimes used.) The Christian gospel is the wonderful news that Jesus Christ came into the world as the Saviour of humankind. God did not just send us good advice (though there is plenty of that in the Bible), but good news. God gives us instruction from the shore about how to cope with the shipwreck, but more importantly God tells us that a lifeboat is ready and waiting. Notice two words which the Bible connects with the gospel – grace and peace. Grace tells us that the gospel comes from the undeserved love of God. Peace tells us how it flows into our hearts, ending the hostility between human beings and God. Grace is the source from which this life-giving river springs; peace is the blessing it brings into our hearts.*

**Lord, I want Your grace and peace to make such a difference in my life that I in turn will want to spread the good news of Jesus Christ to others. Amen.**

## The joy of the Lord is your strength.
### (Nehemiah 8:10)

Blessed is the one whose transgression is forgiven, whose sin is covered (Psalm 32:1). In your presence there is fullness of joy; at your right hand are pleasures for evermore (Psalm 16:11). I rejoice at your word like one who finds great spoil (Psalm 119:162). "Ask, and you will receive, that your joy may be full" (John 16:24). Though the fig tree should not blossom, nor fruit be on the vines, the produce of the olive fail and the fields yield no food, the flock be cut off from the fold and there be no herd in the stalls, yet I will rejoice in the Lord; I will take joy in the God of my salvation (Habakkuk 3:17, 18). Rejoice in the Lord always; again I will say, Rejoice. (Philippians 4:4).

*What's your recipe for happiness? Many of the ingredients are probably things God created for our pleasure in this world – our families, homes, friends, books, games and so on. This is fine, but the test comes when, like the farmer in today's reading, we face a period of 'drought'. When we are deprived of health, money, friends or even liberty – what then? Christians should still be happy and content, because we have a secret reservoir of joy in our lives that others do not. We are to rejoice regardless of our circumstances because God has forgiven our sins and is always with us, answering our prayers and speaking with us from the Bible. Joy is the flag which flies from the heart of the Christian when the King is in residence.*

Lord, I thank You for all of the good things You've given me to enjoy, but please help me always to remember that You Yourself are the true source of my joy. Amen.

**From childhood you have been acquainted with the sacred writings. (2 Timothy 3:15)**

And when Jesus was twelve years old, they went up according to custom. And . . . as they were returning, the boy Jesus stayed behind . . . His parents did not know it . . . After three days they found him in the temple, sitting among the teachers, listening to them and asking them questions. And all who heard him were amazed at his understanding and his answers . . . And his mother said to him, "Son, why have you treated us so? Behold, your father and I have been searching for you in great distress." And he said to them, "Why were you looking for me? Did you not know that I must be in my Father's house?" . . . And he went down with them . . . to Nazareth and was submissive to them . . . And Jesus increased in wisdom and in stature and in favour with God and man (Luke 2:42–52).

*Have you ever been so interested and absorbed in something you were doing, or a book you were reading, that you lost track of time and maybe missed a meal, a train or an appointment? Jesus experienced that, too – but He wasn't absorbed in a game or a television programme. He was completely engrossed in learning about His heavenly Father and doing His will. We know how thoughtful and helpful Jesus was at home, but this story teaches us that no one is too young to learn about and grow closer to God. God wants us from an early age to become partners in his 'business' of trying to make the world a better, happier and more Christian place.*

**Lord, please help me to be more thoughtful and considerate but also to focus on my chief purpose in life – to please You, to do Your will, and to share in Your work. Amen.**

## It is not good that the man should be alone. (Genesis 2:18)

Two are better than one . . . For if they fall, one will lift up his fellow. But woe to him who is alone when he falls and has not another to lift him up! (Ecclesiastes 4:9, 10) A friend loves at all times, and a brother is born for adversity (Proverbs 17:17). Faithful are the wounds of a friend (Proverbs 27:6). There is a friend who sticks closer than a brother (Proverbs 18:24). "Do not urge me to leave you or to return from following you. For where you go I will go, and where you lodge I will lodge. Your people shall be my people, and your God my God. Where you die I will die, and there will I be buried" (Ruth 1:16, 17). Then Jonathan made a covenant with David, because he loved him as his own soul (1 Samuel 18:3). "Greater love has no one than this, that someone lay down his life for his friends" (John 15:13).

*Friendship is one of God's greatest gifts. We all need friends, and however old or independent we grow we cannot really do without them. There is a pathetic little story about Rupert Brooke. Feeling friendless and alone as he boarded a ship for America, he paid a small boy money to wave a handkerchief to him until the ship was out of sight. Friends can be a tremendous source of encouragement to each other – just as Ruth was to Naomi, David to Jonathan, and Paul to Barnabas. We need to be careful that we choose friends who will be honest, supportive and encouraging. We also need to be careful that we don't lose good friends by being selfish, disloyal or neglectful of their interests.*

Thank You, Lord, for my friends. Help me to be a good friend, just as I find encouragement and counsel from them. Amen.

## Repent, for the kingdom of heaven is at hand. (Matthew 4:17)

If my people who are called by my name humble themselves, and pray and seek my face and turn from their wicked ways, then I will hear from heaven and will forgive their sin and heal their land (2 Chronicles 7:14). Turn away from evil and do good; seek peace and pursue it (Psalm 34:14). "Let the wicked forsake his way, and the unrighteous man his thoughts; let him return to the Lord, that he may have compassion on him, and to our God, for he will abundantly pardon" (Isaiah 55:7). Whoever conceals his transgressions will not prosper, but he who confesses and forsakes them will obtain mercy (Proverbs 28:13). God . . . commands all people everywhere to repent (Acts 17:30).

*Repentance does not just mean saying we are sorry. Rather, it means 'coming to our senses' (like the prodigal son in Luke 15:17). The result is a change of heart and mind about sin. Repentance is a condition of forgiveness, because God cannot forgive the sins that we will not forsake. A defeated French admiral was once led on to Nelson's quarterdeck. He went forward with his hand outstretched, waiting to make friends with his conqueror. But Nelson turned his back on him and said, 'Sir, I want your sword first.' There could be no friendship until that symbol of enmity had been surrendered. Friendship with God can only begin when we turn away from everything that we know to be sinful and wrong and dedicate ourselves, with His help, to living our lives according to His perfect will.*

Lord, please help me to practice true repentance. Help me not just to say that I'm sorry, ask forgiveness, and then do the same things all over again. With Your strength I want to declare war on everything that is hurtful or displeasing to You. Amen.

## "I have come to do your will, O God." (Hebrews 10:7)

"I seek not my own will but the will of him who sent me" (John 5:30). Meanwhile the disciples were urging him, saying, "Rabbi, eat." But he said to them, "I have food to eat that you do not know about." So the disciples said to one another, "Has anyone brought him something to eat?" Jesus said to them, "My food is to do the will of him who sent me and to accomplish his work" (John 4:31–34). "For I have come down from heaven, not to do my own will but the will of him who sent me" (John 6:38). Then Jesus said to them, "My soul is very sorrowful, even to death" . . . And going a little farther he fell on his face and prayed, saying, "My Father, if it be possible, let this cup pass from me; nevertheless, not as I will, but as you will" (Matthew 26:38, 39). "I desire to do your will, O my God; your law is within my heart" (Psalm 40:8).

*Sometimes we ask what makes a person tick. In other words, what is the force that drives his or her life? What made Jesus tick? Doing the will of God was the one business that occupied Him, the food that sustained Him, the ambition that inspired Him and the pleasure that refreshed Him. Doing the will of God ran like a thread right through His life – from childhood until His death – holding together everything He did. The will of God was the gauge by which He tested every suggestion put to Him and every decision He had to make. And this resolve to do God's will, regardless of where it leads or how much it costs, is the Christian's secret of a happy life. As Dante put it, 'In His will is our peace.'*

'Your way, not mine, O Lord, however dark it be; lead me by Your own hand, choose out my path for me.' Amen.

### What is man . . . ? (Psalm 8:4)

Then God said, "Let us make man in our image, after our likeness. And let them have dominion over . . . all the earth" . . . So God created man in his own image, in the image of God he created him; male and female he created them (Genesis 1:26, 27). What is man that you are mindful of him, and the son of man that you care for him? Yet you have made him a little lower than the heavenly beings and crowned him with glory and honour. You have given him dominion over the works of your hands; you have put all things under his feet (Psalm 8:4–6). "Bring my sons from afar and my daughters from the end of the earth, everyone who is called by my name, whom I created for my glory, whom I formed and made . . . The people whom I formed for myself that they might declare my praise" (Isaiah 43:6, 7, 21).

*The Bible doesn't tell us exactly how God made us, but it does say three very important things about our creation. First, we were* made by God. *Human beings are not the result of blind chance, but the creations of an infinitely wise and loving Creator. Secondly, we were* made like God. *This doesn't mean that we bear any outward or physical resemblance to God, and in that respect we are perhaps more 'like the beasts that perish' (Psalm 49:12). But God did make us with hearts and minds with which we can know God, a conscience to tell good from evil, and a will to choose the right and refuse the wrong. Thirdly, we have been* made for God. *Just as a painting brings credit and renown to its artist, so God created human beings to display and proclaim the wisdom, power and love of God.*

**Thank You, Lord, that You have made me for Yourself. Help me to commit to You all my powers of body and mind, and to live to Your glory. Amen.**

## As the mountains surround Jerusalem, so the Lord surrounds his people. (Psalm 125:2)

I lift up my eyes to the hills. From where does my help come? My help comes from the Lord, who made heaven and earth. He will not let your foot be moved; he who keeps you will not slumber. Behold, he who keeps Israel will neither slumber nor sleep. The Lord is your keeper; the Lord is your shade on your right hand. The sun shall not strike you by day, nor the moon by night. The Lord will keep you from all evil; he will keep your life. The Lord will keep your going out and your coming in from this time forth and for evermore (Psalm 121).

*Hills and mountains played an incredibly important part in the history of God's people. God gave Moses the Ten Commandments on Mount Sinai; Jesus was transfigured and His glory was revealed on Mount Hermon; Jesus went to the Mount of Olives to rest and pray; and, most important of all, He suffered and died for us all on the green hill outside the city wall. But hills themselves cannot help us, and this psalm should really start with a question, 'Shall I lift up my eyes . . . ?' The answer is 'No, because inspiring though the hills may be, it is the Lord, the maker of the hills, who alone can come to our aid.' And notice how completely He does so. He keeps body and soul; He watches over us day and night; and He guards our coming and going.*

**Hide me, O Lord, under the shadow of Your wings. Help me to remember that You are my strength in every situation. Amen.**

### Sin will have no dominion over you.
### (Romans 6:14)

Count it all joy, my brothers, when you meet trials of various kinds, for you know that the testing of your faith produces steadfastness. And let steadfastness have its full effect, that you may be perfect and complete, lacking in nothing (James 1:2–4). The Lord knows how to rescue the godly from trials (2 Peter 2:9). The Lord is faithful. He will establish you and guard you against the evil one (2 Thessalonians 3:3). You have delivered my soul from death, yes, my feet from falling, that I may walk before God in the light of life (Psalm 56:13). Keep back your servant also from presumptuous sins; let them not have dominion over me! (Psalm 19:13). Blessed is the man who remains steadfast under trial (James 1:12). Thanks be to God, who gives us the victory through our Lord Jesus Christ (1 Corinthians 15:57).

*Doesn't temptation bring the risk of failure and sin? Then why should we welcome it? For the same reason that the keen mountaineer approaches a difficult rock face, or the boxer a strong sparring partner. These challenges provide opportunities to test the power that is in them and to gain experience for even more demanding tasks in the future. So Christians are to welcome trials, temptations and difficulties as they require us to practice drawing from the power of Christ living within us to triumph over every attack and emerge victorious. Then, when the next attack comes, we will be in an even stronger position to meet and resist it.*

**O God, forasmuch as without You we are not able to please You, mercifully grant that Your Holy Spirit may in all things direct and rule our hearts, through Jesus Christ our Lord. Amen.**

**Christ has been raised from the dead, the first-fruits of those who have fallen asleep.**
**(1 Corinthians 15:20)**

Behold! I tell you a mystery. We shall not all sleep, but we shall all be changed, in a moment, in the twinkling of an eye, at the last trumpet. For the trumpet will sound, and the dead will be raised imperishable, and we shall be changed. For this perishable body must put on the imperishable, and this mortal body must put on immortality . . . Then shall come to pass the saying that is written: "Death is swallowed up in victory. O death, where is your victory? O death, where is your sting?" The sting of death is sin, and the power of sin is the law. But thanks be to God, who gives us the victory through our Lord Jesus Christ. Therefore, my beloved brothers, be steadfast, immovable, always abounding in the work of the Lord (1 Corinthians 15:51–58).

*Death is not the end, but a junction. Our journey doesn't finish at death but changes. We exchange our mortal, perishable bodies for ones suited for an altogether different kind of existence. We could compare our present earthly life to that of a caterpillar, which after a while undergoes a great change and emerges from the torpid, death-like state of the chrysalis into the new, free, airborne life of the moth or the butterfly. Jesus was the first person to experience this great metamorphosis, and because He gained victory over death we know that all who trust in Him will share that experience and enjoy everlasting life. This hope, Paul tells us, should be the motive for steadfast, active Christian living.*

**Help us, Lord, to live as those who believe and trust in the resurrection to eternal life. Please strengthen our faith and hope every day, through the love of Your Son, Jesus Christ our Saviour. Amen.**

## I desire then that in every place the men should pray. (1 Timothy 2:8)

"Now I was cupbearer to the king . . . I took up the wine and gave it to the king. Now I had not been sad in his presence. And the king said to me . . . 'What are you requesting?' So I prayed to the God of heaven. And I said to the king . . ." (Nehemiah 1:11–2:5). Daniel . . . went to his house where he had windows in his upper chamber open toward Jerusalem. He got down on his knees three times a day and prayed and gave thanks (Daniel 6:10). Then Jonah prayed to the Lord his God from the belly of the fish (Jonah 2:1). And rising very early in the morning, while it was still dark, Jesus departed and went out to a desolate place, and there he prayed (Mark 1:35). Peter went up on the housetop . . . to pray (Acts 10:9). For from the rising of the sun to its setting my name will be great among the nations, and in every place incense will be offered to my name, and a pure offering. For my name will be great among the nations, says the Lord of hosts (Malachi 1:11).

*Most Christians try to set aside specific times each day for prayer, but these passages remind us that we can also speak to God in prayer at any moment of the day or night, and in any place. God is always available, and the line is always open and He always answers. As C. S. Lewis says, 'God has all eternity to answer the split second prayer of a pilot whose aeroplane is crashing in flames.' And, if we take the world as a whole, it is probably true to say in the words of John Ellerton's classic hymn, 'the voice of prayer is never silent, nor dies the strain of praise away.' Have you a favourite place for prayer?*

**Thank You, Lord, that You are always listening to our prayers, and that You are far more ready to hear than we are to pray. Amen.**

## The Spirit of truth. (John 14:17)

"I will ask the Father, and he will give you another Helper, to be with you forever, even the Spirit of truth" (John 14:16, 17). "It is to your advantage that I go away, for if I do not go away, the Helper will not come to you. But if I go, I will send him to you" (John 16:7). "But when the Helper comes . . . he will bear witness about me" (John 15:26). "He will convict the world concerning sin" (John 16:8). "He will teach you all things and bring to your remembrance all that I have said to you" (John 14:26). "He will glorify me, for he will take what is mine and declare it to you" (John 16:14). When the day of Pentecost arrived, they were all together in one place. And suddenly there came from heaven a sound like a mighty rushing wind, and it filled the entire house where they were sitting . . . And they were all filled with the Holy Spirit (Acts 2:1–4).

*Imagine what it would be like if someone in your town, office, college or school became famous all at once because of some discovery or achievement. Reporters, sightseers and visitors swarm into the area, and life comes to a standstill. Then the BBC comes to the rescue and whisks our hero away by helicopter to the TV studios. You might feel cheated that this great person was snatched away from you. But you would probably understand if the person appeared on TV that night to speak to the whole nation and even the world. This person, you would realize, had been taken from the few to be given back to the many. That is a picture of what happened to Jesus. On Ascension Day He was taken from the few, and on the Day of Pentecost He was given back in the person of His Holy Spirit, so that everyone, everywhere and always, could enjoy His presence and power as if He were physically present.*

**Thank You, Lord, that You are not only alive but also still in the world and able to help all who trust You. Amen.**

## If possible, so far as it depends on you, live peaceably with all. (Romans 12:18)

"You shall love your neighbour as yourself" (Leviticus 19:18). Children, obey your parents in everything, for this pleases the Lord (Colossians 3:20). "Greater love has no one than this, that someone lay down his life for his friends" (John 15:13). "But I say to you, Love your enemies and pray for those who persecute you" (Matthew 5:44). To the contrary, "if your enemy is hungry, feed him; if he is thirsty, give him something to drink" (Romans 12:20). Let every person be subject to the governing authorities. For there is no authority except from God, and those that exist have been instituted by God (Romans 13:1). Be subject for the Lord's sake to every human institution (1 Peter 2:13). Honour everyone. Love the brotherhood. Fear God. Honour the emperor (1 Peter 2:17).

*'No man is an island.' In some way or another we are all connected with each other – because we live in the same school, town, country or family. And we owe something to everyone with whom we come in contact. To our neighbours – the people we meet in the course of daily life – we owe the kindness and consideration we expect from them. To our friends we owe loyalty, even to the point of sacrifice. We are in debt even to our enemies, because we owe them our help and understanding, with the hope of turning them from enemies into friends. Our parents have a right to expect obedience while we're still young. All of us must respect 'authority' and treat God Himself with reverence and fear. If everyone observed these rules, what a happy place the world would be!*

**Lord, help me to be an easy person for others to live with. Amen.**

## Clothe yourselves, all of you, with humility.
## (1 Peter 5:5)

"Come to me . . . Take my yoke upon you, and learn from me, for I am gentle and lowly in heart, and you will find rest for your souls" (Matthew 11:28–29). Have this mind among yourselves, which is yours in Christ Jesus, who, though he was in the form of God, did not count equality with God a thing to be grasped . . . he humbled himself by becoming obedient to the point of death, even death on a cross (Philippians 2:5–8). Humble yourselves, therefore, under the mighty hand of God so that at the proper time he may exalt you (1 Peter 5:6). It is better to be of a lowly spirit with the poor than to divide the spoil with the proud (Proverbs 16:19). For though the Lord is high, he regards the lowly, but the haughty he knows from afar (Psalm 138:6). God opposes the proud, but gives grace to the humble (James 4:6).

What is humility? *It is not pretending that we are bad at something at which we happen to excel. Rather, it is forgetting that we are very good. Some soldiers wear medals on their greatcoats, but in the British army soldiers wear medals on their tunics so they are hidden when covered with a greatcoat. That should be the Christian's attitude – to achieve as much as we can, and to talk about it as little as possible.* Why is humility important? *It is important because Jesus, who is our example, was humble – and God calls us to be like Him. It is important because God cannot tolerate pride and keeps His distance from proud people. It is important because humility brings happiness and peace – things which those who are always striving for recognition and promotion never achieve. Finally, it is important because God only uses humble people, who depend completely upon Him, in His service.*

Lord, please keep me humble and help me to succeed without conceit and to fail without complaint. Amen.

**Your adversary the devil. (1 Peter 5:8)**

The Lord said to Satan, "From where have you come?" Satan answered the Lord and said, "From going to and fro on the earth, and from walking up and down on it" (Job 1:7). Be sober-minded; be watchful. Your adversary the devil prowls around like a roaring lion, seeking someone to devour. Resist him, firm in your faith (1 Peter 5:8, 9). So that we would not be outwitted by Satan; for we are not ignorant of his designs (2 Corinthians 2:11). Satan disguises himself as an angel of light (2 Corinthians 11:14). The God of peace will soon crush Satan under your feet (Romans 16:20). And the great dragon was thrown down, that ancient serpent, who is called the devil and Satan, the deceiver of the whole world – he was thrown down to the earth, and his angels were thrown down with him (Revelation 12:9).

*It seems likely that Satan was once an angel of God who rebelled against Him and set up a rival kingdom which has been at war ever since with the kingdom of heaven. Satan's chief aim is to try to stop people from crossing the frontier that separates the two kingdoms, and to harass those who have succeeded in doing so. We need to study his tactics carefully. Sometimes he attacks with the subtle cunning of a serpent or snake, sometimes with the ferocity of a hungry lion. To resist him we need courage and faith. But he is a defeated foe, mortally wounded upon the cross, and God is able to deal with him both in the short term by giving us victory over him, and in the long term when God will finally cast him out and destroy him.*

'Lord, may I always watch and pray, and feel that I am frail; that if the tempter cross my way, yet he may not prevail.' Amen.

## A good soldier of Christ Jesus. (2 Timothy 2:3)

Therefore take up the whole armour of God, that you may be able to withstand in the evil day, and having done all, to stand firm. Stand therefore, having fastened on the belt of truth, and having put on the breastplate of righteousness, and, as shoes for your feet, having put on the readiness given by the gospel of peace. In all circumstances take up the shield of faith, with which you can extinguish all the flaming darts of the evil one; and take the helmet of salvation, and the sword of the Spirit, which is the word of God, praying at all times in the Spirit, with all prayer and supplication. To that end keep alert with all perseverance (Ephesians 6:13–18).

*This passage portrays the Christian as a Roman soldier, armed and prepared for battle. Notice first* the enemy, *described here as 'the evil one' – that is Satan, or the devil, of whom we thought yesterday. We could find many names for the 'flaming darts' he hurls at us – pride, greed, doubt, anger and so on. But notice also* our equipment. *God arms Christians at every point. Our helmets guard our minds against Satan's suggestions, and our breastplates and shields protect our hearts against evil desires. Finally, notice* his exercise. *We are not only to be on guard, but we are to be in action, constantly praying for victory for ourselves and others. And 'as shoes for your feet' we are to 'put on the readiness given by the gospel of peace'. In other words, we are to be on our toes to bring the good news of Jesus Christ to those who have never heard it.*

Help me, Lord, not to be ashamed to confess the faith of Christ crucified, but to fight bravely under His banner against sin, the world and the devil. Amen.

## Be content . . . (Hebrews 13:5)

I have learned in whatever situation I am to be content. I know how to be brought low, and I know how to abound. In any and every circumstance, I have learned the secret of facing plenty and hunger, abundance and need (Philippians 4:11, 12). Now there is great gain in godliness with contentment, for we brought nothing into the world, and we cannot take anything out of the world. But if we have food and clothing, with these we will be content (1 Timothy 6:6–8). "Look at the birds of the air: they neither sow nor reap nor gather into barns, and yet your heavenly Father feeds them. Are you not of more value than they?" (Matthew 6:26). Be content with what you have, for he has said, "I will never leave you nor forsake you" (Hebrews 13:5). Soldiers also asked him [John the Baptist], "And we, what shall we do?" And he said to them . . . "Be content with your wages" (Luke 3:14).

*There is a sense, of course, in which all Christians should be discontented – with their progress, with the state of the world in which they live. But there is another very important sense in which Christians should be the most contented people in the world. Why? Because the valuable things in life are spiritual and not material. We can't buy any of them, yet they're the only things we really 'possess' – peace, joy, inner strength and so on. Secondly we should be content because Christ is with us and we can say with David, 'The Lord's my Shepherd, I shall not want.' When we have Christ, we have all that really matters. Finally, we have a loving heavenly Father watching over us and taking care of us every day, so we never need to be anxious or envious.*

**Lord, help me to trust You completely and find my contentment in You. Amen.**

## Paul, a servant of Christ Jesus. (Romans 1:1)

Now as Paul went on his way, he approached Damascus, and suddenly a light from heaven flashed around him. And falling to the ground he heard a voice saying to him, "Saul, Saul, why are you persecuting me?" And he said, "Who are you, Lord?" And the Lord said, "I am Jesus, whom you are persecuting. But rise and enter the city, and you will be told what you are to do" (Acts 9:3–6). "He is a chosen instrument of mine to carry my name before the Gentiles and kings and the children of Israel" (Acts 9:15).

*On January 25th the Church of England has always commemorated the conversion of Paul, that great event which turned the fiercest enemy of Christ into one of His most stalwart champions. His conversion had three stages. Halt! God suddenly stopped Saul's wild career of persecution against the Christians. But this may not have happened quite as suddenly as it seems, because it's possible that a voice in his conscience had been nagging him ever since Stephen's martyrdom. About turn! A Christian is someone whose life follows a completely new direction. I am no longer the guide, the director and the master of my heart and mind – Christ is. Quick march! From that point on Paul poured out all his great ability and energy for Christ, and he devoted his whole life to advancing the faith he had tried to destroy and to supporting those he had formerly persecuted.*

**Lord, please fill me with something of the courage and devotion with which Paul followed and served You. Amen.**

## Stay with us. (Luke 24:29)

For thus says the One who is high and lifted up, who inhabits eternity, whose name is Holy: "I dwell in the high and holy place, and also with him who is of a contrite and lowly spirit" (Isaiah 57:15). "Behold, I stand at the door and knock. If anyone hears my voice and opens the door, I will come in to him and eat with him, and he with me" (Revelation 3:20). I bow my knees before the Father, that . . . He may grant you to be strengthened with power through his Spirit in your inner being, so that Christ may dwell in your hearts through faith – that you, being rooted and grounded in love (Ephesians 3:14–17). A dwelling place for God by the Spirit (Ephesians 2:22). Jesus acted as if he were going farther, but they urged him strongly, saying, "Stay with us, for it is toward evening and the day is now far spent." So he went in to stay with them (Luke 24:28, 29). "They shall call his name Immanuel" (which means, God with us) (Matthew 1:23).

*Our lives are like houses with many different rooms – one for work, one for friends, sport, pastimes and so on. As we grow up, we add new wings or storeys to the house – career, family, business. Most of us aren't very good 'housekeepers,' and our lives become dusty and dirty over the years with sin and wrongdoing. Holman Hunt's picture 'The Light of the World' shows Jesus standing at the door, ready to come in and fill the house with His light and love. When someone asked Hunt why there was no handle on the outside of the door, he replied, 'The door at which Christ stands is the door of the human heart. Outside that door there is no handle. The only handle is on the inside.' In other words, Christ waits for us to say, 'Stay with me . . .'*

**Come into my heart, Lord Jesus, and fill it with Your light and make it Your home and palace and headquarters. Amen.**

## The Lord is my light and my salvation.
## (Psalm 27:1)

The grace of God has appeared, bringing salvation for all people (Titus 2:11). "Sirs, what must I do to be saved?" And they said, "Believe in the Lord Jesus, and you will be saved" (Acts 16:30, 31). For by grace you have been saved through faith. And this is not your own doing; it is the gift of God, not a result of works, so that no one may boast (Ephesians 2:8, 9). How shall we escape if we neglect such a great salvation? (Hebrews 2:3) "And there is salvation in no one else, for there is no other name under heaven given among men by which we must be saved" (Acts 4:12). Jesus said . . . "I am the way" (John 14:6). "The way of salvation" (Acts 16:17).

*In this reading you will notice three very important words, each with five letters. The first word is* saved. *Nowadays people more often refer to being 'rescued' or 'delivered', and these words remind us that we are by nature the prisoners of sin and need to be set free from its guilt and power.* Grace *describes the undeserved love of God which He bestows upon us all the time, but chiefly of course in sending His Son, Jesus Christ, to die on the cross as a sacrifice for our sins.* Faith *(and the verb that goes with it – believe) describes the simple act of trust by which we receive the gift of salvation that God offers to each one of us – our empty, outstretched hand taking what He wants to give us.*

Lord, 'thank You for the love that drew salvation's plan, the grace that brought it down to man, and the mighty gulf which You did span at Calvary'. Give me faith and courage to receive and to enjoy all that You have done for me. Amen.

## Not rich toward God. (Luke 12:21)

"Do not lay up for yourselves treasures on earth, where moth and rust destroy and where thieves break in and steal, but lay up for yourselves treasures in heaven, where neither moth nor rust destroys and where thieves do not break in and steal. For where your treasure is, there your heart will be also" (Matthew 6:19–21). He has caused us to be born again . . . to an inheritance that is imperishable, undefiled, and unfading, kept in heaven for you (1 Peter 3, 4). As for the rich in this present age, charge them not to be haughty, nor to set their hopes on the uncertainty of riches, but on God, who richly provides us with everything to enjoy. They are to do good, to be rich in good works, to be generous and ready to share, thus storing up treasure for themselves as a good foundation for the future, so that they may take hold of that which is truly life (1 Timothy 6:17–19). A good name is to be chosen rather than great riches, and favour is better than silver or gold (Proverbs 22:1).

*There is a story about a rich banker who died. At his funeral mourners sang the famous hymn 'Guide me O Thou great Redeemer', one line of which runs, 'Land me safe on Canaan's side.' Unfortunately there was a misprint, and the hymn read, 'Land my safe on Canaan's side.' That is the one thing we cannot do – but many rich people, who have made accumulating wealth their chief aim in life, no doubt wish they could. Such people are 'paupers in the sight of God'. Who are the wealthy people in God's eyes? They are those who have set their hearts upon Him, who have spent their lives serving others, and who have earned a name for generosity, integrity and humility. They are the truly rich people – the spiritual millionaires.*

**Lord, help me to seek the true wealth in life, and to remember that to know and serve You is better than any earthly treasure. Amen.**

## The splendour of holiness. (Psalm 29:2)

Strive for . . . holiness without which no one will see the Lord (Hebrews 12:14). Put off your old self, which belongs to your former manner of life and is corrupt through deceitful desires, and . . . be renewed in the spirit of your minds, and . . . put on the new self, created after the likeness of God in true right-eousness and holiness (Ephesians 4:22–24). For God has not called us for impurity, but in holiness (1 Thessalonians 4:7). Who shall ascend the hill of the Lord? And who shall stand in his holy place? He who has clean hands and a pure heart, who does not lift up his soul to what is false and does not swear deceitfully (Psalm 24:3, 4). He chose us . . . that we should be holy and blameless before him. In love (Ephesians 1:4). "Speak to all the congregation of the people of Israel and say to them, you shall be holy, for I the Lord your God am holy" (Leviticus 19:2).

*'Holiness' is one of those words which has had what we might call 'a bad press'. People often associate it with weakness and false piety. But in fact it is a fine, strong word and is related to the word 'healthy', for just as a healthy person is fit and free from infection, so a holy person is one whose heart and life are unpolluted by sin. A holy person is morally and spiritually healthy. There are two reasons why we need to pursue holiness. First, it is a straightforward com-mand from God – 'You shall be holy'. Secondly, it is the one qualifi-cation we must have if we are to 'ascend the hill of the LORD' – to live in His presence now and in the next life.*

**Lord, cleanse the thoughts of my heart by the inspiration of Your Holy Spirit so I can perfectly love You and worthily magnify Your holy name. Amen.**

### Serve the Lord. (Romans 12:11)

"Your God, whom you serve continually" (Daniel 6:16). Whatever you do, work heartily, as for the Lord and not for men, knowing that from the Lord you will receive the inheritance as your reward. You are serving the Lord Christ (Colossians 3:23, 24). "Serving the Lord with all humility" (Acts 20:19). For a day in your courts is better than a thousand elsewhere. I would rather be a doorkeeper in the house of my God than dwell in the tents of wickedness (Psalm 84:10). Serve the Lord with gladness! (Psalm 100:2) I will most gladly spend and be spent for your souls (2 Corinthians 12:15). "But I do not account my life of any value nor as precious to myself, if only I may finish my course and the ministry that I received from the Lord Jesus" (Acts 20:24) Therefore let us be grateful for receiving a kingdom that cannot be shaken, and thus let us offer to God acceptable worship, with reverence and awe (Hebrews 12:28).

*Not all service that we render to God is acceptable to Him. How can we be sure to please Him in what we try to do for Him? We need to serve* continually. *Like ambassadors, we are always under observation, and the way we do the ordinary things in life will commend our King to others. We must serve* humbly. *If we remember that we are serving Christ, then the lowliest task will seem worthwhile and take on a new importance. We also need to serve* gladly. *No task seems unbearable or even difficult if we do it for someone we really love, and that is the kind of service God wants – the service of a friend or a loving child.*

**Teach me, Lord, to serve You as You deserve, to give and not to count the cost, to fight and not to notice the wounds, to toil and not to look for rest, to labour and not to expect any reward except knowing that I do Your will. Amen.**

## He satisfies the longing soul. (Psalm 107:9)

"Come, everyone who thirsts, come to the waters; and he who has no money, come, buy and eat! Come, buy wine and milk without money and without price. Why do you spend your money for that which is not bread, and your labour for that which does not satisfy? Listen diligently to me, and eat what is good, and delight yourselves in rich food. Incline your ear, and come to me; hear, that your soul may live . . . Seek the Lord while he may be found; call upon him while he is near; let the wicked forsake his way, and the unrighteous man his thoughts; let him return to the Lord, that he may have compassion on him, and to our God, for he will abundantly pardon" (Isaiah 55: 1–7).

*This is one of those passages in the Bible which is worth learning by heart – not just because it happens to be a beautiful piece of poetry, but because of the truth it contains. It tells us what we find over and over again in other parts of the Bible – that God does two things for those who seek Him. He pardons and He provides. If we turn from what we know to be wrong and seek Him with all our hearts, then He will erase the sins we have committed and not remember them any more. We do the forsaking and He will do the forgiving. Then He will provide us with true, deep and lasting satisfaction. Many people look for these things in money, success, adventure, pleasure, sex and so on. But only Christ Himself can supply in unlimited quantity the spiritual bread, water, wine and milk which really satisfy.*

**Lord, please save me from wasting time, money and energy on the things that don't really satisfy, and help me to find true happiness in knowing and serving You. Amen.**

## Whoever does the will of God abides forever. (1 John 2:17)

"I know the plans I have for you, declares the Lord, plans for wholeness and not for evil, to give you a future and a hope" (Jeremiah 29:11). "It is not the will of my Father who is in heaven that one of these little ones should perish" (Matthew 18:14). The Lord is . . . patient toward you, not wishing that any should perish, but that all should reach repentance (2 Peter 3:9). This is the will of God, your sanctification (1 Thessalonians 4:3). Give thanks in all circumstances; for this is the will of God in Christ Jesus for you (1 Thessalonians 5:18). For this is the will of God, that by doing good you should put to silence the ignorance of foolish people (1 Peter 2:15). Understand what the will of the Lord is (Ephesians 5:17). That you may stand mature and fully assured in all the will of God (Colossians 4:12). That by testing you may discern what is the will of God, what is good and acceptable and perfect (Romans 12:2).

*God has two plans for His people – a general plan for all who call themselves Christians, and a personal plan for each individual follower. Our reading today concerns the former, and it deals with what applies to all Christians everywhere and at all times. It is God's will that we should turn to Him in repentance and faith, and that our lives thereafter should be holy, grateful and influential for good. Christians also find in experience that true happiness and rest of mind come to those who are living at the very centre of God's will, walking in His ways and thinking His thoughts after Him. Not only is this the secret of true peace, but we discover for ourselves that the will of God is 'good, acceptable and perfect'.*

**Lord, when I am tempted to turn from the paths of righteousness, help me to echo Your prayer – 'Not my will, but Yours be done.' Amen.**

## The love of Christ controls us.
## (2 Corinthians 5:14)

And now, behold, I am going to Jerusalem, constrained by the Spirit, not knowing what will happen to me there, except that the Holy Spirit testifies to me in every city that imprisonment and afflictions await me. But I do not account my life of any value nor as precious to myself, if only I may finish my course and the ministry that I received from the Lord Jesus, to testify to the gospel of the grace of God . . . And now I commend you to God and to the word of his grace, which is able to build you up and to give you the inheritance among all those who are sanctified. I coveted no one's silver or gold or apparel. You yourselves know that these hands ministered to my necessities and to those who were with me. In all things I have shown you that by working hard in this way we must help the weak and remember the words of the Lord Jesus, how he himself said, "It is more blessed to give than to receive" (Acts 20:22–24, 32–35).

*This is part of a talk which Paul gave to the church leaders he had called together at a place called Miletus, on the coast of what is now Turkey. We hear a lot these days, don't we, about retirement and pay? But neither of these matters found a place in Paul's thinking. For him there was no cosy period of retirement to look forward to, for he was determined to go on spreading the gospel right to the end of his life, in spite of persecution and even the threat of death. And what did he get for all this? He spent his spare time working at making tents in order to support himself on his missionary journeys. But, far from being resentful, he liked it this way. It made him happier to give than to receive. When Paul became a Christian he was 'arrested' by Jesus and became His 'prisoner'. But he never tried to escape, because the bonds and bars that held him were made of love.*

**Lord Jesus, give me something of Paul's courage, determination and love, that I too may serve You as You deserve to be served. Amen.**

## You shall not steal. (Exodus 20:15)

A false balance is an abomination to the Lord, but a just weight is his delight (Proverbs 11:1). Let the thief no longer steal, but rather let him labour, doing honest work with his own hands, so that he may have something to share with anyone in need (Ephesians 4:28). And Zacchaeus stood and said to the Lord, "Behold, Lord, the half of my goods I give to the poor. And if I have defrauded anyone of anything, I restore it fourfold" (Luke 19:8). The getting of treasures by a lying tongue is a fleeting vapour and a snare of death (Proverbs 21:6).

*Most decent people, whether Christians or not, would never dream of taking what doesn't belong to them – of stealing. But while we may dismiss stealing from the door, we are sometimes apt to entertain some of its unpleasant relations. Travelling without a ticket, fiddling with income tax returns, tinkering with the scales, borrowing without any intention of returning – all of these are first cousins of theft and we need to take care to avoid them. This country was once called 'a nation of shopkeepers', but now I am afraid it almost deserves to be called 'a nation of shoplifters', because millions of pounds' worth of goods are stolen from shops and supermarkets every year. Christians will be known for their honesty in everything to do with money and will be the sort of people in whom others can place complete trust. Christians know that stealing in any form is hateful to God and can bring no permanent pleasure.*

**Lord, keep my eyes from coveting what is not mine, and my hands from picking and stealing, for Christ's sake. Amen.**

## Your kingdom come . . . (Matthew 6:10)

The God of heaven will set up a kingdom that shall never be destroyed (Daniel 2:44). Your kingdom is an everlasting kingdom, and your dominion endures throughout all generations (Psalm 145:13). The kingdom of God is not coming with signs to be observed, nor will they say, "Look, here it is!" or "There!" for behold, the kingdom of God is in the midst of you (Luke 17:20–21). Jesus answered, "My kingdom is not of this world. If my kingdom were of this world, my servants would have been fighting, that I might not be delivered over to the Jews. But my kingdom is not from the world" (John 18:36). For the kingdom of God is not a matter of eating and drinking but of righteousness and peace and joy in the Holy Spirit (Romans 14:17). "Unless one is born again he cannot see the kingdom of God . . . he cannot enter the kingdom of God" (John 3:3–5). He has delivered us from the domain of darkness and transferred us to the kingdom of his beloved Son (Colossians 1:13).

*The kingdom of God is different from all other kingdoms in two important respects. First, it is spiritual and not material. Its size is not measured in acres, nor its strength in armies, but it exists wherever there are Christian people who are bound together by their love for, and loyalty to, Christ. To enter it people have to be 'born again' – that is to say, they must commit their lives to Christ as their King and Saviour. Second, it is eternal and not temporal. It will outlast every earthly kingdom that has ever been set up, for:*

*'The kingdoms of the world go by in purple and in gold,*
*They rise, they flourish and they die, and all their tale is told.*
*One kingdom only is divine, one banner triumphs still,*
*Its King a Servant, and its sign, a gibbet on a hill.'*

**May Your kingdom come O Lord, and may I do all I can to extend its frontiers into other people's lives. Amen.**

### David strengthened himself in the Lord his God. (1 Samuel 30:6)

"Only be strong and very courageous, being careful to do according to all the law that Moses my servant commanded you. Do not turn from it to the right hand or to the left, that you may have good success wherever you go" (Joshua 1:7). "Be strong, and let us use our strength for our people and for the cities of our God, and may the Lord do what seems good to him" (1 Chronicles 19:13). Then David said to Solomon his son, "Be strong and courageous and do it. Do not be afraid and do not be dismayed" (1 Chronicles 28:20). "Have I not commanded you? Be strong and courageous. . . . for the Lord your God is with you wherever you go" (Joshua 1:9). Wait for the Lord; be strong, and let your heart take courage; wait for the Lord! (Psalm 27:14) The brothers there, when they heard about us, came . . . to meet us. On seeing them, Paul thanked God and took courage (Acts 28:15).

*How often we need courage! We need courage to face some great difficulty and to 'behave ourselves valiantly', but we also need courage just to do some dull, routine, even boring piece of work without flagging or complaining. Where does this courage come from? First, it comes from the presence of Christ with us in our daily lives. After one of his bitterest battles Napoleon had a medal struck to commemorate his victory, and on it were the three words, 'J'y étais'. 'I was there'. It was his presence in the front line that inspired and encouraged his soldiers. But courage also comes from other people. Solomon was encouraged by David, and even Paul (who had himself encouraged so many people) was heartened and strengthened by the Christian friends he met on his last long journey to Rome. Is there anyone you can encourage today? Or to whom you yourself can look for courage?*

**Lord, make me courageous to stand for You as a Christian, to face difficulties and dangers without shrinking, and to do my duty without shirking. Amen.**

## "David . . . a man after my heart." (Acts 13:22)

"I have exalted one chosen from the people. I have found David, my servant . . . my hand shall be established with him; my arm also shall strengthen him" (Psalm 89:19–21). David said to the Philistine, "You come to me with a sword and with a spear and with a javelin, but I come to you in the name of the Lord of hosts" (1 Samuel 17:45). So David prevailed over the Philistine with a sling and with a stone (1 Samuel 17:50). David said to Saul . . . "Behold, this day your eyes have seen how the Lord gave you today into my hand in the cave. And some told me to kill you, but I spared you. I said, 'I will not put out my hand against my lord, for he is the Lord's anointed'" (1 Samuel 24:9, 10). David said to Nathan, "I have sinned against the Lord." And Nathan said to David, "The Lord also has put away your sin" (2 Samuel 12:13). David did what was right in the eyes of the Lord and did not turn aside from anything that he commanded him all the days of his life, except in the matter of Uriah the Hittite (1 Kings 15:5).

*What a remarkable man David was! He was a shepherd by trade, a poet, musician, courtier, soldier, fugitive and finally king. Few can have lived such an exciting and varied life. All this appeals to us, but what qualities especially appealed to God and made him 'a man after God's own heart'? The first such quality was his* audacity. *With nothing more than a sling he tackled the most formidable champion of the day. He did so because he had a secret weapon – his trust in God. The second quality was his* generosity. *At least twice he had the chance to kill Saul – to put an end to his own troubles and seize the throne. Saul deserved such a fate, but David refused to take advantage of his opportunity to revenge himself. The third quality was his* humility. *There was one terrible failure in his life ('the matter of Uriah the Hittite'), but when it was pointed out to him he admitted his sin at once and, in Psalm 51, showed how truly sorry he was.*

**Lord, make me, like David, a person after Your own heart. Amen.**

## "You shall love . . . your neighbour as yourself." (Luke 10:27)

Jesus replied, "A man was going down from Jerusalem to Jericho, and he fell among robbers, who stripped him and beat him and departed, leaving him half dead. Now by chance a priest was going down that road, and when he saw him he passed by on the other side. So likewise a Levite, when he came to the place and saw him, passed by on the other side. But a Samaritan, as he journeyed, came to where he was, and when he saw him, he had compassion. He went to him and bound up his wounds, pouring on oil and wine. Then he set him on his own animal and brought him to an inn and took care of him. And the next day he took out two denarii and gave them to the innkeeper, saying, 'Take care of him, and whatever more you spend, I will repay you when I come back'" (Luke 10:30–35).

*Jesus told this story in answer to the question, 'Who is my neighbour?' It teaches us that our neighbour is not just the friendly person who lives next door, but any stranger and even enemy (for the Jews and Samaritans hated each other) who happens to be in need. On this occasion the church ('a priest') and the law ('a Levite') failed miserably in their duty, and it was left to this Samaritan to show true Christian love and come to the rescue. Notice how he loved. He loved with his* heart *(for 'he had compassion on him'), with his* strength *(for he more or less carried him to safety) and with his* mind *(for he made careful plans for his welfare). Can you think of anyone to whom you might be 'a good Samaritan' today? Perhaps the chance will come quite unexpectedly, as it did to this man.*

Lord, help me not to be unconcerned or merely curious about those in need, but to see, to feel and to act. Amen.

## Walk in a manner worthy of the Lord, fully pleasing to him. (Colossians 1:10)

Blessed is the man who walks not in the counsel of the wicked, nor stands in the way of sinners (Psalm 1:1). Let us walk in the light of the Lord (Isaiah 2:5). Walk as children of light (Ephesians 5:8). If we walk in the light, as he is in the light, we have fellowship with one another, and the blood of Jesus his Son cleanses us from all sin (1 John 1:7). And walk in love, as Christ loved us (Ephesians 5:2). He has told you, O man, what is good; and what does the Lord require of you but to do justice, and to love kindness, and to walk humbly with your God? (Micah 6:8) Teach me your way, O Lord, that I may walk in your truth (Psalm 86:11). No good thing does he withhold from those who walk uprightly (Psalm 84:11).

*Are there people you can recognize not just by their voice, but by their walk? Some jobs seem to produce a certain kind of walk – the slow, measured tread of the policeman, the quick purposeful steps of the nurse, and so on. It is quite natural, therefore, that the Bible should use the idea of walking as a picture or metaphor of how we live, and our reading today shows us how a Christian should be easily recognized by his or her manner of life. You would not think much of a soldier slouching along with his hands in his pockets, and if we Christians are to be worthy of the King we serve then we need to walk in the light. We are to avoid all we know to be sinful and wrong so that we can be loving, humble and upright.*

**O Lord, help me to live in such a way as to please You, and to show others that I am a good soldier of Jesus Christ. Amen.**

### "Which one of you convicts me of sin?" (John 8:46)

For we do not have a high priest who is unable to sympathize with our weaknesses, but one who in every respect has been tempted as we are, yet without sin (Hebrews 4:15). Holy, innocent, unstained, separated from sinners (Hebrews 7:26). "I have sinned by betraying innocent blood" (Matthew 27:4). "This man has done nothing wrong" (Luke 23:41). "I find no guilt in this man" (Luke 23:4). "Certainly this man was innocent!" (Luke 23:47) "He committed no sin, neither was deceit found in his mouth" (1 Peter 2:22). For our sake God made him to be sin who knew no sin (2 Corinthians 5:21). In him there is no sin (1 John 3:5). And all spoke well of him and marvelled at the gracious words that were coming from his mouth (Luke 4:22). And they were astonished beyond measure, saying, "He has done all things well" (Mark 7:37). And a voice came from heaven, "You are my beloved Son; with you I am well pleased" (Luke 3:22).

*It does not usually take us very long to find some fault with people we get to know well; and the press and mass media are quick to point an accusing finger at important public people in whose character they detect some weakness. But no one at all could find fault with Jesus. His enemies (Pilate, Judas, His executioner and His fellow victim) could find nothing wrong. His friends (Peter, Paul and John) agreed that He was free of sin. The ordinary people who heard Him preach and saw His miracles had nothing but praise; while God Himself expressed unqualified pleasure in His Son. Of course, Jesus knew what it was like to be tempted. He did not escape the attacks of Satan, as we know. But He never gave in, and to the end of His life He remained absolutely sinless and was therefore able to offer His life as a sacrifice for our sins.*

Lord, I thank You for the wonderful life You lived, and for offering it as a sacrifice for my own sinful one. Amen.

## Come into his presence with thanksgiving.
## (Psalm 95:2)

Then one of them, when he saw that he was healed, turned back, praising God with a loud voice; and he fell on his face at Jesus' feet, giving him thanks. Now he was a Samaritan. Then Jesus answered, "Were not ten cleansed? Where are the nine? Was no one found to return and give praise to God except this foreigner?" (Luke 17:15–18) Giving thanks always and for everything to God (Ephesians 5:20). And when Paul had said these things, he took bread, and giving thanks to God in the presence of all he broke it and began to eat (Acts 27:35). Thanks be to God for his inexpressible gift! (2 Corinthians 9:15) Thanks be to God, who gives us the victory through our Lord Jesus Christ (1 Corinthians 15:57). And they were to stand every morning, thanking and praising the LORD, and likewise at evening (1 Chronicles 23:30). Bless the Lord, O my soul, and forget not all his benefits (Psalm 103:2).

*Would you not agree that ingratitude is one of the hardest things to bear – the gift, the letter, the good turn for which someone fails to say 'Thank you'? Jesus must have felt like that, when only one of the ten – ten percent – of those He had healed of leprosy took the trouble to return to thank Him. Let us be very careful not to forget God's goodness to us. Rather, we should try to count up each morning and evening the benefits He has bestowed upon us – the smaller things, like food and clothing and shelter, and the enormous gift of sending of His Son into the world to bring us forgiveness and victory. And remember, the best way of showing gratitude to God is by trying to please Him day by day. Thanksgiving must become 'thanksliving'.*

**I thank You, Lord, for my creation, preservation and all the blessings of this life, but above all I thank You for Your inestimable gift in the redemption of the world by our Lord Jesus Christ. Amen.**

## She loved much. (Luke 7:47)

Now when Jesus was at Bethany in the house of Simon the leper, a woman came up to him with an alabaster flask of very expensive ointment, and she poured it on his head as he reclined at table. And when the disciples saw it, they were indignant, saying, "Why this waste? For this could have been sold for a large sum and given to the poor." But Jesus, aware of this, said to them, "Why do you trouble the woman? For she has done a beautiful thing to me. For you always have the poor with you, but you will not always have me. In pouring this ointment on my body, she has done it to prepare me for burial. Truly, I say to you, wherever this gospel is proclaimed in the whole world, what she has done will also be told in memory of her" (Matthew 26:6–13)

*A very expensive and lovely gift of flowers would perhaps be a modern, western way of doing what this woman did to Jesus. What made the disciples so wrong when they said it was a waste? They forgot to whom the gift was given. It was a present to Jesus, the Son of God, and He is worthy of the very best we can produce. They also forgot why it was given. This woman had been a sinner but, because she had been so generously forgiven by Jesus, 'she loved much' and wanted to show her gratitude in this way. Nothing is ever wasted that is given to Jesus with love. Many people would never have heard of Jesus if some Christian men and women had not been willing to 'waste' their lives in some remote corner of the world in order to bring them the good news. They may not earn much money or gain promotion, but their reward, like this woman's, is that they are remembered with gratitude by those they have served.*

**Lord, make me willing to spend and be spent in Your service. Amen.**

## He learned obedience through what he suffered. (Hebrews 5:8)

Out of the depths I cry to you, O Lord! (Psalm 130:1) "But when I hoped for good, evil came, and when I waited for light, darkness came. My inward parts are in turmoil and never still; days of affliction come to meet me" (Job 30:26–27). "Now is my soul troubled. And what shall I say? 'Father, save me from this hour'? But for this purpose I have come to this hour" (John 12:27). So to keep me from being too elated by the surpassing greatness of the revelations, a thorn was given me in the flesh, a messenger of Satan to harass me, to keep me from being too elated (2 Corinthians 12:7). And after you have suffered a little while, the God of all grace, who has called you to his eternal glory in Christ, will himself restore, confirm, strengthen, and establish you (1 Peter 5:10). So we do not lose heart. Though our outer nature is wasting away, our inner nature is being renewed day by day. For this slight momentary affliction is preparing for us an eternal weight of glory beyond all comparison (2 Corinthians 4:16–17). Many are the afflictions of the righteous, but the Lord delivers him out of them all (Psalm 34:19).

*Why does God allow suffering? That is one of the oldest questions there is, and it has never been fully answered. Some suffering, of course, we bring upon ourselves by our own stupidity and sin, but there is a great deal which seems completely undeserved. Does God allow it, do you think, to teach us a greater faith in Himself? It is interesting to note that few, if any, great Bible characters escaped suffering of some sort, and in today's reading we see how trials afflicted David, Job, Jesus and Paul. Again, we must remember that this life is not all there is, and as Christians we look forward to a time when we will understand things fully. Perhaps this alone will compensate for the sorrow, the sickness and the misfortune which pursue us all through this earthly life.*

**O Lord, give me the faith to trust You even when I cannot understand, and to believe that all things work together for good to those who love You. Amen.**

## Fellowship of the Holy Spirit.
## (2 Corinthians 13:14)

Behold, how good and pleasant it is when brothers dwell in unity! (Psalm 133:1) "A new commandment I give to you, that you love one another: just as I have loved you, you also are to love one another. By this all people will know that you are my disciples, if you have love for one another" (John 13:34–35). And they devoted themselves to the apostles' teaching and fellowship, to the breaking of bread and the prayers . . . And all who believed were together and had all things in common. And they were selling their possessions and belongings and distributing the proceeds to all, as any had need (Acts 2:42, 44–45). Eager to maintain the unity of the Spirit in the bond of peace (Ephesians 4:3). Then those who feared the Lord spoke with one another (Malachi 3:16). Therefore encourage one another and build one another up, just as you are doing (1 Thessalonians 5:11).

*Christians are members of the same family, whose Father is God, and members of the same army, whose King is Christ. There should therefore exist between them a great bond of unity, or fellowship. Their love for Christ should override any differences in class or colour that there may be between them, and knit them together as one body. They should enjoy talking with each other about their experience as Christians, praying together, encouraging each other, and even sharing their possessions. But this kind of unity doesn't happen automatically. We must be 'eager to maintain' it and not allow prejudice or personal feelings to destroy it. Behold, how bad and unpleasant a thing it is when Christians quarrel and fight!*

**Lord, I thank You for other Christians who have helped me, and I ask that I may in my turn be an encouragement to them. Amen.**

## The Lord has led me in the way. (Genesis 24:27)

Teach me your way, O Lord, and lead me on a level path because of my enemies (Psalm 27:11). Your word is a lamp to my feet and a light to my path (Psalm 119:105). And your ears shall hear a word behind you, saying, "This is the way, walk in it," when you turn to the right or when you turn to the left (Isaiah 30:21). And Samuel said to the people . . . "I will instruct you in the good and the right way" (1 Samuel 12:20, 23). I will instruct you and teach you in the way you should go; I will counsel you with my eye upon you. Be not like a horse or a mule, without understanding, which must be curbed with bit and bridle, or it will not stay near you (Psalm 32:8–9). That this is God, our God forever and ever. He will guide us forever (Psalm 48:14).

*Does God guide us, or does He leave us to grope our way through life, like the proverbial blind man looking in a dark room for a black cat that isn't there? The answer is that He does guide us, and we can confidently expect Him to help us over the important decisions which we have to make – career, marriage, job, and so on. He uses His Word, the Bible, which is like a map, showing the main roads which we should take. He uses our conscience, like a compass, so that a small but insistent voice begins to say to us, 'This is right', or 'This is wrong'. He uses the advice of older, wiser Christians just as He used Samuel to guide His people long ago. He uses the circumstances of our lives, like signposts, so that generally speaking He will lead us to do things for which we are naturally, temperamentally and educationally suited.*

**Lead me, Lord, in Your righteousness; make Your way plain before my face. Amen.**

## "Man is born to trouble as the sparks fly upward." (Job 5:7)

And to Adam he said . . . "Cursed is the ground because of you; in pain you shall eat of it all the days of your life" (Genesis 3:17). "Man who is born of a woman is few of days and full of trouble" (Job 14:1). What has a man from all the toil and striving of heart with which he toils beneath the sun? For all his days are full of sorrow, and his work is a vexation. Even in the night his heart does not rest. This also is vanity (Ecclesiastes 2:22–23). Therefore, just as sin came into the world through one man, and death through sin, and so death spread to all men because all sinned (Romans 5:12). The creation itself will be set free from its bondage to decay (Romans 8:21). The last enemy to be destroyed is death (1 Corinthians 15:26). "For behold, I create new heavens and a new earth, and the former things shall not be remembered or come into mind" (Isaiah 65:17). According to his promise we are waiting for new heavens and a new earth in which righteousness dwells (2 Peter 3:13).

*Not only is sin the cause of all our sorrow, suffering and death, but it has also dislocated the whole creation, so that the world is hopelessly out of joint. The balance of nature has been destroyed, and humankind is the victim of the twin evils of grinding poverty on the one hand and a super-abundance of wealth on the other. But for the Christian this state of affairs spells hope rather than despair, because we firmly believe that a time will come when God will bring into existence new heavens and a new earth, where righteousness will reign and where there will be no place for sorrow, suffering or death.*

**O Lord, inspired by hope for the future, may I do what I can to meet the needs of the present. Amen.**

## "The Lord also has put away your sin."
## (2 Samuel 12:13)

Have mercy on me, O God, according to your steadfast love; according to your abundant mercy blot out my transgressions. Wash me thoroughly from my iniquity, and cleanse me from my sin! For I know my transgressions, and my sin is ever before me. Against you, you only, have I sinned and done what is evil in your sight . . . Behold, I was brought forth in iniquity, and in sin did my mother conceive me . . . Wash me, and I shall be whiter than snow . . . Hide your face from my sins, and blot out all my iniquities. Create in me a clean heart, O God, and renew a right spirit within me . . . Restore to me the joy of your salvation (Psalm 51:1–12). Whoever conceals his transgressions will not prosper, but he who confesses and forsakes them will obtain mercy (Proverbs 28:13).

*King David had committed a terrible sin. He had engineered the death of one of his generals so that he might take the man's wife for his own. Here we have his prayer for forgiveness after Nathan the prophet opened his eyes to the wickedness of what he had done. It is a wonderful prayer, and it shows us three things about David. First, he* admits sin. *He makes no attempt to conceal or minimize what he did. Second, he* understands sin. *He realizes that it stems from a sinful nature which has been with him from birth, and which only God's Holy Spirit can counteract. Notice the words he uses – 'transgression' means to trespass or break bounds; 'iniquity' means to stray or turn aside; 'sin' means to fall short. Like a bowls ball, we are apt to fail in all three ways. Finally, David* forsakes sin, *asking God to give him a completely new attitude towards it. Don't forget this prayer of David's if ever you have a bad fall into temptation.*

**Create in me a clean heart, O God, and renew a right spirit within me. Amen.**

## Keep your tongue from evil. (Psalm 34:13)

If anyone does not stumble in what he says, he is a perfect man . . . Look at the ships also: though they are so large and are driven by strong winds, they are guided by a very small rudder . . . So also the tongue is a small member, yet it boasts of great things. How great a forest is set ablaze by such a small fire! And the tongue is a fire . . . Every kind of beast . . . can be tamed and has been tamed . . . but no human being can tame the tongue. It is a restless evil, full of deadly poison. With it we bless our Lord . . . and . . . curse people . . . From the same mouth come blessing and cursing. My brothers, these things ought not to be so (James 3:2–10). I said, "I will guard my ways, that I may not sin with my tongue" (Psalm 39:1). Set a guard, O Lord, over my mouth; keep watch over the door of my lips! (Psalm 141:3) Let the words of my mouth . . . be acceptable in your sight, O Lord, my rock and my redeemer (Psalm 19:14).

*What a difficult thing the tongue is to control! It is* very small, *like the rudder of a ship – out of sight most of the time, but governing the course the ship takes. It is like a key which can unlock a great door. It is also* very sharp, *like a sword, and we can hurt people badly by using it to make cutting or wounding remarks. Likewise it is* very strong, *like a wild beast, and liable at any time to break loose and do a great deal of damage. How can we control it? God helped by designing us so that our tongues are behind strong rows of teeth and two lips, but even that is not enough. Our tongues need more than bars – they need a keeper, who will watch the doors of our mouths, and keep our tongues from evil. That keeper is the Lord.*

**Lord, I ask You to save me from using my tongue to say what is unkind, untruthful or unclean. Amen.**

## "Go into all the world and proclaim the gospel." (Mark 16:15)

After this the Lord appointed seventy-two others and sent them on ahead of him, two by two, into every town and place where he himself was about to go. And he said to them, "The harvest is plentiful, but the labourers are few. Therefore pray earnestly to the Lord of the harvest to send out labourers into his harvest. Go your way; behold, I am sending you out as lambs in the midst of wolves" (Luke 10:1–3). The seventy-two returned with joy, saying, "Lord, even the demons are subject to us in your name!" And he said to them, "I saw Satan fall like lightning from heaven. Behold, I have given you authority to tread on serpents and scorpions, and over all the power of the enemy, and nothing shall hurt you. Nevertheless, do not rejoice in this, that the spirits are subject to you, but rejoice that your names are written in heaven" (Luke 10:17–20).

*We read today about the birth of missionary work. We see the great need of the world for the gospel of Jesus Christ, like a harvest waiting to be reaped and gathered. We see the risks that missionaries sometimes run, like lambs among wolves, and the wisdom therefore of working not on their own, but with partners, 'two by two'. We see the threat which all missionary work levels at the strongholds of Satan, challenging his sovereignty. We see the danger of getting overexcited and happy about success that can come and go, and we are reminded of the need to find true joy in the fact that our names are registered in heaven and we are under the constant care of God.*

Lord, I ask You to inspire and equip men and women to take the gospel to places where it has never been heard, and help me to do my part by prayer, by giving and even by going myself. Amen.

## We are sure that we have a clear conscience.
## (Hebrews 13:18)

Give your servant therefore an understanding mind . . . that I may discern between good and evil (1 Kings 3:9). But solid food is for the mature, for those who have their powers of discernment trained by constant practice to distinguish good from evil (Hebrews 5:14). "So I always take pains to have a clear conscience toward both God and man" (Acts 24:16). Holding faith and a good conscience. By rejecting this, some have made shipwreck of their faith (1 Timothy 1:19). The insincerity of liars whose consciences are seared (1 Timothy 4:2). Both their minds and their consciences are defiled (Titus 1:15). They have become callous and have given themselves up to sensuality, greedy to practice every kind of impurity (Ephesians 4:19). Let us draw near with a true heart in full assurance of faith, with our hearts sprinkled clean from an evil conscience (Hebrews 10:22). As an appeal to God for a good conscience (1 Peter 3:21).

*Have you ever used a substance called litmus paper? Its purpose is to tell you the difference between an acid and an alkali. What litmus paper does chemically, our consciences are meant to do morally and spiritually, distinguishing for us between right and wrong. There are three kinds of conscience. The* twisted conscience *does not give the right answer, like a watch which is fast or slow, because it has never been checked and tested by Big Ben. Jesus is the standard by which we must set our consciences. God can cleanse and heal the* troubled conscience *when we ask His forgiveness for what we have done wrong – and perhaps apologize to someone else too. The* trained conscience *is kept alive and sensitive and accurate because it is constantly checked by the life of Jesus and the teachings of the Bible.*

**Give me, O Lord, the strength to choose the good and refuse the evil, and an understanding heart to know the difference. Amen.**

## "I will follow you, Lord, but . . ." (Luke 9:61)

Now great crowds accompanied him, and he turned and said to them, "If anyone comes to me and does not hate his own father and mother and wife and children and brothers and sisters, yes, and even his own life, he cannot be my disciple. Whoever does not bear his own cross and come after me cannot be my disciple. For which of you, desiring to build a tower, does not first sit down and count the cost, whether he has enough to complete it? . . . Or what king, going out to encounter another king in war, will not sit down first and deliberate whether he is able with ten thousand to meet him who comes against him with twenty thousand? . . . So therefore, any one of you who does not renounce all that he has cannot be my disciple" (Luke 14:25–28, 31, 33).

*Of course Jesus did not mean that we should literally 'hate' those we love best, but that we must put Him first. In some Muslim or Communist countries, would-be Christians face expulsion from their homes and family circles. Nor does Jesus expect us to carry a literal cross, or even wear one, wherever we go. This was Jesus' way of telling people that they must not be ashamed of Him but must be ready to be recognized as His disciples. In other words, Jesus is saying, 'I don't want the second place in your life, I want the first; and I don't want a secret place, where no one will see me. I want it to be known that I am living in your heart and life.' It isn't easy to be a Christian, and that is why, if we are wise, we will count the cost very carefully and 'sit down first and deliberate'.*

**Lord, give me the faith to put You first, and the courage to let others see it. Amen.**

## Put off your old self. (Ephesians 4:22)

Therefore, having put away falsehood, let each one of you speak the truth with his neighbour, for we are members one of another. Be angry and do not sin; do not let the sun go down on your anger, and give no opportunity to the devil. Let the thief no longer steal, but rather let him labour, doing honest work with his own hands, so that he may have something to share with anyone in need. Let no corrupting talk come out of your mouths, but only such as is good for building up, as fits the occasion, that it may give grace to those who hear. And do not grieve the Holy Spirit of God, by whom you were sealed for the day of redemption. Let all bitterness and wrath and anger and clamour and slander be put away from you, along with all malice. Be kind to one another, tenderhearted, forgiving one another, as God in Christ forgave you (Ephesians 4:25–32).

*We hear a lot today about the 'standard of living', the material comforts and benefits which people feel they have a right to expect; and in these verses we see that moral 'standard of living' which God expects of those who love Him. Just as we would never dream of hurting the feelings of someone who had come to be our guest, so we must not 'grieve the Holy Spirit' who, if we are true Christians, has come to live in our hearts. We can grieve the Spirit in our* thoughts, *by harbouring bitter, malicious thoughts about people; with dishonest or impure* words; *and by* deeds, *for example by theft. The devil will try to make us do what is wrong, but we must give him no opportunity. When he calls, remember you are 'not at home'.*

**Lord, help me each day to 'put away', out of sight and reach, those things which I know would grieve and disappoint You. Amen.**

## "He has visited and redeemed his people." (Luke 1:68)

"For even the Son of Man came not to be served but to serve, and to give his life as a ransom for many" (Mark 10:45). Who gave himself as a ransom for all (1 Timothy 2:6). Who gave himself for us to redeem us from all lawlessness and to purify for himself a people for his own possession who are zealous for good works (Titus 2:14). Knowing that you were ransomed from the futile ways inherited from your forefathers, not with perishable things such as silver or gold, but with the precious blood of Christ, like that of a lamb without blemish or spot (1 Peter 1:18–19). In him we have redemption through his blood, the forgiveness of our trespasses, according to the riches of his grace (Ephesians 1:7). For the ransom of their life is costly (Psalm 49:8). Let the redeemed of the Lord say so, whom he has redeemed from trouble (Psalm 107:2).

*It used to be necessary to go right back to Richard Coeur de Lion to illustrate the meaning of the word 'ransom', but nowadays, with kidnapping and hijacking, we are all too familiar with the idea. If you like to think of it in this way, Satan has kidnapped the world – you and me and everyone else. We are his prisoners, and the price that has to be paid for our release is the death of Jesus upon the cross. Only in this way can we be 'ransomed, healed, restored, forgiven'. Of course, this is picture language, and we must not think of Satan making a fortune out of our release. That would be pressing the metaphor too far. But Jesus' death made possible our escape from the guilt and power of sin, and in His mercy God gave 'His only Son Jesus Christ to suffer death upon the cross for our redemption'.*

**Thank You, Lord, for being good enough to pay the price of sin. Amen.**

### "You will be my witnesses." (Acts 1:8)

But you are . . . a people for his own possession, that you may proclaim the excellencies of him who called you out of darkness into his marvellous light (1 Peter 2:9). The man from whom the demons had gone begged that he might be with him, but Jesus sent him away, saying, "Return to your home, and declare how much God has done for you." And he went away, proclaiming throughout the whole city how much Jesus had done for him (Luke 8:38–39). I will show you my faith by my works (James 2:18). By his good conduct let him show his works in the meekness of wisdom (James 3:13). "Let your light shine before others, so that they may see your good works and give glory to your Father who is in heaven" (Matthew 5:16). That you may be blameless and innocent, children of God without blemish in the midst of a crooked and twisted generation, among whom you shine as lights in the world (Philippians 2:15).

*If you were arrested and charged with being a Christian, and then put on trial, would there be enough evidence to convict you? I remember how that question challenged me when I first heard it; and our reading today reminds us that it is not just by what we say or preach that we spread the gospel and witness for Christ, but by the quality of our lives. If people realize that because we are Christians are we kinder, humbler, more patient and much nicer to know, then they will be attracted towards Christ Himself. Peter sketches a scene in which an unbelieving husband may be won for Christ 'without a word being said', simply by the way in which his wife's behaviour speaks to him. On William Wilberforce's tomb are the words, 'The abiding eloquence of a Christian life'. How we live for Christ speaks more loudly than what we say.*

**Lord, help me to please You throughout every day, in all that I do and in all that I say. Amen.**

## "Your kingdom come." (Luke 11:2)

The Spirit of the Lord God is upon me, because the Lord has anointed me to bring good news to the poor; he has sent me to bind up the brokenhearted, to proclaim liberty to the captives, and the opening of the prison to those who are bound; to proclaim the year of the Lord's favour, and the day of vengeance of our God; to comfort all who mourn; to grant to those who mourn in Zion – to give them a beautiful headdress instead of ashes, the oil of gladness instead of mourning, the garment of praise instead of a faint spirit; that they may be called oaks of righteousness, the planting of the Lord, that he may be glorified (Isaiah 61:1–3). I will greatly rejoice in the Lord; my soul shall exult in my God, for he has clothed me with the garments of salvation; he has covered me with the robe of righteousness (Isaiah 61:10).

*This beautiful passage from Isaiah describes the kingdom of God. It began to be fulfilled with the coming of Christ, and it will reach its climax when He returns to establish His kingdom on earth. The health and greatness of any country depend upon two things – the happiness and holiness of its people. The kingdom of God is no exception. Christ came to bring happiness to people, and the depressed and downhearted may find new hope and joy in knowing and serving Him. He came also to set new standards of righteousness, and to clothe people not only with ordinary wearing apparel, but also with 'the garments of salvation'. Just as the kilt is the national dress for the Scottish, and the sari for the women of India, so righteousness is what members of God's kingdom wear.*

Lord, make me a worthy member of Your kingdom, that others may see Whose I am and the One I serve. Amen.

## The haughty he knows from afar. (Psalm 138:6)

"Take care lest you forget the Lord your God . . . lest, when you
have eaten and are full and have built good houses and live in
them . . . and your silver and gold is multiplied and all that
you have is multiplied, then your heart be lifted up, and you
forget the Lord your God, who brought you out of . . . the
house of slavery" (Deuteronomy 8:11–14). The Lord hates . . .
haughty eyes (Proverbs 6:16–17). Everyone who is arrogant in
heart is an abomination to the Lord (Proverbs 16:5). Pride goes
before destruction, and a haughty spirit before a fall (Proverbs
16:18). Those who walk in pride he is able to humble (Daniel
4:37). God opposes the proud but gives grace to the humble.
Humble yourselves, therefore, under the mighty hand of God
so that at the proper time he may exalt you (1 Peter 5:5–6).

*Pride was the first sin for, as you will remember, it was their desire
to be like God, and to know everything, that proved the undoing of
Adam and Eve. It is also perhaps the worst sin, because the proud
person is really setting him or herself up against God. Pride is unreasonable, because everything we possess – material property, natural
ability – is given to us by God. Pride is also undesirable, because it
is abominable in God's eyes and so often leads to tragic failure and
destruction. We need to guard against four kinds of pride: pride of
race (looking down on other people), pride of face (conceit about our
appearance), pride of place (a larger house, a bigger car than others)
and pride of grace (imagining that we are better than others).*

Lord, keep me humble and save me from becoming a snob,
a swank or a prig. Amen.

## Stand in awe of him. (Psalm 22:23)

There is none like you, O Lord; you are great, and your name is great in might. Who would not fear you, O King of the nations? For this is your due; for among all the wise ones of the nations and in all their kingdoms there is none like you (Jeremiah 10:6–7). The fear of the Lord is hatred of evil (Proverbs 8:13). Fear God and keep his commandments, for this is the whole duty of man (Ecclesiastes 12:13). "I will put the fear of me in their hearts, that they may not turn from me" (Jeremiah 32:40). The fear of the Lord is the beginning of knowledge (Proverbs 1:7). My son, if you receive my words . . . then you will understand the fear of the Lord and find the knowledge of God (Proverbs 2:1, 5). Oh, fear the Lord, you his saints, for those who fear him have no lack! (Psalm 34:9)

*'What does it mean to fear God?' I remember being asked that question when I was standing by the sea, and so I pointed towards it and said, 'I love the sea. I enjoy being beside it. I like being on it. I adore being in it. But I have learned to respect it deeply. I know something of its awful majesty and power, and I would never take liberties with it.' You could say the same about fire – so warm and welcoming at home on a cold day, but how fearsome when raging through a forest! So our love for God must always be tinged with awe. We must not allow ourselves to become flippant or familiar, and we must never use His name lightly, as a kind of oath. Fear is love, lined with reverence and respect.*

**'O how I fear You, living God, with deepest, tenderest fears; and worship You with trembling hope, and penitential tears.' Amen.**

## "Take care then how you hear." (Luke 8:18)

Jesus said to them: "Listen! A sower went out to sow. And as he sowed, some seed fell along the path, and the birds came and devoured it. Other seed fell on rocky ground, where it did not have much soil, and immediately it sprang up, since it had no depth of soil. And when the sun rose it was scorched, and since it had no root, it withered away. Other seed fell among thorns, and the thorns grew up and choked it, and it yielded no grain. And other seeds fell into good soil and produced grain, growing up and increasing and yielding thirtyfold and sixtyfold and a hundredfold." And he said, "He who has ears to hear, let him hear" (Mark 4:2–9).

*This story illustrates four different kinds of people and the way they listen to the message of Jesus. The* light-hearted *enjoy the talk or sermon but never think it over seriously and, almost immediately, other matters come crowding in like a flock of birds and the seed is snatched away and the message forgotten. The* faint-hearted *also enjoy what they hear and put it into practice for a time, but then things get difficult. They are teased for being religious and one or two friends drop them. The sun is too hot, and they wither away. The* half-hearted *show some promise, and for a time go well, but then other things begin to compete with the seed – money, business concerns, the garden, the latest hobby, and slowly the message is choked. The* whole-hearted *really mean business. They think over what they have heard. They count the cost. They give it priority. They grow into strong, mature Christians. Which sort of soil are you?*

Lord, when You speak to me, help me to chase away the birds, pick out the stones and cut back the thorns so that Your word may take root in my heart and bear fruit. Amen.

## Seek the Lord and His strength. (1 Chronicles 16:11)

That you may know what is the hope to which he has called you, what are the riches of his glorious inheritance in the saints, and what is the immeasurable greatness of his power toward us who believe, according to the working of his great might that he worked in Christ when he raised him from the dead (Ephesians 1:18–20). May you be strengthened with all power, according to his glorious might, for all endurance and patience with joy (Colossians 1:11). But he said to me, "My grace is sufficient for you, for my power is made perfect in weakness." Therefore I will boast all the more gladly of my weaknesses, so that the power of Christ may rest upon me. For the sake of Christ, then, I am content with weaknesses, insults, hardships, persecutions, and calamities. For when I am weak, then I am strong (2 Corinthians 12:9–10). Finally, be strong in the Lord and in the strength of his might (Ephesians 6:10). You then, my child, be strengthened by the grace that is in Christ Jesus (2 Timothy 2:1). I can do all things through him who strengthens me (Philippians 4:13). Blessed are those whose strength is in you (Psalm 84:5).

*I often think that Christians are like cars. We need two kinds of power – the power of the brake and of the accelerator. In other words, we need a power that will drag us back when we are in danger of falling into temptation, and we need a power that will drive us forward to accept a challenge, complete a demanding task or face a difficult situation. We cannot find this power within ourselves, for we have no power to help ourselves. But power belongs to God, and as we link ourselves to Him by faith His power will flow into our lives so that we can do all the things He means us to through Christ who strengthens us. But we must remember that it is only weakness that can receive strength. The Lord says to us, as we might say to someone we were trying to rescue from the sea, 'Don't fight in your own strength. Take hold of my strength.'*

**Lord, I thank You that You have promised power – 'power to all who ask, power to conquer Satan, power for every task'. Amen.**

## I have slain them by the words of my mouth. (Hosea 6:5)

For the word of God is living and active, sharper than any two-edged sword, piercing to the division of soul and of spirit, of joints and of marrow, and discerning the thoughts and intentions of the heart. And no creature is hidden from his sight, but all are naked and exposed to the eyes of him to whom we must give account (Hebrews 4:12–13). From his mouth came a sharp two-edged sword (Revelation 1:16). The sword of the Spirit, which is the word of God (Ephesians 6:17). He made my mouth like a sharp sword (Isaiah 49:2). Let all the house of Israel therefore know for certain that God has made him both Lord and Christ, this Jesus whom you crucified. Now when they heard this they were cut to the heart, and said to Peter and the rest of the apostles, "Brothers, what shall we do?" (Acts 2:36–37)

*God's Word, when it is thoughtfully read or faithfully preached, acts in many ways like a sword, piercing to the very depth of our personality. It reaches the conscience, where it pricks those things which we know to be wrong but which we have perhaps tried to conceal from ourselves and others. It reaches the heart, where it lays bare our innermost thoughts, intentions and desires. But God uses His Word not so much as a weapon as an instrument – more like a surgeon's scalpel than a soldier's sword. He hurts only because He wants to heal. He cuts only so that He may cure. And, if we are wise, we submit to His judgment and allow His Word, whenever we read or hear it, to have free course in our lives.*

Help me, Lord, not to shrink from the sharpness of what You sometimes have to say to me through Your Word, but to allow You to have Your way with me. Amen.

## He will have compassion. (Lamentations 3:32)

Jesus . . . said, "I have compassion on the crowd because they have been with me now three days and have nothing to eat" (Matthew 15:32). For the needy shall not always be forgotten, and the hope of the poor shall not perish forever (Psalm 9:18). When he went ashore he saw a great crowd, and he had compassion on them and healed their sick (Matthew 14:14). In all their affliction he was afflicted, and the angel of his presence saved them (Isaiah 63:9). As he drew near to the gate of the town, behold, a man who had died was being carried out, the only son of his mother, and she was a widow, and a considerable crowd from the town was with her. And when the Lord saw her, he had compassion on her and said to her, "Do not weep" (Luke 7:12–13). Surely he has borne our griefs and carried our sorrows (Isaiah 53:4). When he saw the crowds, he had compassion for them, because they were harassed and helpless, like sheep without a shepherd (Matthew 9:36). He will tend his flock like a shepherd; he will gather the lambs in his arms (Isaiah 40:11).

*The word translated in the New Testament as 'compassion' is an emotional, and not an intellectual, word. It means to be inwardly moved, almost physically affected – so much so that we feel we must do something to help those in need or trouble. Again and again we read that Jesus was 'moved with compassion'. Poverty, suffering, sorrow and oppression stirred Him deeply, and wherever possible He brought comfort and relief. It should be a great comfort to us to know that in Jesus Christ we have someone who understands and shares our problems and is able to help; and it should be a great challenge to us to do all we can to help those who, as the Book of Common Prayer says, 'are in any ways afflicted or distressed, in mind, body, or estate'.*

**Lord, may sorrow and suffering never fail to stir my feelings of pity and concern and spur me into some kind of action. Amen.**

## "Our God whom we serve is able to deliver us." (Daniel 3:17)

For because he himself has suffered when tempted, he is able to help those who are being tempted (Hebrews 2:18). He is able to save to the uttermost those who draw near to God through him, since he always lives to make intercession for them (Hebrews 7:25). Now to him who is able to keep you from stumbling and to present you blameless before the presence of his glory with great joy (Jude 24). Jesus said to them, "Do you believe that I am able to do this?" They said to him, "Yes, Lord." Then he touched their eyes, saying, "According to your faith be it done to you" (Matthew 9:28–29). Now to him who is able to do far more abundantly than all that we ask or think, according to the power at work within us, to him be glory in the church and in Christ Jesus throughout all generations, forever and ever. Amen (Ephesians 3:20–21).

*Yesterday we thought about the Lord's willingness to help those in need, and today we read about His power to do so. These two things – willingness and ability – don't always go together. Sometimes there are those who say, 'I would help you if I could, but I can't.' And there are others who say (though not always out loud), 'I could help you if I would, but I won't.' How different is Jesus! He has pity and power, sympathy and strength. The only thing that limits the flow of His power towards us is our faith – just as a doctor can only help us in so far as we trust him. The more we expect Him to do, the more He is able to do. The measure of help He gives is not according to His power, but according to our faith.*

**Lord, give me the faith to believe that You are both willing and able to help me in my daily needs and problems. Amen.**

## Now Samuel died. And all Israel . . . mourned for him. (1 Samuel 25:1)

Now Samuel did not yet know the Lord, and the word of the Lord had not yet been revealed to him (1 Samuel 3:7). And the Lord came and stood, calling as at other times, "Samuel! Samuel!" And Samuel said, "Speak, for your servant hears" (1 Samuel 3:10). And Samuel grew, and the Lord was with him and let none of his words fall to the ground. And all Israel . . . knew that Samuel was established as a prophet of the Lord (1 Samuel 3:19–20). And Samuel said to all the house of Israel, "If you are returning to the Lord with all your heart, then put away the foreign gods . . . from among you and direct your heart to the Lord and serve him only" (1 Samuel 7:3). "As for me, far be it from me that I should sin against the Lord by ceasing to pray for you, and I will instruct you in the good and the right way" (1 Samuel 12:23).

*Samuel has been called 'the last of the Judges of Israel and the first of the Prophets'. The people regarded him as the most important and influential figure since Moses (Jeremiah 15:1). He was a* reformer. *The country at the time of his birth was in a terrible state of chaos and disarray, but he turned the people back again to worship the true God, training prophets to take the message back into the villages, teaching people to fear the Lord, and above all praying for them. He was also a* counsellor. *He was Saul's chief adviser, though Saul did not often heed his advice, and he did much to train David for future leadership. In public and in private Samuel sought to serve the Lord who had called him, when he was still only a child, into a life of friendship with Himself.*

'Lord, give me Samuel's ear, the open ear, O Lord, alive and quick to hear each whisper of Your word; like him to answer at Your call, and to obey You first of all.' Amen.

## "Forgive, and you will be forgiven." (Luke 6:37)

Then Peter . . . said . . . "Lord, how often will my brother sin against me, and I forgive him? As many as seven times?" Jesus said to him, "I do not say to you seven times, but seventy times seven . . . The kingdom of heaven may be compared to a king who wished to settle accounts with his servants . . . One was brought to him who owed him ten thousand talents. And since he could not pay, his master ordered him to be sold . . . and payment to be made . . . So the servant fell on his knees, imploring him, 'Have patience with me, and I will pay you everything.' And out of pity for him the master of that servant . . . forgave him the debt. But when that same servant went out, he found one of his fellow servants who owed him a hundred denarii, and seizing him . . . saying, 'Pay what you owe.' So his fellow servant . . . pleaded with him, 'Have patience with me, and I will pay you.' He refused and went and put him in prison . . . Then his master . . . said to him, 'You wicked servant! I forgave you all that debt . . . should not you have had mercy on your fellow servant, as I had mercy on you?'" (Matthew 18:21–35)

*Whenever we say the Lord's Prayer we use the words, 'Forgive us our sins, as we forgive those who sin against us.' They are easy to say, but it is sometimes very hard to forgive someone who has wronged us in some way. But we must forgive and also give that person the chance to apologize, if we expect God to forgive us the much greater wrongs that we have done to Him. A lake which has an inflow but no outflow quickly becomes stale and stagnant, unfit for swimming or fishing. If God is going to forgive us, then we must be ready to pass on that forgiveness to others.*

**Forgive me my sins, O Lord, even as today I seek to forgive those who sin against me. Amen.**

**And just as it is appointed for man to die once, and after that comes judgment. (Hebrews 9:27)**

"Because God has fixed a day on which he will judge the world in righteousness by a man whom he has appointed; and of this he has given assurance to all by raising him from the dead" (Acts 17:31). For God will bring every deed into judgment, with every secret thing, whether good or evil (Ecclesiastes 12:14). "Nothing is covered up that will not be revealed, or hidden that will not be known" (Luke 12:2). On that day when, according to my gospel, God judges the secrets of men by Christ Jesus (Romans 2:16). For God did not send his Son into the world to condemn the world, but in order that the world might be saved through him. Whoever believes in him is not condemned, but whoever does not believe is condemned already, because he has not believed in the name of the only Son of God (John 3:17–18).

*'We shall all stand before the judgment seat of God', and it seems from the Bible that His judgment of us will be in two stages. First, God will judge us according to what we have done about Jesus Christ – whether we have believed in Him and responded to His call, or whether we have refused Him a place in our lives. Then, if we have believed in Christ and received Him, God will want to know how we have spent our lives. God examines our thoughts, words and deeds, as well as the way in which we have used our time and our talents. How splendid if He can say to us, 'Well done, good and faithful servant . . . enter into the joy of your Lord!'*

**Teach me to live, Lord, that I may rise glorious at that last great day. Amen.**

### Be glad in the Lord, and rejoice. (Psalm 32:11)

Blessed is the one whose transgression is forgiven, whose sin is covered. Blessed is the man against whom the Lord counts no iniquity, and in whose spirit there is no deceit . . . I acknowledged my sin to you, and I did not cover my iniquity; I said, "I will confess my transgressions to the Lord," and you forgave the iniquity of my sin . . . You are a hiding place for me; you preserve me from trouble; you surround me with shouts of deliverance. I will instruct you and teach you in the way you should go; I will counsel you with my eye upon you . . . Many are the sorrows of the wicked, but steadfast love surrounds the one who trusts in the Lord. Be glad in the Lord, and rejoice, O righteous, and shout for joy, all you upright in heart! (Psalm 32:1–2, 5, 7–8, 10–11)

*The word 'blessed' means 'highly favoured', and therefore 'happy', and it is interesting to note that the secret of true happiness is not great wealth, promotion or success, but the forgiveness of our sins. A clear conscience before God and others is a most priceless possession. Notice, too, that God promises to do two things for His people. First, He will hide them. During the World War II bombing of London everyone knew where the nearest air-raid shelter was and would go there in time of trouble. God is our shelter when we are bombarded by temptation, sorrow or suffering. Secondly, God will guide His people. Life is full of perplexing turnings at which, left to ourselves, we could easily lose the way. With God as our guide, we have no excuse for going astray.*

**Keep me, O Lord, as the apple of Your eye, hide me under the shadow of Your wings. Amen.**

### Keep your heart with all vigilance, for from it flow the springs of life. (Proverbs 4:23)

The heart is deceitful above all things, and desperately sick; who can understand it? "I the Lord search the heart and test the mind" (Jeremiah 17:9–10). "For from within, out of the heart of man, come evil thoughts, sexual immorality, theft, murder, adultery" (Mark 7:21). I groan because of the tumult of my heart (Psalm 38:8). A broken and contrite heart, O God, you will not despise (Psalm 51:17). My son, give me your heart (Proverbs 23:26). That Christ may dwell in your hearts through faith (Ephesians 3:17). Let us draw near with a true heart in full assurance of faith, with our hearts sprinkled clean from an evil conscience (Hebrews 10:22). "You shall love the Lord your God with all your heart" (Matthew 22:37). "My servant David, who kept my commandments and followed me with all his heart, doing only that which was right in my eyes" (1 Kings 14:8).

*The word 'heart', when used in the Bible, does not of course refer to the physical organ which pumps the blood round our bodies. Rather, it refers to that inner, central self. It has been well described as 'the parliament' of a person's life, for it is there that his or her wishes are expressed and decisions made. In its natural state the heart is diseased, and there is only one 'heart specialist' who can deal with it – Jesus Christ. He invites us to put our heart into His hands so He can cleanse it from sin, occupy it as its leader and guide, and inspire it with a love for Himself and a desire to follow Him and to walk in His ways.*

Lord, may the government of my life be upon Your shoulder, and from now on may I consult Your wishes and obey Your commands so that Your will may be done. Amen.

### A dwelling place for God by the Spirit.
### (Ephesians 2:22)

Let each one take care how he builds upon it. For no one can lay a foundation other than that which is laid, which is Jesus Christ. Now if anyone builds on the foundation with gold, silver, precious stones, wood, hay, straw – each one's work will become manifest, for the Day will disclose it, because it will be revealed by fire, and the fire will test what sort of work each one has done. If the work that anyone has built on the foundation survives, he will receive a reward. If anyone's work is burned up, he will suffer loss, though he himself will be saved, but only as through fire. Do you not know that you are God's temple and that God's Spirit dwells in you? If anyone destroys God's temple, God will destroy him. For God's temple is holy, and you are that temple (1 Corinthians 3:10–17).

*This passage compares the Christian to a building and suggests three important questions. First,* is the foundation sound? *Some of the foundations which people choose, such as money, pleasure and ambition, will crumble when the real test comes. There is only one foundation which has been proved completely solid and trustworthy – namely, Jesus Christ. Second,* what materials are used? *Having started in the right way, it is important that we should continue to build with the best materials. The gold, silver and fine stones stand for those things which please God, in contrast to the wood, hay and straw, which represent the trivial and temporary concerns of this life. As Paul says elsewhere, 'Can it be that you are so stupid? You started with the spiritual; do you now look to the material to make you perfect?' (Galatians 3:3) Third,* what is the building for? *It is a dwelling place, a temple, for God through His Spirit.*

**Lord, make our hearts Your dwelling place, and more worthy of You. Amen.**

## His Spirit who dwells in you. (Romans 8:11)

"And when he comes, he will convict the world concerning sin and righteousness and judgment: concerning sin, because they do not believe in me; concerning righteousness, because I go to the Father, and you will see me no longer; concerning judgment, because the ruler of this world is judged" (John 16:8–11). "And I will ask the Father, and he will give you another Helper, to be with you forever" (John 14:16). "He will teach you all things and bring to your remembrance all that I have said to you" (John 14:26). "He will guide you into all the truth, for he will not speak on his own authority, but whatever he hears he will speak, and he will declare to you the things that are to come. He will glorify me" (John 16:13–14). "He will bear witness about me" (John 15:26).

*The Holy Spirit is at work in the world in at least four different ways. First, the Spirit works as a* prosecutor. *It is the Spirit who convicts the world of sin, bringing home to a person's mind and heart and conscience that he or she needs Christ as Saviour. The Spirit is also a* helper. *The word literally means 'one who is called alongside to help'. He does not just come to soothe and comfort, but to stimulate Christians into greater activity. (In the Bayeux Tapestry, William of Normandy is prodding one of his soldiers in the backside with a sword, and beneath are the words 'William comforteth one of his soldiers'). The Spirit acts as* instructor *in helping us to understand the truths of the Bible, shining on the printed word just as the sun shines upon a sundial, giving it meaning and sense. In His role as* ambassador, *the Spirit represents Jesus in the heart of the Christian believer, bearing witness to the Saviour's majesty and giving Him the glory and credit.*

**Lord, may Your Spirit be free to work in my heart, my mind, my conscience and my will. Amen.**

## Fight the good fight of the faith. (1 Timothy 6:12)

Put on the whole armour of God, that you may be able to stand against the schemes of the devil. For we do not wrestle against flesh and blood, but against . . . spiritual forces of evil . . . all circumstances take up the shield of faith, with which you can extinguish all the flaming darts of the evil one; and take the helmet of salvation, and the sword of the Spirit, which is the word of God (Ephesians 6:11–12, 16–17). Share in suffering as a good soldier of Christ Jesus. No soldier gets entangled in civilian pursuits, since his aim is to please the one who enlisted him (2 Timothy 2:3–4). Wage the good warfare, holding faith and a good conscience (1 Timothy 1:18–19). I have fought the good fight (2 Timothy 4:7). Be sober-minded; be watchful. Your adversary the devil prowls around like a roaring lion, seeking someone to devour (1 Peter 5:8).

*When we become Christians, we enlist in the army of Christ and the big question is, 'How can I be a good soldier?' There are at least three answers to this. First, the Christian soldier is* on parade. *The Christian life will bear close inspection and always 'satisfy the one who has enlisted him'. The Christian soldier is also* in action. *The Christian life is not just a battle, it is a war that will last until finally we take 'the leave that knows no ending'. We must be trained, through Bible reading, prayer and Christian friendship, if we are to withstand the forces of evil in the world. We must 'put on the whole armour of God', especially the shield and the sword. Finally, we must be* on guard. *There will be long periods when we don't feel particularly harassed or tempted, but we must be watchful and on our guard, lest Satan attacks us unawares.*

**Lord, please help me to fight the good fight with all my might. Amen.**

## Blessed is he who trusts in the Lord.
## (Proverbs 16:20)

Blessed is he whose help is the God of Jacob, whose hope is in the Lord his God, who made heaven and earth, the sea, and all that is in them, who keeps faith forever (Psalm 146:5–6). Blessed are the people whose God is the Lord! (Psalm 144:15) Blessed is the one who finds wisdom, and the one who gets understanding (Proverbs 3:13). Blessed is he who is generous to the poor (Proverbs 14:21). Blessed is he who keeps the law (Proverbs 29:18). "Blessed is the one whom God reproves; therefore despise not the discipline of the Almighty" (Job 5:17). Blessed is the man who remains steadfast under trial, for when he has stood the test he will receive the crown of life, which God has promised to those who love him (James 1:12). If you are insulted for the name of Christ, you are blessed, because the Spirit of glory and of God rests upon you (1 Peter 4:14). Behold, we consider those blessed who remained steadfast (James 5:11).

*'The world is so full of a number of things, that I am sure we should all be as happy as kings.' Robert Louis Stevenson was right. Just think of all the things God has provided for our happiness! In spite of all we have done to spoil it, we live in a marvellous world and enjoy our homes, friends, leisure activities, sport and so on. But I sometimes think these things are like sugar cakes compared with the deeply satisfying 'bread of life', which is the knowledge of Christ. It is trusting Him, trying to do His will in the world and fighting His battles which give us really deep happiness (or blessedness) – the joy which Jesus said no one could take from us.*

**Grant, O Lord, that 'among the sundry and manifold changes of the world, our hearts may surely there be fixed where true joys are to be found, through Jesus Christ our Lord'. Amen.**

## You have been born again. (1 Peter 1:23)

A man . . . named Nicodemus . . . came to Jesus by night and said to him, "Rabbi, we know that you are a teacher come from God, for no one can do these signs that you do unless God is with him." Jesus answered him, "Truly, truly, I say to you, unless one is born again he cannot see the kingdom of God." Nicodemus said to him, "How can a man be born when he is old? Can he enter a second time into his mother's womb and be born?" Jesus answered, "Truly, truly, I say to you, unless one is born of water and the Spirit, he cannot enter the kingdom of God. That which is born of the flesh is flesh, and that which is born of the Spirit is spirit. Do not marvel that I said to you, 'You must be born again.' The wind blows where it wishes, and you hear its sound, but you do not know where it comes from or where it goes. So it is with everyone who is born of the Spirit" (John 3:1–8).

*In this passage Jesus teaches us that a Christian is not just someone who is a little more religious than the person next door, someone who has 'turned over a new leaf'. Rather, a Christian is someone who has been 'born again' and begun a new life. This mysterious and marvellous miracle takes place in those who receive Christ as their Saviour and Friend (John 1:12). They become new people, with a new nature, new desires, new prospects and a completely new outlook on life. To borrow an illustration from science, what takes place is not just a physical change (water into steam), which is reversible, but a chemical change (when a new substances is born), which cannot be reversed.*

**Lord, help me to understand what it means to be a true Christian. Amen.**

## "If anyone serves me, he must follow me." (John 12:26)

While walking by the Sea of Galilee, he saw two brothers, Simon (who is called Peter) and Andrew his brother, casting a net into the sea, for they were fishermen. And he said to them, "Follow me . . ." Immediately they left their nets and followed him. And going on . . . James . . . and John his brother, in the boat . . . mending their nets, and he called them. Immediately they left the boat . . . and followed him (Matthew 4:18–22). Jesus . . . saw a man called Matthew sitting at the tax booth, and he said to him, "Follow me." And he rose and followed him (Matthew 9:9). "My servant Caleb . . . has followed me fully" (Numbers 14:24). "My servant David . . . followed me with all his heart" (1 Kings 14:8). And Peter was following him at a distance (Matthew 26:58). And a scribe came up and said to him, "Teacher, I will follow you wherever you go." And Jesus said to him, "Foxes have holes, and birds of the air have nests, but the Son of Man has nowhere to lay his head" (Matthew 8:19–20).

*Perhaps you are a follower of a particular cricket or football team, or a political party. If so, you give that team or party your close attention, loyalty and support. That is what Jesus expects of all those who, like the early disciples, have responded to his call, 'Follow me'. What does it mean in practice? We follow with our eyes, making Him our daily example and, whenever in doubt, saying to ourselves, 'What would Jesus do?' We follow with our ears, alive and quick to hear each whisper of His word as He speaks to us through the Bible or our own conscience. This means keeping close – and not making Peter's sad mistake of following from a distance.*

'Jesus, grant that we may follow in the path Your steps have trod; may Your kindness and Your patience be our pattern, Son of God.' Amen.

**That you may know that you have eternal life.
(1 John 5:13)**

"If anyone hears my voice and opens the door, I will come in to him" (Revelation 3:20). "Whoever comes to me I will never cast out" (John 6:37). "I give them eternal life, and they will never perish, and no one will snatch them out of my hand" (John 10:28). Therefore, if anyone is in Christ, he is a new creation. The old has passed away; behold, the new has come (2 Corinthians 5:17). "Instead of the thorn shall come up the cypress; instead of the brier shall come up the myrtle; and it shall make a name for the Lord, an everlasting sign that shall not be cut off" (Isaiah 55:13). Whoever believes in the Son of God has the testimony in himself (1 John 5:10). The Spirit himself bears witness with our spirit that we are children of God (Romans 8:16).

*Uncertainty is a horrid thing. Waiting for the result of an exam or an operation, for example, is a nerve-wracking experience. But many people live in a sort of spiritual twilight. They say, 'I have asked Jesus Christ into my heart, and committed my life to Him, but how can I be sure that He has come and has accepted me?' First, we must hold on to His promises to come in if we ask Him and never to leave us. These promises are like a birth certificate, proving that we really belong to Him. Secondly, we begin to experience the difference He can make: a new desire to conquer temptation, a new love for the Bible – flowers instead of thorns. Thirdly, as time goes on, his Holy Spirit will bring the inner certainty that we are His and He is ours for ever.*

**Help me, O Lord, to trust Your promises, and then to prove in my daily experience that You are my Saviour and Friend. Amen.**

## Children of God without blemish.
## (Philippians 2:15)

O Lord, who shall sojourn in your tent? Who shall dwell on your holy hill? He who walks blamelessly and does what is right and speaks truth in his heart; who does not slander with his tongue and does no evil to his neighbour, nor takes up a reproach against his friend; in whose eyes a vile person is despised, but who honours those who fear the Lord; who swears to his own hurt and does not change; who does not put out his money at interest and does not take a bribe against the innocent. He who does these things shall never be moved (Psalm 15).

*It has been said that this psalm describes the perfect Christian gentleman – that is, the kind of person the Lord would enjoy having to live with Him on His holy hill, and who would feel at home in His presence. You may recognize him (or her) in three ways. The first way is by the* talk he enjoys. *He hates lies and gossip and will not fight for his rights or make rash promises which he cannot keep, thus letting people down. The second way to recognize this person is by the* people he admires. *You can often tell a lot about a person by the company he keeps, and the Christian is always happiest with those who, like him, fear and love the Lord. The third characteristic this Christian will exhibit has to do with the* money he gets. *He won't stoop to dishonest methods of making money such as bribes, and he will even make money available to those in need without expecting interest. What a high standard!*

**Lord, help me each day to walk blamelessly, so that even those who may want to find fault with my life will be unable to do so. Amen.**

### "Let not the rich man boast in his riches."
### (Jeremiah 9:23)

As for the rich in this present age, charge them not to be haughty, nor to set their hopes on the uncertainty of riches, but on God, who richly provides us with everything to enjoy. They are to do good, to be rich in good works, to be generous and ready to share (1 Timothy 6:17–18). Do not toil to acquire wealth; be discerning enough to desist. When your eyes light on it, it is gone, for suddenly it sprouts wings, flying like an eagle toward heaven (Proverbs 23:4–5). But those who desire to be rich fall into temptation, into a snare . . . For the love of money is a root of all kinds of evils. It is through this craving that some have wandered away from the faith and pierced themselves with many pangs (1 Timothy 6:9–10). If riches increase, set not your heart on them (Psalm 62:10). And Jesus looked around and said to his disciples, "How difficult it will be for those who have wealth to enter the kingdom of God" (Mark 10:23)!

*There is nothing wrong with money, and nowhere in the Bible is a man criticized simply for being rich. Wealth, like nuclear power, is a neutral thing, and in the right hands it can be used to do an enormous amount of good. Many rich people have used their money in the wisest and most generous ways. The trouble starts when we being to crave it. First, this is foolish because nothing is more uncertain than riches, and fortunes have been lost overnight. Secondly, it is fatal. The desire for money can make people haughty and proud. It can lead people into debt and into serious forms of dishonesty. Saddest of all, perhaps, it can twine itself round our hearts like ivy and become such an obsession that it starves and chokes our Christian faith.*

Lord, in times of poverty make me perfectly content, and in times of wealth make me generous and liberal. Amen.

## We are members one of another. (Ephesians 4:25)

"This is my commandment, that you love one another as I have loved you" (John 15:12). "By this all people will know that you are my disciples, if you have love for one another" (John13:35). Bear one another's burdens, and so fulfil the law of Christ (Galatians 6:2). We who are strong have an obligation to bear with the failings of the weak, and not to please ourselves. Let each of us please his neighbour for his good, to build him up. For Christ did not please himself (Romans 15:1–3). And let us consider how to stir up one another to love and good works, not neglecting to meet together, as is the habit of some, but encouraging one another (Hebrews 10:24–25). Pray for one another (James 5:16). Be kind to one another, tenderhearted, forgiving one another, as God in Christ forgave you (Ephesians 4:32).

*You sometimes meet a very fine sportsman who is a very bad team player because he always plays for himself and never tries to work with others. The Christian must beware of that danger. As individuals, of course, we must be blameless, but we are also members of a team – the Christian church. Others will look to us eagerly for sympathy, support and prayers, and discovering how much we owe to the stimulating encouragement of fellow Christians will keep us humble. Try not to go it alone as a Christian, but link up with others in your place of work or education and find mutual benefit in your fellowship with each other.*

**Lord, I thank You for the help that other Christians are to me, and I ask that they may find great encouragement in my friendship. Amen.**

**Come, let us walk in the light of the Lord.
(Isaiah 2:5)**

This is the message we have heard from him and proclaim to
you, that God is light, and in him is no darkness at all. If we
say we have fellowship with him while we walk in darkness,
we lie and do not practice the truth. But if we walk in the light,
as he is in the light, we have fellowship with one another, and
the blood of Jesus his Son cleanses us from all sin. If we say we
have no sin, we deceive ourselves, and the truth is not in us. If
we confess our sins, he is faithful and just to forgive us our
sins and to cleanse us from all unrighteousness (1 John 1:5–9).

*It often happened that one side of the street on which I used to live
was in dark shadow while the other was in bright sunshine – and so
I could choose which side to take. If a friend wanted to walk on the
sunny side, and I insisted on the shady side, then obviously there
could be no fellowship or conversation between us. So it is that if we
call ourselves friends of Jesus, and deliberately take the path opposite
to Him, it makes a mockery of that friendship. We must be careful to
'walk in the light' – that is to say, always to do those things which
we know will please Him. Then we will enjoy true fellowship with
Him and even if at times we do stumble or stray, He has promised to
help and we can be sure of His forgiveness.*

**Lord, when I stumble or slip, please restore me; and if I am
tempted to walk in darkness, restrain me. Amen.**

## Unstained from the world. (James 1:27)

Do you not know that friendship with the world is enmity with God? Therefore whoever wishes to be a friend of the world makes himself an enemy of God (James 4:4). Do not love the world or the things in the world. If anyone loves the world, the love of the Father is not in him. For all that is in the world – the desires of the flesh and the desires of the eyes and pride in possessions – is not from the Father but is from the world. And the world is passing away along with its desires, but whoever does the will of God abides forever (1 John 2:15–17). Do not be conformed to this world, but be transformed by the renewal of your mind (Romans 12:2). If then you have been raised with Christ, seek the things that are above, where Christ is, seated at the right hand of God. Set your minds on things that are above, not on things that are on earth (Colossians 3:1–2).

*The Bible uses the word 'world' in three ways. It describes the created universe (Hebrews 1:2); the people in it – that is, humankind in general (John 3:16); and, as in the verses we read today, it also describes society, which has no place for God in its thinking and is ruled by Satan, 'the prince of this world'. The hallmarks of the world in this sense are its materialism and its transience. It is chiefly and almost entirely concerned with fleeting pleasures like money, excitement and sex. Every Christian has to spend much time in the world, but we must take care not to be contaminated or polluted by it. A nurse must live in the midst of sickness, but she must not succumb to it. A ship must be in the water, but the water must not get into the ship. We can't help being in the world, but we must not allow it to mould us into its pattern.*

**I ask, O Lord, not to be taken out of the world, but to be kept from its evil influences. Amen.**

## "Will God indeed dwell on the earth?"
## (1 Kings 8:27)

"Behold, the virgin shall conceive and bear a son, and they shall call his name Immanuel" (Matthew 1:23). "Therefore the child to be born will be called holy – the Son of God" (Luke 1:35). And the Word became flesh and dwelt among us, and we have seen his glory, glory as of the only Son from the Father (John 1:14). And behold, a voice from heaven said, "This is my beloved Son" (Matthew 3:17). Jesus said to them, "But who do you say that I am?" Simon Peter replied, "You are the Christ, the Son of the living God" (Matthew 16:15–16). Thomas answered him, "My Lord and my God!" (John 20:28) His Son . . . was declared to be the Son of God in power . . . by his resurrection from the dead, Jesus Christ our Lord (Romans 1:3–4). For in him the whole fullness of deity dwells bodily (Colossians 2:9).

*It is a very great mistake to suppose that Jesus was just a very good man who was promoted, so to speak, to be Son of God much in the same way as a person may be promoted to the House of Lords for services to the country. Jesus was God Himself. He came into this world to reveal Himself to us in space and time, and in terms which we could understand. He was like a playwright, coming on to the stage to take the part of one of his characters, or like the rainbow which breaks up the unapproachable light of the sun into the colours of the spectrum which we can see and enjoy. That was what Jesus meant when He said 'Whoever has seen me has seen the Father' (John 14:9).*

**Lord Jesus, I honour and worship and adore You as the Son of God most high. Amen.**

**Wait for the Lord; be strong, and let your heart take courage; wait for the Lord! (Psalm 27:14)**

To whom then will you compare me, that I should be like him? says the Holy One. Lift up your eyes on high and see: who created these? He who brings out their host by number, calling them all by name, by the greatness of his might, and because he is strong in power not one is missing . . . Have you not known? Have you not heard? The Lord is the everlasting God, the Creator of the ends of the earth. He does not faint or grow weary; his understanding is unsearchable. He gives power to the faint, and to him who has no might he increases strength. Even youths shall faint and be weary, and young men shall fall exhausted; but they who wait for the Lord shall renew their strength; they shall mount up with wings like eagles; they shall run and not be weary; they shall walk and not faint (Isaiah 40:25–26, 28–31).

*This lovely passage reminds us that the power of God, which created and now sustains the universe, is also available to individual people like us. And don't we need Him badly? Again and again when faced with some temptation or difficult task we realize that we have 'no power of ourselves to help ourselves'. Even the young, with all their energy and enthusiasm, cannot cope. But how does this power come to us? It comes simply by 'waiting upon the Lord'. As we spend time with Him in prayer, Bible reading and thought, our spiritual batteries are recharged. We can then surmount our problems and meet the daily challenges of life with fresh confidence and zeal.*

**Lord, save me from being so busy or hurried that I have no time to wait upon You. Amen.**

## Have faith in God. (Mark 11:22)

For by grace you have been saved through faith (Ephesians 2:8). Therefore, since we have been justified by faith, we have peace with God through our Lord Jesus Christ (Romans 5:1). And this is the victory that has overcome the world – our faith (1 John 5:4). Who by God's power are being guarded through faith for a salvation ready to be revealed in the last time (1 Peter 1:5). Then the disciples came to Jesus privately and said, "Why could we not cast it out?" He said to them, "Because of your little faith. For truly, I say to you, if you have faith like a grain of mustard seed, you will say to this mountain, 'Move from here to there,' and it will move" (Matthew 17:19–20). The apostles said to the Lord, "Increase our faith!" (Luke 17:5). So faith comes from hearing, and hearing through the word of Christ (Romans 10:17).

*Do you know what a 'master key' is? It will unlock every room in a building, even though each individual lock is different. Faith is like a master key. It is the key to our salvation, for those who believe in Christ find forgiveness and life. It is the key to victory, for as we trust Him He will give us the power we need to overcome our temptations. It is the key for coping with the mountains of difficulties, disappointment, suffering or sorrow that we face from time to time. But how do we get faith? In the same way as we get faith in a doctor, or lawyer, or coach or teacher. We hear about Him – what He has done for others and what He promises to do for us. Hearing will lead to trusting, and trusting will lead to personal experience.*

**Lord, in the time of temptation, in the hour of difficulty, in the day of sorrow, help me to have complete faith in You. Amen.**

## Christ in you, the hope of glory. (Colossians 1:27)

Jesus answered him, "If anyone loves me, he will keep my word, and my Father will love him, and we will come to him and make our home with him" (John 14:23). "Behold, I stand at the door and knock. If anyone hears my voice and opens the door, I will come in to him and eat with him, and he with me" (Revelation 3:20). That Christ may dwell in your hearts through faith (Ephesians 3:17). It is . . . Christ who lives in me. And the life I now live in the flesh I live by faith in the Son of God, who loved me and gave himself for me (Galatians 2:20). If the Spirit of him who raised Jesus from the dead dwells in you, he who raised Christ Jesus from the dead will also give life to your mortal bodies through his Spirit who dwells in you (Romans 8:11). Little children, you are from God and have overcome them, for he who is in you is greater than he who is in the world (1 John 4:4).

*I suppose all of us have listened to a great pianist, or watched a great gymnast or golfer, and wished that we could reach that standard. We have their example, and perhaps if we are lucky we have their advice, through some book or lesson; but somehow it isn't enough. 'It's no good,' we say, 'I can't do it. It isn't in me.' That is the trouble – 'it isn't in us'. But for the Christian the wonderful thing (our 'hope of glory') is that Jesus offers us much more than His example or His advice, valuable as they are. He offers us His presence, and in the Person of His Holy Spirit He will actually come and live within us, giving us the help we need and working out through us His own great will and purpose.*

**Abide with me, O Lord, for I need Your presence every passing hour. Amen.**

**"And I, when I am lifted up from the earth, will draw all people to myself." (John 12:32)**

The people spoke against God . . . Then the Lord sent fiery serpents . . . and they bit the people, so that many . . . died. And the people came to Moses and said, "We have sinned, for we have spoken against the Lord and against you. Pray to the Lord, that he take away the serpents from us." So Moses prayed for the people. And the Lord said to Moses, "Make a fiery serpent and set it on a pole, and everyone who is bitten, when he sees it, shall live." So Moses made a bronze serpent and set it on a pole. And if a serpent bit anyone, he would look at the bronze serpent and live (Numbers 21:5–9). And as Moses lifted up the serpent in the wilderness, so must the Son of Man be lifted up, that whoever believes in him may have eternal life (John 3:14–15).

*Like so many incidents in the Old Testament, this one illustrates a New Testament truth. Just as the Israelites were cured by looking at the bronze serpent, so by looking in faith to Jesus bearing our sins (even, as Paul says, 'made sin for us') on the cross we find forgiveness and life. In the National Gallery there is a painting by Rubens that depicts this scene. Moses is shown standing before the bronze serpent, pointing to it with one hand and, with the other hand, beckoning for people to look. Once we ourselves have been cleansed from sin, that becomes our privilege and duty – to point to Jesus as the Saviour of the world, and to beckon others to come and look and live.*

**Lord, I thank You for the wonderful cure You made possible for me on the cross. Please help me in my turn to beckon to others and point them to You. Amen.**

## And Mary said, "Behold, I am the servant of the Lord." (Luke 1:38)

And the angel answered Mary, "The Holy Spirit will come upon you, and the power of the Most High will overshadow you; therefore the child to be born will be called holy – the Son of God" (Luke 1:35). And Mary said, "My soul magnifies the Lord, and my spirit rejoices in God my Saviour, for He has looked on the humble estate of his servant. For behold, from now on all generations will call me blessed; for He who is mighty has done great things for me, and holy is his name (Luke 1:46–49)". And Simeon blessed them and said to Mary . . . "Behold, this child is appointed for the fall and rising of many in Israel, and for a sign that is opposed (and a sword will pierce through your own soul also)" (Luke 2:34–35).

*Never, before or since, has God used anyone for such a wonderfully privileged task as that of bringing His Son, our Lord and Saviour Jesus Christ, into this world. It is worth asking ourselves what qualified Mary for this great responsibility. She had faith, to believe that the promise made to her would be fulfilled. She needed courage, because there were going to be times of doubt, misunderstanding and in the end bitter anguish. But perhaps above all she possessed humility. Because she was low, God could lift her; because she was empty, He could fill her; because she was humble, God could use her. It is tempting sometimes to think that God uses us because of our gifts; but I think more often than not He has to use us in spite of them.*

**Lord, give me faith, courage and especially humility for the things You want me to do for You today. Amen.**

### "You are the salt of the earth." (Matthew 5:13)

"Blessed are the poor in spirit, for theirs is the kingdom of heaven. Blessed are those who mourn, for they shall be comforted. Blessed are the meek, for they shall inherit the earth. Blessed are those who hunger and thirst for righteousness, for they shall be satisfied. Blessed are the merciful, for they shall receive mercy. Blessed are the pure in heart, for they shall see God. Blessed are the peacemakers, for they shall be called sons of God. Blessed are those who are persecuted for righteousness' sake, for theirs is the kingdom of heaven. Blessed are you when others revile you and persecute you and utter all kinds of evil against you falsely on my account. Rejoice and be glad, for your reward is great in heaven" (Matthew 5:3–12).

*Sometimes we describe a person as 'the salt of the earth', meaning his or her influence is wholly for good, and today we read of such people in detail. Like salt, they give flavour to society, they prevent further corruption, and they even make others thirst for the kingdom of God. But what strange people they are! They are not the 'getters', but the 'givers'; not the 'climbers', but the 'stoopers'; not the 'masters', but the 'servants'. 'All the land you can see is mine', said a wealthy landowner, waving his hand towards magnificent scenery. 'Yes', replied his companion, 'but the landscape is mine.' That is what Paul meant when he said, 'Having nothing, and yet possessing all things' and what Jesus meant when He said that by losing our lives we find them. So true happiness comes to the humble, the gentle, the contented, the non-aggressive. In the long run they are not the 'losers' but the 'winners'.*

**Help me to remember, O Lord, that it is better to give than to get, better to stoop than to climb, better to serve than to be served. Amen.**

## "Love your enemies." (Matthew 5:44)

"You have heard that it was said, 'You shall love your neighbour and hate your enemy.' But I say to you, Love your enemies and pray for those who persecute you" (Matthew 5:43–44). Do not rejoice when your enemy falls, and let not your heart be glad when he stumbles (Proverbs 24:17). "If you meet your enemy's ox or his donkey going astray, you shall bring it back to him" (Exodus 23:4). If your enemy is hungry, feed him; if he is thirsty, give him something to drink . . . Do not be overcome by evil, but overcome evil with good (Romans 12:20–21). And Jesus said, "Father, forgive them, for they know not what they do." (Luke 23:34). And as they were stoning Stephen . . . he cried out with a loud voice, "Lord, do not hold this sin against them" (Acts 7:59–60). At my first defence no one came to stand by me [Paul], but all deserted me. May it not be charged against them! (2 Timothy 4:16)

*I suppose all of us have enemies of some sort or another – people who we feel are out to 'do us down' or 'get the better of us'. The easy thing to do, and the thing that comes naturally to us, is to try somehow to 'get our own back', to 'level the score'. But that is not the Christian way. Jesus taught us to pray for such people, and when we get the chance to do them a good turn. This may melt them, and change their attitude towards us, and it will almost certainly help us to see them in a new light. To pray for our enemies and do good to them is the quickest and best way of helping us to regard them in future no longer as enemies, but as friends.*

**Lord, give me the chance today of doing good for someone I find hard to like. Amen.**

## For you were called to freedom (Galatians 5:13)

"The Spirit of the Lord is upon me, because he has anointed me to proclaim good news to the poor. He has sent me to proclaim liberty to the captives and recovering of sight to the blind, to set at liberty those who are oppressed" (Luke 4:18). "You will know the truth, and the truth will set you free." They answered him, "We . . . have never been enslaved to anyone. How is it that you say, 'You will become free'?" Jesus answered them, "Truly, truly, I say to you, everyone who commits sin is a slave to sin. So if the Son sets you free, you will be free indeed" (John 8:32–34, 36). But thanks be to God, that you who were once slaves of sin have become obedient from the heart to the standard of teaching to which you were committed, and, having been set free from sin, have become slaves of righteousness (Romans 6:17–18). For freedom Christ has set us free; stand firm therefore, and do not submit again to a yoke of slavery (Galatians 5:1).

*'Man is born free and everywhere he is in chains.' So said the eighteenth-century French philosopher Rousseau, and in a sense he was right. For at that time millions were born into the world only to become slaves – either literally or to things like poverty and disease. Socially this may have been true but spiritually, of course, it is the exact opposite of the truth. Human beings are born with a built-in bias, like a bowls ball, towards sin. We are born in prison, and the great purpose of Christ's coming was to offer us freedom from the guilt and power of sin. Freedom from sin, but freedom for – what? Not just a self-pleasing life, but a life devoted to the cause of Jesus Christ, 'whose service is perfect freedom'.*

**Lord, I thank You for the liberty Your death on the cross made possible for me. Help me to use it to serve You with all my heart. Amen.**

## "I have loved you with an everlasting love." (Jeremiah 31:3)

And we know that for those who love God all things work together for good, for those who are called according to his purpose. What then shall we say to these things? If God is for us, who can be against us? He who did not spare his own Son but gave him up for us all, how will he not also with him graciously give us all things? Who shall separate us from the love of Christ? Shall tribulation, or distress, or persecution, or famine, or nakedness, or danger, or sword? No, in all these things we are more than conquerors through him who loved us. For I am sure that neither death nor life, nor angels nor rulers, nor things present nor things to come, nor powers, nor height nor depth, nor anything else in all creation, will be able to separate us from the love of God in Christ Jesus our Lord (Romans 8:28, 31–32, 35, 37–39).

*A famous bishop of Durham once had to preach in a village where there had been a terrible mining disaster. He could not think what to say, but as he went into the pulpit there fluttered from his Bible a text worked on a card in wool or silk by his small daughter. He picked it up, and then the inspiration came. He held it to the congregation back to front, and all they saw was a tangled mass of wool, matching their own feelings of horror and anguish at what had happened. Then he turned it around, and in strong, clear letters they read the words, 'God is love'. That is what Paul is saying here, for even trouble, sorrow and suffering can be among the 'all things' that the loving purpose of God is able to work together for our good.*

**Although the path is sometimes dark and hard to understand, Lord, give me faith through joy or pain to trace Your loving hand. Amen.**

### But by the grace of God I am what I am.
### (1 Corinthians 15:10)

For the grace of God has appeared, bringing salvation for all people (Titus 2:11). For by grace you have been saved through faith. And this is not your own doing; it is the gift of God (Ephesians 2:8). In him we have redemption through his blood, the forgiveness of our trespasses, according to the riches of his grace, which he lavished upon us (Ephesians 1:7–8). And are justified by his grace as a gift (Romans 3:24). And God is able to make all grace abound to you, so that having all sufficiency in all things at all times, you may abound in every good work (2 Corinthians 9:8). But he said to me, "My grace is sufficient for you, for my power is made perfect in weakness" (2 Corinthians 12:9). And his grace toward me was not in vain. On the contrary, I worked harder than any of them, though it was not I, but the grace of God that is with me (1 Corinthians 15:10).

*The word 'grace' is one of the most important in the New Testament. It means God's favour freely bestowed upon those who have done nothing to deserve it. It is what we might call a 'one-way word'. That is, it can only flow downwards. The Queen can be gracious to me, but I can't be gracious to her. I can be respectful and courteous, but grace can only move in once direction – from high to low, from plenty to poverty, from rich to poor. God shows His grace to us chiefly in sending Jesus to die for us upon the cross and bring us salvation. He shows further grace in giving us the strength and help which we need every moment of our lives so we can be useful and effective Christians.*

**Lord, help me to grow in grace by experiencing Your power to direct and control my life more and more each day. Amen.**

## "How the mighty have fallen!" (2 Samuel 1:19)

Kish . . . had a son whose name was Saul, a handsome young man. There was not a man among the people of Israel more handsome than he. From his shoulders upward he was taller than any of the people (1 Samuel 9:1–2). When Samuel saw Saul, the Lord told him, "Here is the man of whom I spoke to you! He it is who shall restrain my people" (1 Samuel 9:17). Then Samuel . . . said . . . "The Spirit of the Lord will rush upon you, and you will . . . be turned into another man" (1 Samuel 10:1, 6). Saul . . . reigned . . . over Israel (1 Samuel 13:1). Then Samuel said to Saul, "Stop! I will tell you what the Lord said to me . . . ." And Samuel said, "Though you are little in your own eyes, are you not the head of the tribes of Israel? The Lord anointed you king over Israel. Why then did you not obey the voice of the Lord?" (1 Samuel 15:16–19) Then Saul said, "I have sinned . . . I have acted foolishly, and have made a great mistake" (1 Samuel 26:21). Saul was afraid of David because the Lord was with him but had departed from Saul (1 Samuel 18:12).

*The dictionary defines a tragedy as a 'Drama with an unhappy ending', and perhaps the word applies to no one in the Bible more suitably than to King Saul, whose 'decline and fall' is outlined in today's reading. At the start he showed great promise and appeared to be every inch a king – not only physically, but spiritually as well. Then the trouble started and, if we could read the whole story, we would find the slippery downward steps he took – pride, arrogance, disobedience. How carefully we need to watch these dangers when we find ourselves in any position of authority! And it is worth reading the advice given about kings in Deuteronomy 17:14–20. Do you remember a much happier epitaph that another 'Saul' wrote for himself? Look up 2 Timothy 4:7.*

**Keep me humble, Lord, if I am promoted, and if power is put in my hands may I use it wisely and well. Amen.**

**And he appointed twelve . . . that they might be with him. (Mark 3:14)**

"Whoever does not bear his own cross and come after me cannot be my disciple" (Luke 14:27). Joseph of Arimathea . . . a disciple of Jesus, but secretly for fear of the Jews (John 19:38). "For whoever is ashamed of me and of my words, of him will the Son of Man be ashamed when he comes in his glory and the glory of the Father and of the holy angels" (Luke 9:26). So Jesus said to the Jews who had believed in him, "If you abide in my word, you are truly my disciples" (John 8:31). When Barnabas came and saw the grace of God, he was glad, and he exhorted them all to remain faithful to the Lord with steadfast purpose (Acts 11:23). "By this all people will know that you are my disciples, if you have love for one another" (John 13:35). Beloved, if God so loved us, we also ought to love one another (1 John 4:11). "By this my Father is glorified, that you bear much fruit and so prove to be my disciples" (John 15:8). "You will recognize them by their fruits" (Matthew 7:16).

*A disciple was like an apprentice. He worked alongside his master, learning from him by watching him and asking him questions. Jesus trained twelve men for this purpose 'so that they might be with him, and he might send them out' (Mark 3:14). Just as silver has certain hallmarks which show it to be genuine, so there are certain ways in which you can recognize a true disciple – the real thing – just as the fruit it bears will show you what sort of tree you have in your garden. What, then, are the hallmarks of a genuine disciple? There are three, and we see them in today's reading. A true disciple takes a fearless stand for Christ, continues faithfully with Him and maintains friendly relationships with other Christians.*

**Lord, make me a true disciple of Yours – not in word only, but in the way I live for You and witness to others. Amen.**

## "I am the good shepherd." (John 10:14)

"The sheep hear his voice, and he calls his own sheep by name and leads them out. When he has brought out all his own, he goes before them, and the sheep follow him, for they know his voice. A stranger they will not follow, but they will flee from him, for they do not know the voice of strangers." So Jesus again said . . . "I am the good shepherd. The good shepherd lays down his life for the sheep. He who is a hired hand and not a shepherd, who does not own the sheep, sees the wolf coming and leaves the sheep and flees, and the wolf snatches them and scatters them. He flees because he is a hired hand and cares nothing for the sheep. I am the good shepherd. I know my own and my own know me, just as the Father knows me and I know the Father; and I lay down my life for the sheep" (John 10:3–5, 7, 11–15).

*'Sheep without a shepherd', as Jesus once described the people He was trying to help, face a twofold danger – distraction and destruction. Satan either acts like a thief, trying to entice them from the right path, or like a wolf, trying to force them off the path. What a difference the good shepherd makes! He knows us through and through – our needs, troubles and problems. He cares so deeply that He was prepared to sacrifice His life for the sake of the sheep. He leads, because He knows the way we should take and will choose the 'green pastures' and 'the paths of righteousness' through which He wants us to travel. Are you able to say 'the Lord is my shepherd'?*

**'Loving Shepherd, ever near, teach me now Your voice to hear, suffer not my steps to stray from the strait and narrow way.' Amen.**

**Thus the Lord used to speak to Moses face to face, as a man speaks to his friend. (Exodus 33:11)**

Now the man Moses was very meek, more than all people who were on the face of the earth (Numbers 12:3). By faith Moses, when he was grown up, refused to be called the son of Pharaoh's daughter, choosing rather to be mistreated with the people of God than to enjoy the fleeting pleasures of sin. He considered the reproach of Christ greater wealth than the treasures of Egypt (Hebrews 11:24–26). Moreover, the man Moses was very great in the land of Egypt, in the sight of Pharaoh's servants and in the sight of the people (Exodus 11:3). By faith he left Egypt, not being afraid of the anger of the king, for he endured as seeing him who is invisible (Hebrews 11:27). And he said, "My presence will go with you, and I will give you rest" (Exodus 33:14).

*Many who aspire to be great in office look to Moses' example and qualities with admiration. Viscount Montgomery described him as the greatest leader of all time and Churchill has a very favourable essay on him in* Thoughts and Adventures. *He was indeed very great. But his greatness was not just due to many fine human qualities like courage, patience and endurance, but also to his faith in God and the knowledge that His promise made at the burning bush stood firm – 'I will be with you.' Moses was also very meek. Greatness and meekness don't always go together, but they did with Moses, as with Jesus Himself. He might have had an easy, comfortable life and might even have become Pharaoh, but he gave it all up to help his people. And small thanks he received! For forty years he had to put up with their ingratitude, obstinacy and even rebellion. Yet he never abandoned them and humbly prepared the way for Joshua his successor.*

**Lord, keep me humble when others praise me and when they abuse me. Amen.**

## "Our Father in heaven." (Matthew 6:9)

But to all who did receive him, who believed in his name, he gave the right to become children of God (John 1:12). "Therefore go out from their midst, and be separate from them, says the Lord, and touch no unclean thing; then I will welcome you, and I will be a Father to you, and you shall be sons and daughters to me, says the Lord Almighty" (2 Corinthians 6:17–18). As a father shows compassion to his children, so the Lord shows compassion to those who fear him (Psalm 103:13). "Therefore do not be anxious, saying, 'What shall we eat?' or 'What shall we drink?' or 'What shall we wear?' For . . . your heavenly Father knows that you need them all" (Matthew 6:31–32). My son, do not regard lightly the discipline of the Lord, nor be weary when reproved by him. For the Lord disciplines the one he loves, and chastises every son whom he receives (Hebrews 12:5–6).

*Not everyone is a child of God or can say 'Our Father in heaven'. That privilege belongs to those who, separating themselves from all that is sinful, have received Jesus Christ as their Saviour and Lord. God sets a pattern for all earthly parents by looking after us in two ways. First,* He protects us. *With loving care He provides for our daily needs. Where we are weak, He strengthens us, and where we are fearful, He encourages us. Second,* He corrects us. *Temptation, disappointment, failure – these are some of the ways in which He often tries to check our faults and even punish us when we have disobeyed Him and turned from His ways.*

**'Our Father in heaven, hallowed be your name. Your kingdom come, your will be done, on earth as it is in heaven' (Matthew 6:9–10). Amen.**

**Behold, I was brought forth in iniquity.**
**(Psalm 51:5)**

The Lord God called to the man and said to him, "Have you eaten of the tree of which I commanded you not to eat?" The man said, "The woman whom you gave to be with me, she gave me fruit of the tree, and I ate" (Genesis 3:9, 11–12). Therefore . . . sin came into the world through one man, and death through sin (Romans 5:12). The Lord saw that the wickedness of man was great in the earth, and that every intention of the thoughts of his heart was only evil continually (Genesis 6:5). "Behold . . . the heavens are not pure in his sight; how much less one who is abominable and corrupt, a man who drinks injustice like water!" (Job 15:15–16) As it is written: "None is righteous, no, not one; no one understands; no one seeks for God. All have turned aside; together they have become worthless; no one does good, not even one . . . There is no fear of God before their eyes" . . . all have sinned and fall short of the glory of God (Romans 3:10–12, 18, 23).

*We are often reminded these days of the danger we face from pollution. The air, soil, rivers and coastal waters are all, to some extent, infected and contaminated. In the same way, there is no part of anyone's life which has not been spoiled by sin, which has crept like some horrible moral oil slick into our actions, thoughts and even our imagination. 'All the perfumes of Arabia will not sweeten this little hand', cried the murderess Lady Macbeth – and there is no detergent which can deal with the problem of human sin. But it was this very problem which Jesus came into the world to solve through His death upon the cross. 'The blood of Jesus Christ, God's Son, cleanses us from all sin.'*

**'Create in me a clean heart, O God; and renew a right spirit within me. Purge me with hyssop, and I shall be clean; wash me, and I shall be whiter than snow.' Amen.**

## Far be it from me to boast except in the cross of our Lord Jesus Christ. (Galatians 6:14)

Christ Jesus . . . humbled himself by becoming obedient to the point of death, even death on a cross (Philippians 2:5, 8). Who for the joy that was set before him endured the cross, despising the shame, and is seated at the right hand of the throne of God (Hebrews 12:2). For Christ did not send me to baptize but to preach the gospel, and not with words of eloquent wisdom, lest the cross of Christ be emptied of its power . . . We preach Christ crucified, a stumbling block to Jews and folly to Gentiles, but to those who are called, both Jews and Greeks, Christ the power of God and the wisdom of God (1 Corinthians 1:17–18, 23–24). For I decided to know nothing among you except Jesus Christ and him crucified (1 Corinthians 2:2).

*Sometimes you see a perfectly ordinary, perhaps even ugly, house bearing a plaque indicating that some famous person lived or died there. Immediately that house is charged with a new importance, a new significance – even a new beauty. So it was with the cross. What turned that terrible instrument of torture into the symbol of the Christian faith, respected all over the world, was the fact that it was on a cross that Jesus suffered death for our salvation. It was there that He bore the burden and the guilt of human sin, to bring us back into relationship with God from whom that sin had separated us. That is why the cross was so central to Paul's preaching. It showed the love of God, the power of God and the wisdom of God.*

**'Forbid it Lord, that I should boast, save in the cross of Christ my God.' Amen.**

## But some doubted. (Matthew 28:17)

When John heard in prison about the deeds of the Christ, he sent word by his disciples and said to him, "Are you the one who is to come, or shall we look for another?" And Jesus answered them, "Go and tell John what you hear and see: the blind receive their sight and the lame walk" (Matthew 11:2–5). Peter got out of the boat and walked on the water and came to Jesus. But when he saw the wind, he was afraid, and beginning to sink he cried out, "Lord, save me." Jesus immediately . . . took hold of him, saying . . . "O you of little faith, why did you doubt?" (Matthew 14:29–31) Thomas said . . . "Unless I see . . . I will never believe" . . . Then Jesus said to Thomas, "Put your finger here, and see my hands; and put out your hand, and place it in my side. Do not disbelieve, but believe" (John 20:25, 27).

*Most Christians have doubts at some time or other. Is Jesus really who He claimed to be? Is He alive in the world today? Is He able to help me with the problems and difficulties I have to face? Can these questions be answered in the affirmative, 'beyond all reasonable doubt'? I find three things help me to overcome doubts. First, there is the record in the Bible of what Jesus taught and did, which we are bound to accept unless we believe that He was a fraud or a lunatic. Then there is the tremendous impact the gospel has had on the world, as well as the growth of the Christian church. Finally, there is what I myself have experienced of His love and power, as have any number of my friends and people I know.*

Lord, through what I read, and what I see, and what I experience, please increase my faith and dispel my doubts. Amen.

## "The Lord has risen indeed!" (Luke 24:34)

The angel said to the women, "Do not be afraid, for I know that you seek Jesus who was crucified. He is not here, for he has risen, as he said. Come, see the place where he lay" (Matthew 28:5–6). But in fact Christ has been raised from the dead, the firstfruits of those who have fallen asleep (1 Corinthians 15:20). After these things he appeared in another form to two of them, as they were walking into the country (Mark 16:12). And he said to them . . . "Was it not necessary that the Christ should suffer these things and enter into his glory?" And beginning with Moses and all the Prophets, he interpreted to them in all the Scriptures the things concerning himself (Luke 24:25, 26, 27). He was raised on the third day in accordance with the Scriptures (1 Corinthians 15:4). On the evening of that day . . . Jesus came and stood among them and said to them, "Peace be with you." When he had said this, he showed them his hands and his side. Then the disciples were glad when they saw the Lord (John 20:19–20).

*Someone once called the resurrection of Jesus 'the best attested fact in history', and today we read of three important pieces of evidence to support that claim. First, there was the empty tomb. No one had both opportunity and motive for removing the body, and the only sensible explanation was the one given to the women, 'He is risen'. Secondly, there was the testimony of the Scriptures which pointed forward to His death and resurrection. Thirdly, there was the witness of those who actually met Him and talked with Him after He was risen from the dead. That is why the resurrection is one of the foundation stones of the Christian faith.*

I thank You, Lord Jesus, that You rose again from the dead, and that You are alive for evermore. Amen.

## My God the rock of my refuge. (Psalm 94:22)

He who dwells in the shelter of the Most High will abide in the shadow of the Almighty. I will say to the Lord, "My refuge and my fortress, my God, in whom I trust." For he will deliver you from the snare of the fowler and from the deadly pestilence. He will cover you with his pinions, and under his wings you will find refuge; his faithfulness is a shield and buckler. You will not fear the terror of the night, nor the arrow that flies by day, nor the pestilence that stalks in darkness, nor the destruction that wastes at noonday . . . Because you have made the Lord your dwelling place – the Most High, who is my refuge – no evil shall be allowed to befall you, no plague come near your tent (Psalm 91:1–6, 9–10).

*This psalm, which was once recommended by an eminent physician as the best preservative against cholera, has been a great favourite in wartime and has brought comfort to thousands. But has the Christian any right to expect immunity from danger and disease and death? It is a moot point; but nothing will stop us from believing that God is able to preserve us from being in terror of these things, or from finding great confidence in the fact that we are saved from the final judgment and, in the meantime, nothing can harm us without the Lord's permission. 'Under His shadow' there is calm, and 'under His wings', comfort.*

**Lord, You are my habitation, but help me not to use You simply as a visitor might, but as a resident. Amen.**

## "In my flesh I shall see God." (Job 19:26)

How can some of you say that there is no resurrection of the dead? . . . But in fact Christ has been raised from the dead, the firstfruits of those who have fallen asleep (1 Corinthians 15:12, 20). Jesus said . . . "I am the resurrection and the life. Whoever believes in me, though he die, yet shall he live, and everyone who lives and believes in me shall never die" (John 11:25–26). But someone will ask, "How are the dead raised? With what kind of body do they come?" . . . What you sow is not the body that is to be, but a bare kernel, perhaps of wheat or of some other grain. But God gives it a body as he has chosen . . . So is it with the resurrection of the dead. What is sown is perishable; what is raised is imperishable. It is sown in dishonour; it is raised in glory. It is sown in weakness; it is raised in power. It is sown a natural body; it is raised a spiritual body (1 Corinthians 15:35, 37–38, 42–44).

*Today's verses ask and answer two questions. First, we base our belief in life after death not on any doubtful psychical arguments, but upon the solid fact of Christ's resurrection. Because He lives, we believe that we shall also live. Secondly, we must not think of ourselves as disembodied spirits flapping aimlessly about in space, nor as being merged in the next life into some sort of vague world-soul, losing our identities like a raindrop in a puddle or a blackberry in a pot of bramble jelly. Like the moth emerging from its chrysalis of sleep, we shall be given a new body perfectly adapted to a new kind of existence. It will be a spiritual body, individual and identifiable.*

**Help me, O Lord, to live as one who believes in the resurrection to everlasting life, and strengthen this hope in me all the days of my life. Amen.**

## The Lord worked with them. (Mark 16:20)

Now the eleven disciples went to Galilee, to the mountain to which Jesus had directed them (Matthew 28:16). When they had come together, they asked him, "Lord, will you at this time restore the kingdom to Israel?" He said to them, "It is not for you to know times or seasons that the Father has fixed by his own authority. But you will receive power when the Holy Spirit has come upon you, and you will be my witnesses . . . to the end of the earth" (Acts 1:6–8). "All authority in heaven and on earth has been given to me. Go therefore and make disciples of all nations, baptizing them in the name of the Father and of the Son and of the Holy Spirit, teaching them to observe all that I have commanded you. And behold, I am with you always, to the end of the age" (Matthew 28:18–20).

*The disciples hoped that this was the moment when Jesus would set up some sort of earthly kingdom but this was not to be, for what He wanted to establish was the kingdom of God, not the kingdom of Israel. 'To the end of the earth'. In a sense that command has been obeyed, for there is probably no country in the world without a Christian witness today. 'To the end of time'. Although Jesus was soon to leave them and return to heaven, His Holy Spirit would take His place in their hearts, giving them the power they needed for the tremendous missionary task He had entrusted to them. So, as He said goodbye to His disciples, Jesus gave them a great command, 'Go . . .', and a great promise, 'I am with you.'*

Lord, make me obedient to Your command to spread the gospel, and confident in Your promise to be with me always. Amen.

## I am already being poured out. (2 Timothy 4:6)

I appeal to you therefore, brothers, by the mercies of God, to present your bodies as a living sacrifice, holy and acceptable to God, which is your spiritual worship (Romans 12:1). But whatever gain I had, I counted as loss for the sake of Christ. Indeed, I count everything as loss because of the surpassing worth of knowing Christ Jesus my Lord. For his sake I have suffered the loss of all things and count them as rubbish, in order that I may gain Christ (Philippians 3:7–8). I was ship-wrecked . . . adrift at sea . . . in danger . . . in toil and hardship . . . in hunger and thirst . . . in cold and exposure. And, apart from other things, there is the daily pressure on me of my anxiety for all the churches (2 Corinthians 11:25–28). "Whoever finds his life will lose it, and whoever loses his life for my sake will find it" (Matthew 10:39).

*Garibaldi, Italy's great liberator, used to complain that he could find many people who were prepared to shed their last drop of blood for him, but very few who were prepared to shed their first. He had many friendly well-wishers, but not very many who were prepared for the toil, tears, sweat and blood which was all he had to offer his follow-ers. I wonder whether Jesus is sometimes disappointed in that way. Am I an easy-going Christian, not ready to be offered up as a sacrifice in the service of Christ? Or am I like Paul, prepared to give and not to count the cost, to fight and not heed the wounds, to toil and not to seek for rest, to labour and not to ask for any reward? By los-ing oneself in this way one finds true happiness and peace.*

'Which do I really want, dear Lord, which do I most desire, a short life in the saddle, or a long one by the fire?' Amen.

**Thanks be to God, who gives us the victory through our Lord Jesus Christ.
(1 Corinthians 15:57)**

Let no one say when he is tempted, "I am being tempted by God," for God cannot be tempted with evil, and he himself tempts no one. But each person is tempted when he is lured and enticed by his own desire (James 1:13–14). For I know that nothing good dwells in me, that is, in my flesh. For I have the desire to do what is right, but not the ability to carry it out. For I do not do the good I want, but the evil I do not want is what I keep on doing (Romans 7:18–19). For the desires of the flesh are against the Spirit, and the desires of the Spirit are against the flesh, for these are opposed to each other, to keep you from doing the things you want to do (Galatians 5:17). I can do all things through him who strengthens me (Philippians 4:13). Strengthened with power through his Spirit in your inner being (Ephesians 3:16).

*Imagine a parliament in which there are two almost equally strong parties opposed to each other – Flesh and Spirit. There is a third very small party led by a man named Will Power which can never hope to win on its own but which, by allying itself with Flesh or Spirit, can ensure the victory of one or the other. That is our position, and the secret of victory is this: whenever any issue is debated we need to give our vote to the Spirit and so keep 'the government upon his shoulders'. Our 'constitution' is such that we shall never be able to eliminate the opposition, but Jesus can prevent its assuming power if we will let Him. 'In your hearts enthrone Him, there let Him subdue all that is not holy, all that is not true.' If we crown Him, He will crush the enemy.*

**Lord, help me to give You my vote every time I am tempted to do what in my innermost heart I know to be wrong. Amen.**

## A new creation. (2 Corinthians 5:17)

And they came, bringing to him a paralytic carried by four men. And when they could not get near him because of the crowd, they removed the roof above him, and . . . let down the bed on which the paralytic lay. And when Jesus saw their faith, he said to the paralytic, "My son, your sins are forgiven." Now some of the scribes were sitting there, questioning in their hearts, "Why does this man speak like that? He is blaspheming! Who can forgive sins but God alone?" And . . . Jesus . . . said to them, "Why do you question these things in your hearts? . . . But that you may know that the Son of Man has authority on earth to forgive sins" – he said to the paralytic – "I say to you, rise, pick up your bed, and go home." And he rose and immediately picked up his bed and went out before them all (Mark 2:3–12).

*What did this man take home with him besides the stretcher on which he had been carried to Jesus?* Pardon. *He had not expected this. He had come to have his body healed, but Jesus' 'kind but searching glance can scan the very wounds that shame would hide', and He saw that the man's chief need was for forgiveness.* Power. *Limbs which had long been useless were suddenly filled with new life and strength.* Purpose. *We can easily imagine the new life that opened up in front of him – work he had long since abandoned, leisure activities he was eager to take up. Jesus still offers these three gifts to all who come to Him. If we have found them ourselves, are there others we can introduce to Him, perhaps with the help of our friends? Jesus' touch still has its ancient power.*

**Lord, keep me alive and quick to see the need of others for Your help. Amen.**

## Against you, you only, have I sinned. (Psalm 51:4)

"You say . . . 'I have not sinned'" (Jeremiah 2:35). Sin is law-lessness (1 John 3:4). The power of sin is the law (1 Corinthians 15:56). If it had not been for the law, I would not have known sin. I would not have known what it is to covet if the law had not said, "You shall not covet" (Romans 7:7). All wrongdoing is sin (1 John 5:17). The devising of folly is sin (Proverbs 24:9). Whoever knows the right thing to do and fails to do it, for him it is sin (James 4:17). Whatever does not proceed from faith is sin (Romans 14:23). "When he [the Holy Spirit] comes, he will convict the world concerning sin . . . because they do not believe in me" (John 16:8–9). "If I had not come and spoken to them, they would not have been guilty of sin, but now they have no excuse for their sin" (John 15:22). "Father, I have sinned against heaven and before you" (Luke 15:18).

*Sometimes you read of a court case where a man is charged with one offence and 'others are taken into consideration'. It is rather like that with us. What we are condemned for in God's sight is the breaking of His law in thought, word and deed but, like a disease, sin has a number of very serious side effects, including the fact that 'we have left undone those things which we ought to have done' and not allowed Jesus Christ His rightful place in our hearts and lives. What can we do about it? The first thing to do is to 'plead guilty', like David in the psalm and the Prodigal Son in the story. For such people there is good news – a gospel – because through His death Jesus is able to blot out and cancel the charges against us.*

Lord, we have erred and strayed from Your ways like lost sheep. We have offended against Your holy laws. Have mercy upon us, as we confess our faults to You. Amen.

## The name that is above every name.
## (Philippians 2:9)

His name shall be called Wonderful Counsellor, Mighty God, Everlasting Father, Prince of Peace (Isaiah 9:6). "He will be great and will be called the Son of the Most High" (Luke 1:32). O Lord, our Lord, how majestic is your name in all the earth! (Psalm 8:1) "Behold, the virgin shall conceive and bear a son, and they shall call his name Immanuel" (which means, God with us) (Matthew 1:23). The Word became flesh and dwelt among us . . . full of grace and truth (John 1:14). "She will bear a Son, and you shall call his name Jesus, for he will save his people from their sins" (Matthew 1:21). The Father has sent his Son to be the Saviour of the world (1 John 4:14). Oh, magnify the Lord with me, and let us exalt his name together! (Psalm 34:3) Ascribe to the Lord the glory due his name (1 Chronicles 16:29).

*'What's in a name?' we sometimes ask, implying that it doesn't very much matter what a person is called. There is, however, a great deal in a name. First, names give us identity. A name tells us who a person is, and the many different names given to Jesus remind us of what He came to do – to redeem and reign, to counsel and to comfort. Second, there is dignity in a name. People are often rightly proud of possessing some ancient and honourable name – and the names of Jesus are majestic and unique. There is no one else 'of that name'. A name also implies integrity. We talk of a firm 'having a good name', meaning that their promises can be trusted and we can take them at their word. It is like that with Jesus. Finally, a name can carry authority. 'Use my name', we sometimes say, knowing that it will carry weight with some shop or person. That is why we often end our prayers to God 'in the name of Jesus' or 'for His name's sake'.*

**Lord, help me never to take Your name in vain by using it thoughtlessly or as a swear word. Amen.**

## Alive to God. (Romans 6:11)

As Christ was raised from the dead by the glory of the Father, we too might walk in newness of life . . . So you also must consider yourselves dead to sin and alive to God in Christ Jesus. Let not sin therefore reign in your mortal bodies, to make you obey their passions. Do not present your members to sin as instruments for unrighteousness, but present yourselves to God as those who have been brought from death to life, and your members to God as instruments for righteousness. For sin will have no dominion over you . . . Thanks be to God, that you . . . having been set free from sin, have become slaves of righteousness (Romans 6:4, 11–14, 17–18).

*Imagine a Frenchman who has become a naturalized Englishman but wants to be completely 'anglicized'. How does he do it? First, he reckons himself dead as a Frenchman. He does nothing which might feed his old, French nature. He is deaf to its language and blind to its literature. At the same time, he yields himself to everything English – English friends, books and influences, until he almost feels that he has the mind of an Englishman and begins to think in English. Do you see how that applies to us in the Christian life? We must treat that old nature, called the 'flesh', as if it were dead and do nothing to encourage or enliven it. At the same time we must do all we can to cultivate our new nature (the spirit) so that it becomes increasingly 'alive to God' and sensitive to His will until, in fact, we have 'the mind of Christ'.*

**Lord, make me hard towards sin – 'not at home' when it calls and 'deaf' to its most enticing invitations. Amen.**

## The power . . . of our Lord Jesus Christ.
## (2 Peter 1:16)

Now when the sun was setting, all those who had any who were sick with various diseases brought them to him, and he laid his hands on every one of them and healed them (Luke 4:40). The power of the Lord was with him to heal (Luke 5:17). [Jesus Christ] was declared to be the Son of God in power . . . by his resurrection from the dead (Romans 1:4). That I may know him and the power of his resurrection (Philippians 3:10). Therefore I will boast all the more gladly of my weaknesses, so that the power of Christ may rest upon me (2 Corinthians 12:9). Strengthened with all power, according to his glorious might (Colossians 1:11). "Then will appear in heaven the sign of the Son of Man, and then all the tribes of the earth will mourn, and they will see the Son of Man coming on the clouds of heaven with power and great glory" (Matthew 24:30).

*There are two words in the New Testament for power – exousia, which means authority, and dunamis (cf. dynamite) which means strength. We are concerned with the second of these today, and these verses describe four occasions when the divine power of Jesus is displayed. In His wonderful healing work He showed that He had power over disease of every kind. By rising again from the grave He displayed His power over death. In the daily life of the Christian He exercises power over the devil. And one day, on His return to this earth to set up His kingdom, He will reveal His power over the destiny of humankind. At that time, every other power must submit to Him.*

'Worthy are you, our Lord and God, to receive glory and honour and power, for you created all things, and by your will they existed and were created' (Revelation 4:11). Amen.

**I have stored up your word in my heart, that I might not sin against you. (Psalm 119:11)**

Your word is a lamp to my feet and a light to my path (Psalm 119:105). The unfolding of your words gives light; it imparts understanding to the simple (Psalm 119:130). Like newborn infants, long for the pure spiritual milk, that by it you may grow up to salvation – if indeed you have tasted that the Lord is good (1 Peter 2:2–3). How sweet are your words to my taste, sweeter than honey to my mouth! (Psalm 119:103) And take . . . the sword of the Spirit, which is the word of God (Ephesians 6:17). For the word of God is living and active, sharper than any two-edged sword, piercing to the division of soul and of spirit, of joints and of marrow, and discerning the thoughts and intentions of the heart (Hebrews 4:12). Then Jesus said to him, "Be gone, Satan! For it is written . . ." (Matthew 4:10).

*A torch to find the way, food to feed the body, and a weapon to fight the enemy! That is how the Christian soldier is equipped for his or her adventurous journey through life. What these things can do for us in ordinary life, the Bible is able to do for us in our spiritual pilgrimage. That is why it is so important to become a regular reader of the Bible. Try, whenever you do read it, to let it help you in these ways. Look for a verse that can guide you in the often perplexing decisions you have to make; another that you can feed on in your heart and that will strengthen your faith; and another that will be like a sword in your hand when Satan attacks, enabling you to say, 'Be gone, Satan! For it is written . . .'*

**Lord, may I delight in Your word. Please help me to find new truths there every day, and clearer light to live by. Amen.**

## "I urge you to take heart." (Acts 27:22)

And some people brought to him a paralytic, lying on a bed. And when Jesus saw their faith, he said to the paralytic, "Take heart, my Son; your sins are forgiven" (Matthew 9:2). And in the fourth watch of the night Jesus came to them, walking on the sea. But when the disciples saw him walking on the sea, they were terrified . . . and they cried out in fear. But immediately Jesus spoke to them, saying, "Take heart; it is I. Do not be afraid" (Matthew 14:25–27). The following night the Lord stood by him and said, "Take courage, for as you have testified to the facts about me in Jerusalem, so you must testify also in Rome" (Acts 23:11). "I have said these things to you, that in me you may have peace. In the world you will have tribulation. But take heart; I have overcome the world" (John 16:33).

*People are always cheered by good news – a place won in a team, an exam passed, an exciting holiday planned, and so on. The Christian ought therefore to be the most cheerful person in the world, because the gospel was not just 'glad tidings of great joy' two thousand years ago, it is also 'good news for modern people'. What could be more exciting than to hear of a Saviour who has died to forgive sins, to blot them out for ever? Or the news of a Friend who will be with us in times of fear and loneliness to guide and encourage? Or to hear about a King who, in spite of all appearances, has overcome the forces of evil in the world and will one day reign supreme? Feeling downhearted this April morning? Then 'I exhort you to cheer up!'*

O Lord, may the remembrance of Your pardon, Your presence and Your power banish every shadow of gloom from my heart. Amen.

**That we may present everyone mature in Christ. (Colossians 1:28)**

All Scripture is breathed out by God and profitable for teaching, for reproof, for correction, and for training in righteousness, that the man of God may be competent, equipped for every good work (2 Timothy 3:16–17). Until we all attain to the unity of the faith and of the knowledge of the Son of God, to mature manhood, to the measure of the stature of the fullness of Christ (Ephesians 4:13). And after you have suffered a little while, the God of all grace, who has called you to his eternal glory in Christ, will himself restore, confirm, strengthen, and establish you (1 Peter 5:10). Now may the God of peace . . . equip you with everything good that you may do his will, working in us that which is pleasing in his sight, through Jesus Christ (Hebrews 13:20–21).

*Does this idea of maturity really mean that we are expected to be absolutely flawless? No! Sinless perfection is, I am afraid, far beyond the reach of every Christian. We must wait for that till we get to heaven, where sin will be excluded for ever. We need to think in terms of becoming 'adult', or spiritually 'grown up'. Two things play an important part in this maturing process – the Scriptures and suffering. To get good roses, you must nourish and prune. For the Christian, it is the Scriptures that do the nourishing, strengthening and deepening of our faith in Christ and our usefulness to Him. Suffering, in the form perhaps of temptation or persecution, does the pruning. In this way the child of God grows into the mature godly adult.*

**Help me to see, O Lord, in the disappointments and troubles which You allow, part of Your plan to make me more like Yourself. Amen.**

## God said to Moses, "I AM WHO I AM." (Exodus 3:14)

"I am the bread of life; whoever comes to me shall not hunger" (John 6:35). "I am the light of the world. Whoever follows me will not walk in darkness, but will have the light of life" (John 8:12). "I am the door. If anyone enters by me, he will be saved and will go in and out and find pasture" (John 10:9). "I am the good shepherd. The good shepherd lays down his life for the sheep" (John 10:11). "I am the resurrection and the life. Whoever believes in me, though he die, yet shall he live" (John 11:25). "I am the vine; you are the branches. Whoever abides in me and I in him, he it is that bears much fruit, for apart from me you can do nothing" (John 15:5). "I am the way, and the truth, and the life. No one comes to the Father except through me" (John 14:6).

*Someone has said that 'Jesus Christ was offered to the world, not as a problem, but as a solution', and today we see why. But what tremendous claims He makes for Himself in these verses! If anyone else made them no one would take them seriously, but in His case they are supported by His sinless life and His miraculous work. He sums them up in the last sentence where we see that He has the practical answer to life ('I am the way . . .') – guiding us and guarding us; the intellectual answer ('. . . and the truth . . .'); and the spiritual answer ('. . . and the life'). But Jesus does not just give the answers, He is the answer. To know Him is to find the secret of life: the right pathway through its perplexities; an understanding of its meaning and purpose; and an experience of that new dimension He can give it which we call eternal, or everlasting, life.*

**Lord, show me Your way, teach me Your truth, and give me Your eternal, abundant life. Amen.**

## "Behold, I set before you the way of life and the way of death." (Jeremiah 21:8)

"Enter by the narrow gate. For the gate is wide and the way is easy that leads to destruction, and those who enter by it are many. For the gate is narrow and the way is hard that leads to life, and those who find it are few" (Matthew 7:13–14). There is a way that seems right to a man, but its end is the way to death (Proverbs 14:12). But the path of the righteous is like the light of dawn, which shines brighter and brighter until full day (Proverbs 4:18). For the Lord knows the way of the righteous, but the way of the wicked will perish (Psalm 1:6). You make known to me the path of life; in your presence there is fullness of joy; at your right hand are pleasures for evermore (Psalm 16:11). "I have set before you life and death . . . Therefore choose life" (Deuteronomy 30:19).

*Every driver knows what it is to lose his or her way – to choose what seems to be an easy, attractive short cut, only to get hopelessly lost. Life is like that, and sooner or later we find ourselves facing a fork in the road – one way looks broad, easy and popular, the other narrow, hard and unfrequented. But closer inspection shows that the narrow way is God's way and, though uphill and difficult, it gets brighter and brighter and leads to eternal life. While the broad road of indifference to God and His claims may start pleasantly enough, it ends in disaster and destruction. Have you come to that fork in the road yet? If so, or when you do, study the 'map' carefully and 'choose life'.*

**Lead me, O Lord, in Your righteousness, make Your way clear before my face. Amen.**

## "How can a man be in the right before God?" (Job 9:2)

No human being will be justified in his sight (Romans 3:20). They are justified by his grace as a gift, through the redemption that is in Christ Jesus (Romans 3:24). One act of righteousness leads to justification and life for all men (Romans 5:18). And this is not your own doing; it is the gift of God (Ephesians 2:8). Because of the great love with which he loved us (Ephesians 2:4). Therefore, we have now been justified by his blood (Romans 5:9). For Christ also suffered once for sins, the righteous for the unrighteous, that he might bring us to God (1 Peter 3:18). Therefore, since we have been justified by faith, we have peace with God through our Lord Jesus Christ (Romans 5:1). Who shall bring any charge against God's elect? It is God who justifies. Who is to condemn? (Romans 8:33–34)

*The word 'justify' means to 'count as righteous'. This means that as we stand before God, and in spite of all our sins, the verdict is 'not guilty': not just 'let off', or 'under suspended sentence', but legally acquitted. But how can this possibly be, when we remember that God must punish sin? Its source is in the grace, or undeserved love, of God, who 'desires not the death of a sinner, but rather that he may turn from his wickedness and live'. Its course lies past the cross, where Jesus shed His blood for us, bearing the punishment in our place so that we might go free. Its force is felt in our lives when by faith we believe what Christ has done for us and gratefully receive His wonderful gift of pardon. Has this mighty river of God's love reached you yet?*

Lord Jesus, I thank You today for the love that took You to the cross, so that the charges against me might be dropped. Amen.

**He restores my soul. (Psalm 23:3)**

Now Paul and his companions set sail from Paphos and came
to Perga . . . And John [Mark] left them and returned to
Jerusalem (Acts 13:13). Now Barnabas wanted to take with
them John called Mark. But Paul thought best not to take with
them one who had withdrawn from them in Pamphylia and
had not gone with them to the work (Acts 15:37–38). If you
faint in the day of adversity, your strength is small (Proverbs
24:10). "If you have raced with men on foot, and they have
wearied you, how will you compete with horses?" (Jeremiah
12:5) For I [Paul] am already being poured out as a drink offering, and the time of my departure has come . . . Luke alone is
with me. Get Mark and bring him with you, for he is very useful to me for ministry (2 Timothy 4:6, 11). Formerly he was useless to you, but now he is indeed useful to you and to me
(Philemon 11). He gives power to the faint, and to him who
has no might he increases strength (Isaiah 40:29).

*Can you think of occasions when you have been given a second
chance – perhaps playing for a certain team, or in an exam? How
grateful you have been! God treats us like that. Mark made a pretty
good mess of his first attempt at being a missionary. He found the
going altogether too tough and returned home. Paul and Barnabas
quarrelled about what to do with him on the next journey, but in the
end Mark proved his worth and fought a good fight. Do you remember how Jesus treated Simon Peter in the same way? I find this
encouraging. We are bound to fail at times and let Christ down. But
He won't give up on us. He will 'restore our soul', giving power to
the faint and a new opportunity to prove our loyalty to Him.*

**Lord, I thank You that though Satan may get me down, he
need never keep me down. Amen.**

## The riches of his grace. (Ephesians 1:7)

"The kingdom of heaven is like treasure hidden in a field, which a man found and covered up. Then in his joy he goes and sells all that he has and buys that field. Again, the kingdom of heaven is like a merchant in search of fine pearls, who, on finding one pearl of great value, went and sold all that he had and bought it" (Matthew 13:44–46). Indeed, I count everything as loss because of the surpassing worth of knowing Christ Jesus my Lord. For his sake I have suffered the loss of all things and count them as rubbish, in order that I may gain Christ (Philippians 3:8). In whom are hidden all the treasures of wisdom and knowledge (Colossians 2:3). The unsearchable riches of Christ (Ephesians 3:8). Though you do not now see him, you believe in him and rejoice with joy that is inexpressible and filled with glory (1 Peter 1:8).

*Some great discoveries have been made by chance, when a scientist or explorer has stumbled on some marvellous secret, while others have come as a result of long and painstaking research. So it is with Christ. Some people have drifted almost, it seems, by chance into church or a meeting and have heard of the great 'treasure'. Others, after a long search for life at its best, have at last found 'the pearl of great price'. I have met both kinds of people, and perhaps Jesus was thinking of Gentile listeners in the first instance, and Jewish in the second. The saying about not 'putting all your eggs in one basket' doesn't apply to Christ. Everything we have – time, energy, talents and so on – is worth investing in Him. The capital is secure, and the dividends are rich.*

**Lord, help me to remember that 'all things that may be desired are not to be compared to you'. Amen.**

## Open my eyes, that I may behold wondrous things out of your law. (Psalm 119:18)

Behold, I was brought forth in iniquity, and in sin did my mother conceive me (Psalm 51:5). "Behold, the Lamb of God, who takes away the sin of the world!" (John 1:29) "Behold, I stand at the door and knock. If anyone hears my voice and opens the door, I will come in to him and eat with him, and he with me" (Revelation 3:20). Behold, now is the favourable time; behold, now is the day of salvation (2 Corinthians 6:2). See what kind of love the Father has given to us, that we should be called children of God . . . Beloved, we are God's children now, and what we will be has not yet appeared; but we know that when he appears we shall be like him, because we shall see him as he is. And everyone who thus hopes in him purifies himself as he is pure (1 John 3:1–3).

*The word 'behold' is the old-fashioned word for 'look' or 'take note of', and it occurs many times in the Bible when the writers want to draw the attention of their readers to something of particular importance. Here are five things that we ignore or overlook at our peril. We are reminded that we are born with a sinful nature and are in need of forgiveness if God is to receive us. Christ came into this world to make forgiveness possible through His death upon the cross. He wants to come into our hearts and lives to cleanse and strengthen. We must not lose the opportunity of inviting Him to do so, for to all who receive Him He gives the right to become children of God (John 1:12). These great truths are worth another long, close look.*

**Lord, whenever I read the Bible, open the eyes of my understanding that I may behold wonderful things out of Your Word. Amen.**

## By grace you have been saved. (Ephesians 2:8)

But now in Christ Jesus you who once were far off have been brought near by the blood of Christ (Ephesians 2:13). For through him we . . . have access . . . to the Father (Ephesians 2:18). To the praise of his glorious grace, with which he has blessed us in the Beloved (Ephesians 1:6). For our sake he made him to be sin . . . so that in him we might become the righteousness of God (2 Corinthians 5:21). "They have washed their robes and made them white in the blood of the Lamb" (Revelation 7:14). Jesus said to the Jews who had believed in him . . . "You will know the truth, and the truth will set you free." They answered him, "We are offspring of Abraham and have never been enslaved to anyone. How is it that you say, 'You will become free'?" Jesus answered them . . . "Everyone who commits sin is a slave to sin . . . If the Son sets you free, you will be free indeed" (John 8:31–36).

*Sometimes we talk about someone being 'a self-made man'. We mean someone who, without any special advantages of birth, money, education or background, has risen to the top of his business or profession and made a name for himself. We rightly applaud such people. But the Christian is the exact opposite. Everything we are we owe to God's grace. I can stand in God's presence 'ransomed, healed, restored, forgiven' only because Christ died upon the cross for me. I can enjoy freedom from the ever-present power of sin only because Christ is living within me to give me the strength I need. I have no merit or might of my own. Like Paul I can only say, 'By the grace of God I am what I am'. Amazing grace!*

'Lord, I cannot do without you, I cannot stand alone, I have no power or wisdom, no merit of my own.' Amen.

## Praying at all times. (Ephesians 6:18)

And rising very early in the morning, while it was still dark, he departed and went out to a desolate place, and there he prayed (Mark 1:35). In these days he went out to the mountain to pray, and all night he continued in prayer to God (Luke 6:12). Daniel . . . went to his house . . . He got down on his knees three times a day and prayed and gave thanks before his God (Daniel 6:10). O Lord, in the morning you hear my voice (Psalm 5:3). In the morning my prayer comes before you (Psalm 88:13). I rise before dawn and cry for help (Psalm 119:147). Let my prayer be counted as incense before you, and the lifting up of my hands as the evening sacrifice! (Psalm 141:2) At midnight I rise to praise you (Psalm 119:62). Evening and morning and at noon . . . he hears my voice (Psalm 55:17). They ought always to pray and not lose heart (Luke 18:1). Pray without ceasing (1 Thessalonians 5:17). Continue steadfastly in prayer (Colossians 4:2).

*Most Christians have found that there are two kinds of prayer. First, they find it helpful to have regular fixed times, usually in the morning and the evening. For these times of prayer it is a great help to find a quiet place where we can be apart and alone, and where we can concentrate upon our own needs and the needs of others for whom we want to pray, linking our prayers very often with what we read in the Bible. Second, if Christ is with us all the time then wherever we are, and at any time, we can speak to Him and share a particular problem or pleasure with Him. It is as though we have email contact at fixed times, and a mobile phone for continual, incessant use during the day.*

**Lord, help me to value the privilege of prayer, and to make greater use of it in my daily life. Amen.**

## "Everyone then who hears these words of mine and does them will be like a wise man who built his house on the rock." (Matthew 7:24)

Therefore put away all . . . wickedness and receive with meekness the implanted word, which is able to save your souls. But be doers of the word, and not hearers only, deceiving yourselves. For if anyone is a hearer of the word and not a doer, he is like a man who looks intently at his natural face in a mirror. For he looks at himself and goes away and at once forgets what he was like. But the one who looks into the perfect law, the law of liberty, and perseveres, being no hearer who forgets but a doer who acts, he will be blessed in his doing. If anyone thinks he is religious and does not bridle his tongue but deceives his heart, this person's religion is worthless. Religion that is pure and undefiled before God, the Father, is this: to visit orphans and widows in their affliction, and to keep oneself unstained from the world (James 1:21–27).

*We have all looked into the mirror at times and then forgotten to correct the mistakes it reveals – and that is what we must be careful not to do as we read the Bible. If we read it humbly and thoughtfully, it will frequently remind us of something in our lives which needs cleaning, changing, discarding or improving. We must also, however, be prepared to act upon what it tells us – to be a 'doer' of its teaching and not just a 'hearer'. Notice the very practical things it may speak to us about. Has my tongue been running away with me? Am I taking every opportunity that comes my way to show kindness to those in any sort of need? Am I becoming in any way polluted by the magazines I read or the films I see?*

O Lord, make me a follower of Yours not in word only, but in deed and in truth as well. Amen.

**Thus says the Lord . . . "you are mine."
(Isaiah 43:1)**

It is he who made us, and we are his (Psalm 100:3). Oh come, let us worship and bow down; let us kneel before the Lord, our Maker! For he is our God (Psalm 95:6–7). "Bring my sons from afar and my daughters from the end of the earth, everyone who is called by my name, whom I created for my glory, whom I formed and made" (Isaiah 43:6–7). You are not your own, for you were bought with a price (1 Corinthians 6:19–20). You were ransomed . . . not with perishable things such as silver or gold, but with the precious blood of Christ (1 Peter 1:18–19). But now thus says the Lord, he who created you, O Jacob, he who formed you, O Israel: "Fear not, for I have redeemed you; I have called you by name, you are mine" (Isaiah 43:1). "They shall be mine, says the Lord of hosts, in the day when I make up my treasured possession" (Malachi 3:17).

*Imagine an artist who paints a great masterpiece and then one day, when he is away from home, it is stolen. After many years of fruitless searching, he finds it in a charity shop – disfigured and damaged almost beyond recognition, but unquestionably his picture. He pays for it, takes it home and sets to work to restore it. It now, in a sense, belongs to him twice over. He made it and he bought it. It is his by right of creation and redemption. Do you see how that applies to us? We belong to God because He made us for Himself, but when we had been stolen and damaged by sin, He bought us back at tremendous cost so that now we belong to Him twice over. What is our response to His claim, 'You are mine'? Remember that, unlike the picture, we can say, 'No'.*

**O Lord, You have made me for Yourself, and my heart is empty and restless until it finds repose in You. Amen.**

## I was brutish and ignorant; I was like a beast toward you. (Psalm 73:22)

All we like sheep have gone astray; we have turned every one to his own way (Isaiah 53:6). I have gone astray like a lost sheep (Psalm 119:176). When Jesus saw the crowds, he had compassion for them, because they were harassed and help-less, like sheep without a shepherd (Matthew 9:36). Their fool-ish hearts were darkened (Romans 1:21). For we ourselves were once foolish, disobedient, led astray (Titus 3:3). Be not like a horse or a mule, without understanding, which must be curbed with bit and bridle, or it will not stay near you (Psalm 32:9). Do not now be stiff-necked as your fathers were, but yield yourselves to the Lord (2 Chronicles 30:8). Today, if you hear his voice, do not harden your hearts (Psalm 95:7–8). Whoever hardens his heart will fall into calamity (Proverbs 28:14).

*It is not very flattering, is it, to be compared to a sheep or a mule? But I am afraid we very often behave towards God in a manner which is like those animals.* The sheep is stupid. *It does not think things out for itself but just follows the crowd and gets itself pathetically lost. How easy it is to do that, just drifting with the others along dangerous and forbidden paths!* The mule is stubborn. *Its trouble is not so much blindness of mind, but hardness of heart. Those of us who know what God wants us to do but are unwilling to go His way are like mules. Ignorance and disobedience – these are the two things against which every Christian has to guard him or herself carefully.*

Help me, O Lord, to love You with my mind and my heart: to know what You want me to do, and then to be willing to do it. Amen.

## O Lord, be my helper! (Psalm 30:10)

I have set the Lord always before me; because he is at my right hand, I shall not be shaken (Psalm 16:8). For to this you have been called, because Christ also suffered for you, leaving you an example, so that you might follow in his steps. He committed no sin, neither was deceit found in his mouth (1 Peter 2:21–22). "I have given you an example, that you also should do just as I have done to you" (John 13:15). And your ears shall hear a word behind you, saying, "This is the way, walk in it" (Isaiah 30:21). "The word is very near you. It is in your mouth and in your heart, so that you can do it" (Deuteronomy 30:14). "Like an eagle that stirs up its nest, that flutters over its young, spreading out its wings, catching them, bearing them on its pinions, the Lord alone guided him" (Deuteronomy 32:11–12). "There is none like God . . . who rides through the heavens to your help . . . The eternal God is your dwelling place, and underneath are the everlasting arms" (Deuteronomy 33:26–27). So we can confidently say, "The Lord is my helper" (Hebrews 13:6).

*Can you think back to the time when you first learnt to skate, or swim, or cycle? How did it happen? Probably in three stages. First, you watched someone else doing it and made that person your example. Then he or she explained how to do it and you listened to their advice. But was that enough? Probably not. You needed to go through a third stage. Your helper had to come to you and support you on the ice, in the water or on the bike with his or her strength. In exactly the same way, as you can see from these verses, God helps us in our daily lives. He gives us the perfect example in the life of Jesus. His advice reaches us largely through the Bible. We enjoy His strength when we remember that He is always 'at our right hand'.*

Lord, may I never be too stupid or too stubborn to allow You to help me in every possible way. Amen.

## "What is man, that you make so much of him?" (Job 7:17)

O Lord, our Lord, how majestic is your name in all the earth! ... When I look at your heavens, the work of your fingers, the moon and the stars, which you have set in place, what is man that you are mindful of him, and the son of man that you care for him? Yet you have made him a little lower than the heavenly beings and crowned him with glory and honour. You have given him dominion over the works of your hands; you have put all things under his feet, all sheep and oxen, and also the beasts of the field, the birds of the heavens, and the fish of the sea, whatever passes along the paths of the seas. O Lord, our Lord, how majestic is your name in all the earth! (Psalm 8:1–9)

*Pascal once called man 'the glory and the scandal of the universe'. We have thought often enough of our failure and depravity, but it is worth pausing for a moment to consider what marvellous creations we are. Human beings were intended to be, so to speak, 'amphibious' – that is, equally at home in two worlds. On the one hand we were made so that we could communicate with God, sharing and returning His great love. On the other hand we were made to be God's 'viceroys', controlling and using the earth's resources for the benefit of all. How far have we disappointed our Creator by failing to fulfil His purpose? And how far has our forgetfulness of God been responsible for our being tragic failures as viceroys?*

**Forgive me, O Lord, if the majesty and excellence of Your name are not known, as they should be, throughout the earth. Amen.**

## "If only I may finish my course." (Acts 20:24)

Not that I have already obtained this or am already perfect,
but I press on to make it my own, because Christ Jesus has
made me his own. Brothers, I do not consider that I have made
it my own. But one thing I do: forgetting what lies behind and
straining forward to what lies ahead, I press on toward the
goal for the prize of the upward call of God in Christ Jesus
(Philippians 3:12–14). The crown of righteousness, which the
Lord, the righteous judge, will award to me on that Day
(2 Timothy 4:8). Therefore . . . let us also lay aside every
weight, and sin which clings so closely, and let us run with
endurance the race that is set before us, looking to Jesus, the
founder and perfecter of our faith . . . Consider him . . . so that
you may not grow weary or fainthearted (Hebrews 12:1–3).

Finishing. *The Christian life is like a marathon fun run. At times
the going is easy, but often it is hard – uphill and immensely challenging. It demands courage, patience and stamina, and there are
some who drop out on the way. The prize does not go to the winner,
because there are no outright winners in this race. Rather, the prize
goes to those who endure to the end. Finishing the race requires
courage and perseverance.* Forgetting. *One great secret of success is
not to dwell too much on the past. Its successes may make us com-
placent and its failures can dishearten us. It is the future that matters, and we must run with our eyes upon Jesus. He is the one and
only Champion, whose standard is perfect. He is the Coach, who is
there to encourage and advise. He is the Judge who will one day
award the prizes.*

**Lord, help me to run with patience and determination and,
like Paul, to finish my course with joy. Amen.**

## Abraham, the man of faith. (Galatians 3:9)

By faith Abraham obeyed when he was called to go out to a place that he was to receive as an inheritance. And he went out, not knowing where he was going (Hebrews 11:8). By faith Abraham, when he was tested, offered up Isaac, and he who had received the promises was in the act of offering up his only son . . . He considered that God was able even to raise him from the dead (Hebrews 11:17, 19). Abraham believed God, and it was counted to him as righteousness (Romans 4:3). No distrust made him waver concerning the promise of God, but he grew strong in his faith as he gave glory to God, fully convinced that God was able to do what he had promised (Romans 4:20–21). And the Scripture was fulfilled that says, "Abraham believed God, and it was counted to him as right-eousness" – and he was called a friend of God (James 2:23). Abraham, my friend (Isaiah 41:8).

*With unhesitating obedience, Abraham, now an old man, left the home where he had lived all his life for an unknown destination. Then he prepared to offer up his only son, through whom God had promised to give him many descendants. What amazing faith! He never wavered for a moment. His faith passed two supreme tests. He obeyed God, even though what God asked him to do was (a) beyond his reason and (b) against his wishes. He could not understand, nor did he like, what he was told to do. It is not very often that our faith is put to quite such a severe test, but God may call us to make some big sacrifice for His sake, and we ought to be ready for it. The proof of friendship is obedience.*

**Lord, make me ready to do Your will, cost what it may. Amen.**

### The God of hope fill you with all joy and peace in believing. (Romans 15:13)

Rejoice in the Lord always; again I will say, Rejoice. Let your reasonableness be known to everyone. The Lord is at hand; do not be anxious about anything, but in everything by prayer and supplication with thanksgiving let your requests be made known to God. And the peace of God, which surpasses all understanding, will guard your hearts and your minds in Christ Jesus. Finally, brothers, whatever is true, whatever is honourable, whatever is just, whatever is pure, whatever is lovely, whatever is commendable, if there is any excellence, if there is anything worthy of praise, think about these things. What you have learned and received and heard and seen in me – practice these things, and the God of peace will be with you (Philippians 4:4–9).

*We need to remember that this letter of Paul's, which radiates such joy and peace, was not written from a holiday resort in the south of France, but from captivity in Rome. What accounts for its tone is the little phrase 'the Lord is at hand'. It was the living presence of Christ which gave Paul such joy – in spite of the food, the conditions and the company – and which lined his heart and mind with peace, in spite of the clouded and uncertain future. Notice how positive Paul is. 'Think . . . ' We are to furnish our minds with those things that are honourable and worthy. 'Practice . . . ' Right thinking will lead to right action, but fancy being able to say, 'there is nothing in me which you can't copy'! Which of us would dare to make such a claim?*

Lord, give me that quiet confidence in You which can face disappointment, suffering and even death itself with peaceful joy. Amen.

## "Learn from me, for I am gentle and lowly in heart." (Matthew 11:29)

Have this mind among yourselves, which is yours in Christ Jesus, who, though he was in the form of God, did not count equality with God a thing to be grasped, but made himself nothing, taking the form of a servant, being born in the likeness of men (Philippians 2:5–7). "You will find a baby wrapped in swaddling cloths and lying in a manger" (Luke 2:12). "The Son of Man has nowhere to lay his head" (Matthew 8:20). Then Jesus poured water into a basin and began to wash the disciples' feet and to wipe them with the towel that was wrapped around him (John 13:5). "I am among you as the one who serves" (Luke 22:27). And being found in human form, he humbled himself by becoming obedient to the point of death, even death on a cross (Philippians 2:8). In his humiliation justice was denied him (Acts 8:33). When he was reviled, he did not revile in return; when he suffered, he did not threaten (1 Peter 2:23).

*Paul begins a section of one his letters with the words, 'I beseech you by the meekness of Christ'. In the light of the passage we have just read, what place can there be for pride or self-seeking? Notice the three tremendous steps downwards that Christ took.* He came as a man – *not as an angel, with special privileges, but as a man, with all the human limitations, privations and temptations we experience.* He lived as a servant – *not as a prince, but as a humble village carpenter with no great advantages through birth, money or education.* He died as a criminal – *not as a hero, at the head of an army, but in what was probably the most painful and humiliating manner which ingenious human cruelty has ever devised.*

**Lord, as I think of Your wonderful humility, help me to pour contempt on all my pride. Amen.**

**"This is eternal life, that they know you the only true God, and Jesus Christ whom you have sent." (John 17:3)**

For Christ also suffered once for sins . . . that he might bring us to God (1 Peter 3:18). But now in Christ Jesus you who once were far off have been brought near by the blood of Christ (Ephesians 2:13). Through him we have also obtained access by faith into this grace in which we stand (Romans 5:2). We know that Christ, being raised from the dead, will never die again; death no longer has dominion over him (Romans 6:9). "Behold I am alive for evermore" (Revelation 1:18). "I am going to the Father" (John 14:12). "And I will ask the Father, and he will give you another Helper, to be with you forever, even the Spirit of truth, whom the world cannot receive, because it neither sees him nor knows him. You know him, for he dwells with you and will be in you" (John 14:16–17). "It is to your advantage that I go away, for if I do not go away, the Helper will not come to you. But if I go, I will send him to you" (John 16:7).

*When we talk about 'knowing' someone, we often find ourselves up against one of three barriers. There is sometimes a social barrier, because the person concerned is too exalted, too 'high up' for us to know. Or there is an historical barrier, because the person is dead and lived too 'long ago'. We face the geographical barrier when the person lives too 'far away'. But Jesus has destroyed all of these barriers. On* Good Friday *He demolished the social (perhaps 'moral' would now be a better word) barrier when, through His death, He made it possible for us to be received by a holy and righteous God. On* Easter Day *He destroyed the historical barrier when He rose from the dead to live for evermore. On* Whit Sunday *He destroyed the geographical barrier, because through His Holy Spirit He is (like the wind) available for all His people everywhere and at all times.*

**Lord, I thank You that through Your death, Your resurrection and Your Holy Spirit You have made it possible for me to know God. Amen.**

## Put on the Lord Jesus Christ. (Romans 13:14)

I will greatly rejoice in the Lord . . . for he has clothed me with the garments of salvation; he has covered me with the robe of righteousness (Isaiah 61:10). "I put on righteousness, and it clothed me" (Job 29:14). "The father said to his servants, 'Bring quickly the best robe, and put it on him, and put a ring on his hand, and shoes on his feet'" (Luke 15:22). As shoes for your feet, having put on the readiness given by the gospel of peace (Ephesians 6:15). Put on then, as God's chosen ones . . . compassion, kindness, humility, meekness, and patience . . . And above all these put on love, which binds everything together in perfect harmony (Colossians 3:12,14). Clothe yourselves, all of you, with humility toward one another (1 Peter 5:5). And put on the armour of light (Romans 13:12). That the man of God may be competent, equipped for every good work (2 Timothy 3:17).

*Someone has said that our clothes not only conceal us, they also reveal us. How true that is! For you can often tell a great deal about a person – their nationality, occupation and status – by their dress. Christians have to consider three things. We must be* clothed for life *– wearing the robe of righteousness which God provides to cover up all the rags of sin underneath, and the cloak of love and humility on top of everything else. We must be* equipped for work, *and this is where we need the shoes which stand for a readiness to carry the good news of Christ to others. We must be* armed for battle, *because our great enemy Satan will not leave us in peace for long – Satan is always on the prowl.*

**Lord, keep the clothing of my life in good repair, that I may live humbly for You, work eagerly and fight boldly. Amen.**

### Pilate said to him, "What is truth?" (John 18:38)

And they took hold of Paul and brought him to the Areopagus, saying, "May we know what this new teaching is that you are presenting? For you bring some strange things to our ears. We wish to know therefore what these things mean." Now all the Athenians and the foreigners who lived there would spend their time in nothing except telling or hearing something new (Acts 17:19–21). Always learning and never able to arrive at a knowledge of the truth (2 Timothy 3:7). Jesus said to Thomas, "I am . . . the truth . . . No one comes to the Father except through me" (John 14:6). "You will know the truth, and the truth will set you free" (John 8:32). This is good, and it is pleasing in the sight of God our Saviour, who desires all people to be saved and to come to the knowledge of the truth (2 Timothy 2:3–4).

Truth is a personal thing. *Jesus did not say, 'I will tell you the truth', or 'I will give you a set of propositions'. He said, 'I am the truth'. To know Him is to learn the answer to so many of the riddles that have perplexed people down the ages – What is God like? What is the purpose of life? Truth is a powerful thing. We see this in the political sphere. Once the truth dawns on people living under a political tyranny, they become restless and long to be free. So it is that knowing Jesus is the greatest liberating force in the world. It sets people free from the slavery of sin, the power of Satan and the fear of death. As people watch us and speak to us, is the truth expressed (2 Corinthians 4:2) or suppressed (Romans 1:18)?*

**O Lord, may people learn the truth about You from the way I live and the things I say. Amen.**

**And he is before all things, and in him all things hold together. (Colossians 1:17)**

All look to you, to give them their food in due season . . . when you take away their breath, they die and return to their dust. When you send forth your Spirit, they are created, and you renew the face of the ground (Psalm 104:27, 29–30). "If he should . . . gather to himself his spirit and his breath, all flesh would perish together, and man would return to dust" (Job 34:14–15). "In his hand is the life of every living thing and the breath of all mankind" (Job 12:10). "He himself gives to all mankind life and breath and everything . . . for 'In him we live and move and have our being'" (Acts 17:25, 28). Then Daniel answered and said before the king . . . "O King . . . the God in whose hand is your breath, and whose are all your ways, you have not honoured" (Daniel 5:17–18, 23).

*Some people believe in a God who created the universe, set everything going, and now leaves it like some great and infinite clock to keep itself ticking. But that is not at all the picture of God that the Bible gives us. We see there Someone who is not just the Creator, but the Controller, sustaining and directing everything with love, power and wisdom. Our food, our breath, our very existence depend upon Him, and the knowledge that He is in charge ought to give us great confidence. It ought to have another effect as well, as Daniel reminded King Belshazzar, for a God to whom we owe so much deserves our homage and obedience. He upholds us, that we should uplift Him before others.*

**Lord, knowing that I depend upon You for life and health, may I be kept very humble and very grateful. Amen.**

### "My glory I will not give to another." (Isaiah 48:11)

Thus says the Lord: "Let not the wise man boast in his wisdom, let not the mighty man boast in his might, let not the rich man boast in his riches, but let him who boasts boast in this, that he understands and knows me, that I am the Lord who practices steadfast love, justice, and righteousness in the earth" (Jeremiah 9:23–24). God chose what is foolish in the world to shame the wise; God chose what is weak in the world to shame the strong . . . that no human being might boast in the presence of God . . . Therefore, as it is written, "Let the one who boasts, boast in the Lord" (1 Corinthians 1:27, 29, 31). Not to us, O Lord, not to us, but to your name give glory, for the sake of your steadfast love and your faithfulness! (Psalm 115:1) "Worthy are you, our Lord and God, to receive glory and honour and power, for you created all things, and by your will they existed and were created" (Revelation 4:11). To whom be the glory forever and ever. Amen (Galatians 1:5).

*If you earn something, then perhaps you have reason to congratulate yourself, but if what you receive comes to you as a gift from someone else, then that person deserves the credit and the congratulations. That is how it is with God and us. Everything we have comes from Him – every material blessing as well as every successful step forward we make in the Christian life. As the hymn reminds us, 'every virtue we possess and every victory won and every thought of holiness are His alone'. When people praise us, it is very tempting to pocket the credit for ourselves. But this is really stealing, because it is withholding from God what is rightly due to Him.*

**Lord, You know how much I love the praise of others. Please help me to pass it all on to You, humbly and gratefully. Amen.**

**Christ . . . suffered once for sins, the righteous for the unrighteous, that he might bring us to God. (1 Peter 3:18)**

He was despised and rejected by men; a man of sorrows, and acquainted with grief; and as one from whom men hide their faces he was despised, and we esteemed him not. Surely he has borne our griefs and carried our sorrows; yet we esteemed him stricken, smitten by God, and afflicted. But he was wounded for our transgressions; he was crushed for our iniquities; upon him was the chastisement that brought us peace, and with his stripes we are healed. All we like sheep have gone astray; we have turned every one to his own way; and the Lord has laid on him the iniquity of us all. He was oppressed, and he was afflicted, yet he opened not his mouth; like a lamb that is led to the slaughter, and like a sheep that before its shearers is silent, so he opened not his mouth . . . Yet it was the will of the Lord to crush him (Isaiah 53:3–7, 10).

*These words were written some eight hundred years before Christ and, while they may have had some local and contemporary application, their true meaning and significance only became apparent with the coming of Jesus Himself – for they give us a remarkably detailed picture of the crucifixion. Two little phrases sum up this tremendous event. 'Rejected by men.' Jesus, so sensitive and sinless, became the target for human greed, cruelty and cowardice. Our minds shrink from thinking of all He had to endure physically and mentally. 'Smitten by God.' But there was another, even darker, side to His sufferings – for on the cross He accepted the burden and the punishment of human sin so that we might be set free from its guilt and power. That is why we read that 'it was the will of the Lord to crush Him'.*

**Lord, I thank You for the insults You bore, the pain You suffered and the burden You carried that You might bring me liberty and life. Amen.**

**Blessed is the one whose transgression is forgiven, whose sin is covered. (Psalm 32:1)**

"Come now, let us reason together, says the Lord: though your sins are like scarlet, they shall be as white as snow; though they are red like crimson, they shall become like wool" (Isaiah 1:18). The Lord is merciful and gracious, slow to anger and abounding in steadfast love . . . He does not deal with us according to our sins, nor repay us according to our iniquities. For as high as the heavens are above the earth, so great is his steadfast love toward those who fear him; as far as the east is from the west, so far does he remove our transgressions from us (Psalm 103:8, 10–12). He will again have compassion on us; he will tread our iniquities underfoot. You will cast all our sins into the depths of the sea (Micah 7:19). You have cast all my sins behind your back (Isaiah 38:17). "I, I am he who blots out your transgressions for my own sake, and I will not remember your sins" (Isaiah 43:25).

*The word for 'forgive' comes from a Greek word meaning to 'send away' or 'dismiss', much as you might try to get rid of an unwelcome caller, or a stray dog that was following you. And in these verses we have some vivid word-pictures of the ways in which God deals with our sins and gets rid of them for ever. They are like a blot, or a stain, which He cleanses and puts out of sight. They are like a weight, which He takes from our backs and throws away into the sea, out of reach. They are like a debt, which He refuses to hold against us and puts out of mind. Never again need we feel guilty about sins with which God has so completely and effectively dealt.*

**Thank You, Lord, for dying for me, Thank You, Lord, for setting me free. Thank You, Lord, for giving to me Your great salvation so rich and free. Amen.**

## Keep alert with all perseverance. (Ephesians 6:18)

Clothe yourselves, all of you, with humility toward one another, for "God opposes the proud but gives grace to the humble." Humble yourselves, therefore, under the mighty hand of God so that at the proper time he may exalt you, casting all your anxieties on him, because he cares for you. Be sober-minded; be watchful. Your adversary the devil prowls around like a roaring lion, seeking someone to devour. Resist him, firm in your faith, knowing that the same kinds of suffering are being experienced by your brotherhood throughout the world. And after you have suffered a little while, the God of all grace, who has called you to his eternal glory in Christ, will himself restore, confirm, strengthen, and establish you. To him be the dominion forever and ever. Amen (1 Peter 5:5–11).

*It is interesting to remember that these words were written by Simon Peter, and to compare them with his experience many years before in the Garden of Gethsemane. What a long way he had come since that terrible evening! Then he had been proud, but here he is humble; then he had slept, but here he is watchful; then he had fled, but here he resists firmly. Satan is pictured here as a lion – very angry at being robbed of his followers and very active in the world. Two things will help us to resist and overcome him: faith in God to give us the strength we need day by day; and the friendship, sympathy and help of other Christians fighting the same battles 'throughout the world'. And remember, too, that temptation is one of God's ways of establishing us more firmly in our Christian lives.*

**Lord, keep me humble, keep me vigilant, keep me firm, that I may be victorious over every attack of Satan. Amen.**

## God has highly exalted him. (Philippians 2:9)

And when Jesus had said these things, as they were looking on, he was lifted up, and a cloud took him out of their sight (Acts 1:9). Lift up your heads, O gates! And lift them up, O ancient doors, that the King of glory may come in. Who is this King of glory? (Psalm 24:9–10). Jesus Christ, who has gone into heaven and is at the right hand of God (1 Peter 3:21–22). He sat down at the right hand of the Majesty on high (Hebrews 1:3). "Whom heaven must receive until the time for restoring all the things about which God spoke by the mouth of his holy prophets long ago" (Acts 3:21). For Christ has entered . . . into heaven itself, now to appear in the presence of God on our behalf (Hebrews 9:24). Consequently, he is able to save to the uttermost those who draw near to God through him, since he always lives to make intercession for them (Hebrews 7:25).

*After forty days, during which Jesus had been training His disciples to live by faith and not by sight, He was taken up from them into heaven. They saw Him no more, though ten days later His Holy Spirit came to take His place in the hearts of His followers everywhere and for all time. What is Jesus doing in heaven? He is resting. His great and eternal work of redemption complete, Jesus is seated at the right hand of God's majesty. He is waiting for that moment of destiny when He will return to this earth in great power and glory. He is working. He is, so to speak, our ambassador in the court of heaven. It is He who represents us to God. It is through Him that we pray to God, and it is through Him that God strengthens and helps us.*

Lord Jesus, friend of sinners, help me never to forget that You are also King of glory. Amen.

## But made himself nothing. (Philippians 2:7)

The Word became flesh and dwelt among us . . . full of grace and truth (John 1:14). We see him who for a little while was made lower than the angels, namely Jesus . . . so that by the grace of God he might taste death for everyone (Hebrews 2:9). Who made himself nothing, taking the form of a servant, being born in the likeness of men. And being found in human form, he humbled himself by becoming obedient to the point of death, even death on a cross (Philippians 2:7–8). Christ redeemed us from the curse of the law by becoming a curse for us – for it is written, "Cursed is everyone who is hanged on a tree" (Galatians 3:13). For our sake he made him to be sin who knew no sin, so that in him we might become the righteousness of God (2 Corinthians 5:21). Jesus, whom God made our wisdom and our righteousness and sanctification and redemption (1 Corinthians 1:30).

*These verses deal with two different aspects, or views, of Christianity – history and experience. First, they tell us what Jesus became for us. It was not enough that He should set us an example as the perfect man. In order to rescue us from sin He had to be 'made sin for us', to bear the guilt and punishment for our sin as if it were His own. Secondly, we see what Jesus becomes to us. In God's eyes we are bankrupt and in danger of liquidation but Jesus, out of His great love for us, gives us all that we need for our eternal salvation. As God looked on Jesus, He saw our sin; and as He looks on us, He sees the holiness and righteousness of Jesus. He accepted the curse for us (where the letter 's' can stand for sin and Satan, which He destroyed), so that He might give us the perfect cure.*

**Lord, I thank You again today for the love that brought You from heaven, took You to the cross, and made You enter my heart and life. Amen.**

## We are ambassadors for Christ.
## (2 Corinthians 5:20)

As Jesus was getting into the boat, the man who had been possessed with demons begged him that he might be with him.
And he did not permit him but said to him, "Go home to your
friends and tell them how much the Lord has done for you,
and how he has had mercy on you" (Mark 5:18–19). And he
said to me, "Son of man, go to the house of Israel and speak
with my words to them. For you are not sent to a people of foreign speech and a hard language, but to the house of Israel"
(Ezekiel 3:4–5). Jesus . . . said to them . . . "Go therefore and
make disciples of all nations" (Matthew 28:18–19). And he said
to Paul, "Go, for I will send you far away to the Gentiles" (Acts
22:21). "'To open their eyes, so that they may turn from darkness to light and from the power of Satan to God, that they
may receive forgiveness of sins and a place among those who
are sanctified by faith in me'" (Acts 26:18).

*Ambassadors are those who represent their king or government in
another country. They are foreigners, with different habits and different standards. They are messengers through whom their own
governments communicate with the other country. They are also
representatives, by whom their own countries will be judged. What
a privilege and responsibility! And we are called to be Christ's
ambassadors, to represent Him in the world. He wants ambassadors
everywhere – in our homes, where we are best known and where
sometimes it is hardest to witness for Him; in our own countries,
amongst people with familiar customs and language; and perhaps
'far away', in some distant country, as foreign missionaries.*

**Lord, train me to become a good ambassador for You, and
may I be willing to represent You wherever You may choose
to send me. Amen.**

## What is your life? (James 4:14)

You are a mist that appears for a little time and then vanishes (James 4:14). "Remember that my life is a breath" (Job 7:7). For my days pass away like smoke (Psalm 102:3). The years of our life are seventy, or even by reason of strength eighty; yet their span is but toil and trouble; they are soon gone, and we fly away (Psalm 90:10). O Lord, make me know my end and what is the measure of my days; let me know how fleeting I am! (Psalm 39:4) "For what does it profit a man to gain the whole world and forfeit his life? For what can a man give in return for his life?" (Mark 8:36–37) You are not your own, for you were bought with a price (1 Corinthians 6:19–20). For none of us lives to himself, and none of us dies to himself. If we live, we live to the Lord, and if we die, we die to the Lord. So then, whether we live or whether we die, we are the Lord's (Romans 14:7–8). Your life is hidden with Christ in God (Colossians 3:3). For to me to live is Christ (Philippians 1:21).

*There are two ways of measuring life – physical and spiritual, earthly and heavenly. Life is a passing thing. We are 'like ships that pass in the night' – you see them in the bay at sunset, and the next morning they have disappeared. The Bible often reminds us that 'in the midst of life we are in death'. Life is a precious thing. People will fight for their lives as they will fight for nothing else, and they will make almost any sacrifice to cling to life. But we realize life's true value when we remember what Christ did to redeem it, what He can make of it if we will let Him do so here and now, and what one day it will blossom into in His presence in heaven. And remember too that, for good or ill, depending upon how it is used, life is a powerful thing.*

'So teach me to number my days, O Lord, that I may get a heart of wisdom' (Psalm 90:12). Amen.

### Bearing fruit in every good work.
### (Colossians 1:10)

Blessed is the man who walks not in the counsel of the wicked, nor stands in the way of sinners, nor sits in the seat of scoffers; but his delight is in the law of the Lord, and on his law he meditates day and night. He is like a tree planted by streams of water that yields its fruit in its season, and its leaf does not wither. In all that he does, he prospers. The wicked are not so, but are like chaff that the wind drives away. Therefore the wicked will not stand in the judgment, nor sinners in the congregation of the righteous; for the Lord knows the way of the righteous, but the way of the wicked will perish (Psalm1:1–6).

*A person is often known by the company he or she keeps and by the books he or she reads. They are part of the environment which conditions our lives. Really successful Christians, whose lives are always fresh, fragrant and fruitful, have two secrets. Their best friends are not those who dishonour their Master, but those who help and encourage them in the right way. Their favourite book, however many others they may read, is the Bible, on whose teaching they meditate, or ponder, day and night. Notice in the opening sentence how people slip, often very gradually, into sin. We walk and see temptation; we stand and study it; we sit and sample it. 'Blessed', or happy, is the one who avoids this downward slide, and who is blind and deaf to the enticing voices of sin. Like a tree, the one who does this stands firm for God and bears 'fruit in every good work'.*

**Lord, help me to draw from Your book and from my Christian friends the nourishment I need to prosper and not to perish. Amen.**

## We are God's children now. (1 John 3:2)

But to all who did receive him, who believed in his name, he gave the right to become children of God, who were born, not of blood nor of the will of the flesh nor of the will of man, but of God (John 1:12–13). For in Christ Jesus you are all sons of God, through faith (Galatians 3:26). Everyone who believes that Jesus is the Christ has been born of God (1 John 5:1). No one born of God makes a practice of sinning, for God's seed abides in him, and he cannot keep on sinning because he has been born of God (1 John 3:9). If you know that he is righteous, you may be sure that everyone who practices righteousness has been born of him (1 John 2:29). For everyone who has been born of God overcomes the world (1 John 5:4). Beloved, let us love one another, for love is from God, and whoever loves has been born of God and knows God (1 John 4:7).

*We become children of God not through inheritance, or through our own efforts or those of anyone else, but through faith in Jesus Christ. When we receive Him we are born again into God's family. How do we know that we are members of God's family? First there is the 'birth certificate' in the shape of His promise to accept us. But, as time goes on, the 'family likeness' should also begin to appear and today we read about two important features.* Our attitude towards sin *should be one of implacable hostility – so much so that we should find ourselves saying, 'I cannot do that', just as a mother might say, 'I cannot drop my baby on the ground.'* Our attitude towards other Christians *should also change as we begin to find that our deepest friendships and our closest ties are with those who share our faith in Jesus Christ, our brothers and sisters in Him.*

**Lord, make me a worthy member of Your family, hating the things You hate and loving my fellow family members. Amen.**

### Doers of the word, and not hearers only.
### (James 1:22)

"Not everyone who says to me, 'Lord, Lord,' will enter the kingdom of heaven, but the one who does the will of my Father who is in heaven . . . Everyone then who hears these words of mine and does them will be like a wise man who built his house on the rock. And the rain fell, and the floods came, and the winds blew and beat on that house, but it did not fall, because it had been founded on the rock. And everyone who hears these words of mine and does not do them will be like a foolish man who built his house on the sand. And the rain fell, and the floods came, and the winds blew and beat against that house, and it fell, and great was the fall of it" (Matthew 7:21, 24–27).

*There probably was not much to choose between these two houses so far as their appearance was concerned, and from the outside they both looked comfortable and secure. But the test of a good house, or car, or almost anything else, is not how it looks but how it lasts – and when the full fury of the storm broke upon them the difference was immediately apparent. So it is possible to have two people who profess to be Christians. They attend the same church and seem equally sincere, but when the storm bursts one collapses and the other comes through strong and unscathed. Why? Because the first person built his or her life upon the shifting sands of human ideas and opinions which disintegrate when the real test comes, while the other chose the solid, unshakable foundations of obedience to Christ's teaching.*

**May it be true of me, O Lord, that 'on Christ the solid rock I stand, all other ground is sinking sand'. Amen.**

## They ought always to pray and not lose heart. (Luke 18:1)

And rising very early in the morning, while it was still dark, he departed and went out to a desolate place, and there he prayed. And . . . they found him and said to him, "Everyone is looking for you" (Mark 1:35–37). He went out to the mountain to pray, and all night he continued in prayer to God. And when day came, he called his disciples and chose from them twelve, whom he named apostles (Luke 6:12–13). But now even more the report about him went abroad, and great crowds gathered to hear him and to be healed of their infirmities. But he would withdraw to desolate places and pray (Luke 5:15–16). And he . . . prayed, saying, "Father, if you are willing, remove this cup from me. Nevertheless, not my will, but yours, be done" . . . And being in an agony he prayed more earnestly; and his sweat became like great drops of blood falling down to the ground (Luke 22:41–42, 44).

*What a lot the disciples must have learnt about prayer from just watching Jesus! Every important occasion in His life was bathed in prayer. Look at four of them here.* A great challenge. *He was just about to start His ministry of healing and teaching, and He committed it all to God in prayer 'a great while before day'.* A great decision. *Perhaps the most important decision He ever made was the choice of His apostles, and it was preceded by a whole night of prayer.* A great fame. *At the very height of His popularity, He made a practice of slipping away quietly for prayer – prayer, perhaps, to be kept humble and dependent.* A great agony. *He found the strength to face the final terrible ordeal in prayer to His Father. No wonder He said, 'Men ought always to pray!'*

Lord, help me to turn to You at all times, but especially when I have a decision to make, a temptation to conquer or a challenge to face. Amen.

### Whom shall I fear? (Psalm 27:1)

"Moses my servant is dead. Now therefore arise, go over this Jordan . . . As I was with Moses, so I will be with you. I will not leave you or forsake you . . . Only be strong and very courageous, being careful to do according to all the law that Moses my servant commanded you. Do not turn from it to the right hand or to the left, that you may have good success wherever you go. This Book of the Law shall not depart from your mouth, but you shall meditate on it day and night, so that you may be careful to do according to all that is written in it. For then you will make your way prosperous, and then you will have good success. Have I not commanded you? Be strong and courageous. Do not be frightened, and do not be dismayed, for the Lord your God is with you wherever you go" (Joshua 1:2, 5, 7–9).

*Moses, the commander-in-chief, had at last been relieved of his post and Joshua, for so long the heir apparent, was to take his place. It was a formidable responsibility – a great people to lead, a river to cross and a country to invade. He needed two things in large measure.* Obedience. *The Law, God's detailed instructions to Moses, was his Bible, and Joshua had to be careful not to deviate from its teachings if he wanted success.* Confidence. *But God was not just going to be his commander, He was going to be his companion as well. Joshua would never be left to fight alone. Are you facing some 'Jordan' – some difficult experience ahead which you are dreading? Then perhaps you can learn the secrets of a successful crossing from Joshua.*

**Lord, 'when I tread the verge of Jordan, bid my anxious fears subside'. Amen.**

## "We are well able to overcome." (Numbers 13:30)

Whatever overcomes a person, to that he is enslaved (2 Peter 2:19). "In me you may have peace. In the world you will have tribulation. But take heart; I have overcome the world" (John 16:33). "And they have conquered him [Satan] by the blood of the Lamb and by the word of their testimony" (Revelation 12:11). For everyone who has been born of God overcomes the world. And this is the victory that has overcome the world – our faith (1 John 5:4). Little children, you are from God and have overcome them, for he who is in you is greater than he who is in the world (1 John 4:4). Do not be overcome by evil, but overcome evil with good (Romans 12:21). "The one who conquers, I will grant him to sit with me on my throne, as I also conquered and sat down with my Father on his throne" (Revelation 3:21).

*The opposite of 'overcoming' is 'undergoing'. We often meet people who have 'undergone' such a long period of defeat in temptation, sorrow, anxiety, persecution or depression that they actually become slaves to these things. Perhaps we have even experienced this ourselves. How can we overcome? We must be on the winning side. Jesus has conquered all these things through His death and resurrection, and so we must belong to Him and join His side. Then we must know the winning moves. There are two mentioned here. We must trust Him to give us the victory – the peace or power that we need. We must also be actively engaged in doing good so that we don't give the evil (whatever form it takes) a chance to flourish. That is how we are going to come through victorious, again and again.*

Lord, make me an 'overcomer' and help me to conquer those things like disappointment and temptation that can so easily 'get me down'. Amen.

## "I will pour out my Spirit on all flesh."
## (Acts 2:17)

When the day of Pentecost arrived, they were all together in one place. And suddenly there came from heaven a sound like a mighty rushing wind, and it filled the entire house where they were sitting. And divided tongues as of fire appeared to them and rested on each one of them. And they were all filled with the Holy Spirit and began to speak in other tongues as the Spirit gave them utterance (Acts 2:1–4). Be filled with the Spirit (Ephesians 5:18). Then Peter, filled with the Holy Spirit, said to them . . . (Acts 4:8). Stephen, full of the Holy Spirit, gazed into heaven and saw the glory of God, and Jesus standing at the right hand of God (Acts 7:55). Barnabas was a good man, full of the Holy Spirit and of faith (Acts 11:24). And the disciples were filled with joy and with the Holy Spirit (Acts 13:52).

*There are two ways in which Christians experience the power of the Holy Spirit. An initial pouring. Just as He came upon the early Christians in that dramatic and unforgettable way, so today He can come into the life of every Christian believer. He comes as the ambassador for Christ, to take His place and to strengthen and guide. A continual filling. The fact that we have received the Holy Spirit does not necessarily mean that we are filled with Him. He is very sensitive, and we may have grieved Him in some way. But we see from these verses how important it is – not only for effective Christian service, but also for our own peace of mind and inner joy, that we should continually 'be filled with the Spirit'.*

**'Spirit of the living God, fall afresh on me – break me, melt me, mould me, fill me; Spirit of the living God, fall afresh on me.' Amen.**

## Jacob whom he loves. (Psalm 47:4)

Isaac said, "Your brother came deceitfully, and he has taken away your blessing." Esau said, "Is he not rightly named Jacob ['Cheater']? For he has cheated me these two times" (Genesis 27:35–36). Then Jacob awoke from his sleep and said, "Surely the Lord is in this place, and I did not know it." And he was afraid and said, "How awesome is this place! This is none other than the house of God, and this is the gate of heaven" . . . Then Jacob made a vow, saying, "If God will be with me . . . then the Lord shall be my God" (Genesis 28:16–17, 20–21). And Jacob was left alone. And a man wrestled with him . . . Then he said, "Let me go" . . . But Jacob said, "I will not let you go unless you bless me." And he said to him, "What is your name?" And he said, "Jacob." Then he said, "Your name shall no longer be called Jacob, but Israel ['Prince'], for you have striven with God and with men, and have prevailed" (Genesis 32:24, 26–28).

*I am always so glad I was not at school with Jacob, for he must have been a most unpleasant person – underhanded and deceitful. I think Esau would have been much nicer to know. But the beauty of this story is that it shows that God loves even the most unlovable and can turn the cheater into a prince. No one is beyond His reach to rescue and to remake. How did it happen? Banished from home, lonely and afraid, Jacob caught a glimpse of the holiness and the power of God. Then, in this curious midnight struggle, he refused to let his mysterious adversary go until He had blessed him by bestowing upon him forgiveness and strength. What a lot of people the Lord transformed! And often a change of name indicated a change of heart: Saul became Paul, Simon became Peter, and Jacob became Israel.*

**I thank you, Lord, that Your love is so great that 'the vilest offender who truly believes, that moment from Jesus a pardon receives'. Amen.**

## "You wicked and slothful servant!"
### (Matthew 25:26)

How long will you lie there, O sluggard? When will you arise from your sleep? A little sleep, a little slumber, a little folding of the hands to rest, and poverty will come upon you like a robber, and want like an armed man (Proverbs 6:9–11). The sluggard does not plough in the autumn; he will seek at harvest and have nothing (Proverbs 20:4). Through sloth the roof sinks in, and through indolence the house leaks (Ecclesiastes 10:18). Go to the ant, O sluggard; consider her ways, and be wise (Proverbs 6:6). The hour has come for you to wake from sleep. For salvation is nearer to us now than when we first believed. The night is far gone; the day is at hand. So then let us cast off the works of darkness and put on the armour of light (Romans 13:11–12). Making the best use of the time, because the days are evil (Ephesians 5:16).

*These verses are not attacking sleep itself, which is one of God's greatest gifts to humankind ('He gives to his beloved sleep', Psalm 127:2). But just as it is possible to eat too much and become a glutton, so it is possible to sleep too much and become a sluggard, and it is a danger which perhaps we all need to watch. In other words, these verses condemn laziness in every shape and form: the lazy farmer who neglects to sow his fields; the lazy householder who doesn't repair his roof; and the lazy Christian who doesn't fight temptation and doesn't take every opportunity he gets of doing good. Next time you see an ants' nest, watch them at work for awhile and let them teach you a lesson of continual and purposeful activity.*

**Lord, next time I am tempted to forsake necessary duty for idle pleasure please give me strength to wake up. Amen.**

## The Lord will be your everlasting light.
## (Isaiah 60:20)

"Because of the tender mercy of our God, whereby the sunrise shall visit us from on high to give light to those who sit in darkness and in the shadow of death" (Luke 1:78–79). The people who walked in darkness have seen a great light; those who dwelt in a land of deep darkness, on them has light shined (Isaiah 9:2). "For you who fear my name, the sun of righteousness shall rise with healing in its wings" (Malachi 4:2). Jesus spoke to them, saying, "I am the light of the world. Whoever follows me will not walk in darkness, but will have the light of life" (John 8:12). "I have come into the world as light, so that whoever believes in me may not remain in darkness" (John 12:46). The Lord is my light and my salvation (Psalm 27:1). In your light do we see light (Psalm 36:9).

*The coming of Jesus into the world was like the dawn of a new day, or the switching on of a brilliant light, for those who were 'walking' in darkness trying to find the way, and for those who were 'sitting' in darkness having given up all hope. There are two things which light does in the ordinary way, and which Jesus can do for those who believe in Him and follow Him. First, it reveals danger. If we keep close to Christ in our daily lives, we shall see more clearly the traps and pitfalls that Satan puts in our path. Second, it removes doubt. In the light of His presence the difficult decisions which we make will become clear to us, and we will have confidence in making them. In His light we shall see light.*

**Lighten my darkness, O Lord, and by Your great mercy defend me from the dangers and doubts of daily life. Amen.**

**This poor man cried, and the Lord heard him.
(Psalm 34:6)**

Jesus also told this parable to some who trusted in themselves that they were righteous, and treated others with contempt: "Two men went up into the temple to pray, one a Pharisee and the other a tax collector. The Pharisee, standing by himself, prayed thus: 'God, I thank you that I am not like other men, extortioners, unjust, adulterers, or even like this tax collector. I fast twice a week; I give tithes of all that I get.' But the tax collector, standing far off, would not even lift up his eyes to heaven, but beat his breast, saying, 'God, be merciful to me, a sinner!' I tell you, this man went down to his house justified, rather than the other. For everyone who exalts himself will be humbled, but the one who humbles himself will be exalted" (Luke 18:9–14).

*Two men went into the temple apparently for the same purpose – to pray. Actually, one went to tell God how good he was, and the other to tell God how bad he was. The tax collector stood 'far off', in some distant corner of the temple, but in fact he was much nearer to God than the Pharisee. For 'though God is high, yet he has respect for the lowly; but the proud he knows afar off' – He keeps them at arm's length. As they made their way home from the temple, what was the real difference between these two men? Just this: the Pharisee was satisfied with himself, but the tax collector was justified with God. No one is ever too bad to approach God.*

**Lord, have mercy upon me, cleanse me from my sin, and incline my heart to do Your will. Amen.**

## We are to grow up in every way . . . into Christ. (Ephesians 4:15)

You have been born again . . . through the living and abiding word of God (1 Peter 1:23). Like newborn infants, long for the pure spiritual milk, that by it you may grow up to salvation (1 Peter 2:2). Be imitators of God, as beloved children. And walk in love, as Christ loved us and gave himself up for us (Ephesians 5:1–2). I write to you, young men, because you are strong, and the word of God abides in you, and you have overcome the evil one (1 John 2:14). In your thinking be mature (1 Corinthians 14:20). That the man of God may be competent, equipped for every good work (2 Timothy 3:17). I am writing to you, fathers, because you know him who is from the beginning (1 John 2:13). Grow in the grace and knowledge of our Lord and Saviour Jesus Christ (2 Peter 3:18). Until we all attain . . . to mature manhood, to the measure of the stature of the fullness of Christ (Ephesians 4:13).

*Growth in the Christian life is a slow business and has various stages, each of which is marked in its own special way. The babe is distinguished by its appetite. If an adult were to drink proportionately as much milk as a baby, he or she would have to consume a quart a day, such is its appetite. The young Christian should be just as keen to feed upon God's word, the Bible. The child loves to imitate and much of its learning is done that way – and so the next stage in Christian growth is to follow Jesus' example. The youth, or young man, is known for his strength, and so increasing victory and usefulness in service ought to be the mark of the maturing Christian. Finally, there is the father. To know and understand Christ better is the final stage of Christian development. It is worth testing yourself from time to time to see how you have grown.*

Help me, O Lord, to grow steadily and strongly towards Christian maturity. Please show me if and where I may be underdeveloped. Amen.

## A precious cornerstone. (Isaiah 28:16)

"Behold, I am laying in Zion a stone, a cornerstone chosen and precious, and whoever believes in him will not be put to shame" (1 Peter 2:6). Knowing that you were ransomed from the futile ways inherited from your forefathers, not with perishable things such as silver or gold, but with the precious blood of Christ, like that of a lamb without blemish or spot (1 Peter 1:18–19). He has granted to us his precious and very great promises, so that through them you may . . . escape . . . from the corruption that is in the world (2 Peter 1:4). In this you rejoice, though now for a little while, if necessary, you have been grieved by various trials, so that the tested genuineness of your faith – more precious than gold that perishes though it is tested by fire – may be found to result in praise and glory and honour at the revelation of Jesus Christ (1 Peter 1:6–7).

*What do you regard as the most precious things in life? Money? Health? Happiness? Friendships? Certainly all these things give life a richness and a flavour, but none of them appear in the list Peter gives us in these verses. As he sees it, everything of real value is associated with Jesus Christ. Jesus is the only foundation on which we can safely build our lives. Jesus shed His blood to purchase our freedom – because 'there was no other good enough to pay the price of sin'. Jesus' promises are like stepping stones on a marshy moorland walk. And so, for all these reasons, faith in Him is the most important thing in life. And, to Him, we are the most precious thing in creation (Isaiah 43:4).*

**All that I need is in You, Lord Jesus. Life would be worthless without You. Amen.**

**The grace of the Lord Jesus Christ and the love of God and the fellowship of the Holy Spirit. (2 Corinthians 13:14)**

"The Holy Spirit will come upon you, and the power of the Most High will overshadow you; therefore the child to be born will be called holy – the Son of God" (Luke 1:35). And the Holy Spirit descended on him in bodily form, like a dove; and a voice came from heaven, "You are my beloved Son; with you I am well pleased" (Luke 3:22). When the goodness and loving kindness of God our Saviour appeared, he saved us . . . by the washing of regeneration and renewal of the Holy Spirit, whom he poured out on us richly through Jesus Christ our Saviour (Titus 3:4–6). "Go therefore and make disciples of all nations, baptizing them in the name of the Father and of the Son and of the Holy Spirit" (Matthew 28:19).

*According to the Bible, the Father, the Son and the Holy Spirit are three distinct and yet united Persons – not one person disguising himself in three different ways, not three separate people working as a sort of 'triumvirate' – three Persons in one God. Our minds cannot grasp such a mystery, but illustrations may help. Think, for example, of a book. It can exist in three ways. First, it can exist in the mind of the author – complete, but invisible and unknown. That is like God the Father. Then the book is written and printed – 'the word becomes flesh' – and we can handle it and see it for ourselves. That is like God the Son. Finally, the book exists in the imagination of the reader so that, for me,* Wuthering Heights *and* Treasure Island *are not so much tangible objects on my bookshelf as they are a series of pictures printed upon my mind. That is like God the Holy Spirit.*

**Lord, make me humble enough to believe what I cannot fully understand. Amen.**

JUNE 4

**"Holy, holy, holy, is the Lord God Almighty, who was and is and is to come!" (Revelation 4:8)**

I saw the Lord sitting upon a throne, high and lifted up; and the train of his robe filled the temple. Above him stood the seraphim . . . and one called to another and said: "Holy, holy, holy is the Lord of hosts; the whole earth is full of his glory!" . . . And I said: "Woe is me! For I am lost; for I am a man of unclean lips, and . . . my eyes have seen the King, the Lord of hosts!" Then one of the seraphim flew to me, having in his hand a burning coal that he had taken with tongs from the altar. And he touched my mouth and said: "Behold, this has touched your lips; your guilt is taken away, and your sin atoned for." And I heard the voice of the Lord saying, "Whom shall I send, and who will go for us?" Then I said, "Here am I! Send me." And he said, "Go, and say to this people . . ." (Isaiah 6:1–9).

*The young man Isaiah never forgot this remarkable experience which came to him, as it did to Moses, at the outset of his ministry as a prophet. I saw . . . It began with a vision of God's majestic, awe-inspiring holiness. Only the knowledge of God's infinite greatness would give him the strength to do his immensely difficult work as a prophet. I said . . . For the first time, perhaps, he saw himself as he really was, for even the whitest sheet cannot compare with the dazzling purity of the snow, and he realized that he was guilty, lost and helpless. Confession brought immediate and complete cleansing. I heard . . . It was then that he was ready to receive his great commission and he gave his immediate and whole-hearted response – 'Here am I! Send me.'*

**'Mine are the hands to do the work, my feet shall run for Thee, my lips shall sound the glorious news, Lord, here am I send me!' Amen.**

## Oh, the depth of the riches and wisdom and knowledge of God! (Romans 11:33)

It is he who made the earth by his power, who established the world by his wisdom, and by his understanding stretched out the heavens (Jeremiah 10:12). O Lord, how manifold are your works! In wisdom have you made them all; the earth is full of your creatures (Psalm 104:24). We preach Christ crucified, a stumbling block to Jews and folly to Gentiles, but to those who are called, both Jews and Greeks, Christ the power of God and the wisdom of God (1 Corinthians 1:23–24). But we impart a secret and hidden wisdom of God, which God decreed before the ages (1 Corinthians 2:7). We . . . pray for you, asking that you may be filled with the knowledge of his will in all spiritual wisdom and understanding, so as to walk in a manner worthy of the Lord, fully pleasing to him, bearing fruit in every good work and increasing in the knowledge of God (Colossians 1:9–10).

*We see the wisdom of God in three ways. First, we see His wisdom as* Creator. *As we look at the universe, we observe how God has brought order and beauty out of empty chaos. Everything we see argues in favour of the existence of an infinitely wise Maker. Second, we see God's wisdom as* Redeemer. *The sin of human beings created an insoluble problem: How could a holy God receive rebellious, sinful people? God solved it by punishing sin and bearing its penalty Himself in the person of Jesus Christ. 'O loving wisdom of our God, when all was sin and shame, a second Adam to the fight and to the rescue came.' Third, we see God's wisdom as* Father. *He promises to give His children, in answer to prayer (James 1:5), a share of this wisdom – so that they learn to walk in His ways and do His will.*

Lord, give me the wisdom I need to know what to believe and to know how to distinguish good from evil, and right from wrong. Amen.

## The grace of God has appeared, bringing salvation. (Titus 2:11)

Christ has entered . . . into heaven itself, now to appear in the presence of God on our behalf . . . he has appeared once for all . . . to put away sin by the sacrifice of himself. And . . . Christ . . . will appear a second time, not to deal with sin but to save those who are eagerly waiting for him (Hebrews 9:24, 26, 28). For by grace you have been saved through faith (Ephesians 2:8). The word of the cross is folly to those who are perishing, but to us who are being saved it is the power of God (1 Corinthians 1:18). Who by God's power are being guarded through faith for a salvation ready to be revealed in the last time (1 Peter 1:5). For salvation is nearer to us now than when we first believed. The night is far gone; the day is at hand (Romans 13:11–12).

*A very learned bishop was once approached on a railway platform by a Salvation Army lass who asked him if he was saved. Rather unkindly, he replied in Greek and completely floored her. But he wanted to show that there are three tenses of salvation – past, present and future – and of course he was quite right. We have been saved from the guilt of sin; we are being saved daily from its power; and one day, when Christ appears again, we shall be saved from its presence. We are like someone who has inherited a fortune which comes to him in three stages: an outright gift to settle all his debts and liabilities; a steady income for life; and a generous provision for his old age. That is why the Bible sometimes speaks of us as being 'saved in hope' (Romans 8:24) as well as 'by faith'.*

**Lord, I thank You that You died to redeem me, that You live to renew me day by day, and that one day You will come again to receive me into Your presence. Amen.**

**Jesus ... manifested his glory. And his disciples believed in him. (John 2:11)**

There was a wedding at Cana in Galilee, and the mother of Jesus was there. Jesus also was invited ... with his disciples. When the wine ran out, the mother of Jesus said to him, "They have no wine." And Jesus said to her, "Woman, what does this have to do with me? My hour has not yet come." His mother said to the servants, "Do whatever he tells you" ... Jesus said to the servants, "Fill the jars with water." And they filled them up to the brim. And he said ... "Now draw some out and take it to the master of the feast" ... When the master of the feast tasted the water now become wine ... he called the bridegroom and said to him, "Everyone serves the good wine first, and when people have drunk freely, then the poor wine. But you have kept the good wine until now" (John 2:1–10).

*I can see two miracles in this story. First there is the* miracle of the water. *Isn't it interesting how inanimate objects behaved as if they were alive when Jesus spoke to them – the waves, the loaves and fishes, and now 'the shamefaced water saw its God and blushed'? But miracles of this sort ought not to surprise us. He is Creator of all things, and all things are under His control and answer to His command. Second, though, there is the* miracle of the waiters. *Jesus often found people far less responsive to Him than nature was, but on this occasion the waiters behaved differently and carried out what must have seemed a strange order without question or hesitation. Are we as ready and responsive as they were when He calls us to some task? I can also see a parable in this story, because just as Jesus turned the water into wine, so He can turn the water of ordinary human existence into the sparkling wine of life at its best.*

**Lord, make me quick to hear and ready to do Your will. Amen.**

### "Your accent betrays you." (Matthew 26:73)

Let no corrupting talk come out of your mouths, but only such as is good for building up, as fits the occasion, that it may give grace to those who hear (Ephesians 4:29). Let your speech always be gracious, seasoned with salt, so that you may know how you ought to answer each person (Colossians 4:6). "Let what you say be simply 'Yes' or 'No'; anything more than this comes from evil" (Matthew 5:37). "I tell you, on the day of judgment people will give account for every careless word they speak, for by your words you will be justified, and by your words you will be condemned" (Matthew 12:36–37). Keep your tongue from evil and your lips from speaking deceit (Psalm 34:13). Know this, my beloved brothers: let every person be quick to hear, slow to speak (James 1:19).

*Have you ever thought what a terrible traitor the tongue is? It is always giving us away. It* betrays our health. *Doctors often used to say, 'Let me see your tongue', and from his observation he could get a shrewd idea of whether we were fit or ill. So it is that the person whose speech is larded with swear words or who indulges in lies, gossip and unkind criticism reveals a pretty poor state of spiritual health. The tongue also* betrays our nationality. *However well foreigners may speak another language, they usually betray themselves by their accents. Christians, too, by the truthful, humble, generous way in which they speak, will show that they are citizens of the kingdom of God.*

Set a watch, O Lord, before my mouth; keep the door of my lips. May the words of my mouth be always acceptable in Your sight, O Lord my strength and my redeemer. Amen.

**I will be a father to you, and you shall be sons
and daughters to me, says the Lord Almighty.
(2 Corinthians 6:18)**

When the fullness of time had come, God sent forth his Son
. . . to redeem those who were under the law, so that we might
receive adoption as sons. And because you are sons, God has
sent the Spirit of his Son into our hearts, crying, "Abba!
Father!" So you are no longer a slave, but a son, and if a son,
then an heir through God (Galatians 4:4–7). He predestined us
for adoption through Jesus Christ (Ephesians 1:5). All who are
led by the Spirit of God are sons of God. For you did not
receive the spirit of slavery to fall back into fear, but . . . the
Spirit of adoption as sons, by whom we cry, "Abba! Father!"
The Spirit himself bears witness with our spirit that we are
children of God, and if children, then heirs – heirs of God and
fellow heirs with Christ (Romans 8:14–17). Blameless and
innocent, children of God without blemish (Philippians 2:15).

*Both John and Paul tell us that we are children of God by faith in
Jesus Christ. But while John uses the metaphor of birth, Paul uses
that of adoption – with its suggestion of a loving choice made on the
part of God. There are three things to consider as we think about
being part of God's family. First,* the family relationship. *As
Christians adopted into God's family we begin to look on Him in a
new way – not as a distant Judge, but as a loving Father whom we
can address in almost affectionate terms ('Abba' = 'Daddy'). Second
are* the family riches. *As fellow heirs with Christ we begin to share
in all the wealth that God has prepared for us. Third, we consider* the
family reputation. *For our part, we must begin to live the sort of
life which will bring credit to the name we now bear.*

**Lord, I thank You for adopting me into Your family, and I ask
for Your help to walk worthy of the name by which I am
called. Amen.**

**"The Son of Man came to seek and to save the lost." (Luke 19:10)**

Jesus told them this parable: "What man of you, having a hundred sheep, if he has lost one of them, does not leave the ninety-nine in the open country, and go after the one that is lost, until he finds it? And when he has found it, he lays it on his shoulders, rejoicing. And when he comes home, he calls together his friends and his neighbours, saying to them, 'Rejoice with me, for I have found my sheep that was lost.' Just so, I tell you, there will be more joy in heaven over one sinner who repents than over ninety-nine righteous persons who need no repentance. Or what woman, having ten silver coins, if she loses one coin, does not light a lamp and sweep the house and seek diligently until she finds it? . . . Just so . . . there is joy before the angels of God over one sinner who repents" (Luke 15:3–8, 10).

*In both of these stories we can imagine the sorrow with which the loss was first discovered, the sacrifices of time, energy and perhaps money that were made during the search, and the satisfaction that followed the recovery of that which had been lost. They remind us how precious we are to God and how much He loves us. What a sacrifice Christ made in coming 'to seek and save' us. For 'None of the ransomed ever knew how deep were the waters crossed, nor how dark was the night that the Lord went through, e'er He found His sheep that was lost'. What joy it gives Him when we repent and return to Him (Isaiah 53:11)! The stories are very alike, but there is one interesting little difference. The sheep knew that it was lost and wanted to be found, but the coin was quite unaware of its need. Can you see how that fits into the interpretation?*

**Lord, I thank You for the deep love which made You search so diligently for me. Amen.**

## Rejoice with those who rejoice, weep with those who weep. (Romans 12:15)

Let each of you look not only to his own interests, but also to the interests of others (Philippians 2:4). Bear one another's burdens, and so fulfil the law of Christ (Galatians 6:2). If one member suffers, all suffer together; if one member is honoured, all rejoice together. Now you are the body of Christ and individually members of it (1 Corinthians 12:26–27). Who is weak, and I am not weak? Who is made to fall, and I am not indignant? (2 Corinthians 11:29) "If you were in my place . . . I could strengthen you with my mouth, and the solace of my lips would assuage your pain" (Job 16:4–5). Anxiety in a man's heart weighs him down, but a good word makes him glad (Proverbs 12:25). "These things I [Jesus] have spoken to you, that my joy may be in you, and that your joy may be full" (John 15:11). Jesus . . . said, "I have compassion on the crowd" (Matthew 15:32). Jesus wept (John 11:35).

*'Sympathy' literally means to 'suffer with' someone – to enter into and share their feelings, whether of sorrow or of joy. This quality ought to be apparent, and especially in any sort of Christian community. Why? First, because it is part of 'the law of Christ' that we should love one another. Secondly, because Jesus Himself set such a wonderful example in this respect. He was the most welcome guest at a wedding at the start of His ministry, and at a funeral at the end of it. Thirdly, Christians are bound together like a body and, when one part of that body is damaged or diseased, the natural thing is for the rest of it to desire and hasten its complete recovery. Christians form a family – the fortunes of one member are followed with eager sympathy by the others.*

I thank You, Lord, for those whose words and actions have helped me at times of disappointment or trouble. Make me, in my turn, a source of comfort to others. Amen.

**"Come to me . . . that your soul may live."
(Isaiah 55:3)**

At that time Jesus declared, "I thank you, Father, Lord of heaven and earth, that you have hidden these things from the wise and understanding and revealed them to little children; yes, Father, for such was your gracious will. All things have been handed over to me by my Father, and no one knows the Son except the Father, and no one knows the Father except the Son and anyone to whom the Son chooses to reveal him. Come to me, all who labour and are heavy laden, and I will give you rest. Take my yoke upon you, and learn from me, for I am gentle and lowly in heart, and you will find rest for your souls. For my yoke is easy, and my burden is light" (Matthew 11:25–30).

*If you have ever played 'hide and seek' with a small child you will know how you have to reveal yourself if the little one is to find you – a toe here, a bulge behind a curtain, a slight noise. So it is only when God reveals Himself to us that we can find Him. Notice how Christ offers three things that everyone needs. First,* an education – *'Learn . . .'* To the very end of our lives we shall be learners, understanding more and more of what God reveals to us. Second, an occupation – *'Take . . .'* 'There's a work for Jesus none but you can do.' It's so important to find out what that is, and to use up every ounce of energy doing it! The third thing we need for a full life is recreation – *'You will find rest'. Perfect rest and peace for the Christian are found in the presence of Christ.*

**Lord, You came that I might have life, and have it more abundantly; help me to find that fullness and satisfaction in Your friendship and Your service. Amen.**

## "Behold, I am making all things new." (Revelation 21:5)

Therefore, if anyone is in Christ, he is a new creation. The old has passed away; behold, the new has come (2 Corinthians 5:17). Put off your old self, which belongs to your former manner of life . . . and . . . be renewed in the spirit of your minds, and . . . put on the new self, created after the likeness of God in true righteousness and holiness (Ephesians 4:22–24). We were buried therefore with him by baptism into death, in order that, just as Christ was raised from the dead by the glory of the Father, we too might walk in newness of life (Romans 6:4). "I will give you a new heart, and a new spirit I will put within you . . . I will put my Spirit within you, and cause you to walk in my statutes" (Ezekiel 36:26–27). He put a new song in my mouth, a song of praise to our God. Many will see and fear, and put their trust in the Lord (Psalm 40:3).

*'Under new management'. You sometimes see that notice outside a shop or café which perhaps for months has been standing empty, forlorn and derelict, and it is not very long before you begin to notice the difference both inside and out. The Christian is someone who has come under new management, and in whom Christ has begun the great work of renovation. Inside we have a new heart with new desire and ambitions, and a new mind to begin to see things from God's point of view. Outside, too, there is a difference which 'many shall see'. Our 'standard of living' takes a marked turn for the better, and people begin to notice a new kindness, a new humility and a new joy.*

'Create in me a clean heart, O God, and renew a right spirit within me.' Amen.

**The Lord is good, a stronghold in the day of trouble; he knows those who take refuge in him. (Nahum 1:7)**

Make a joyful noise to the Lord, all the earth! Serve the Lord with gladness! Come into his presence with singing! Know that the Lord, he is God! It is he who made us, and we are his; we are his people, and the sheep of his pasture. Enter his gates with thanksgiving, and his courts with praise! Give thanks to him; bless his name! For the Lord is good; his steadfast love endures forever, and his faithfulness to all generations (Psalm 100:1–5).

*This lovely little psalm, which used often to be sung in Anglican churches as part of the morning service, radiates happiness and confidence. 'Be joyful . . .' One of the great tragedies of modern times is that people equate religion with gloom and not with gladness. But for the true Christian, of course, as for the devout Israelite of old, faith in God is the source of tremendous joy and satisfaction. 'Be sure . . .' This joy springs from the knowledge that we belong to God. He is our Creator and Shepherd. He understands exactly how we work, where we are liable to go wrong, and how to put us right. In His hands – the Maker's hands – we are absolutely safe and secure. 'Be thankful . . .' How grateful we should be to God for all that He has done for us! But notice the interesting way in which we are to show that gratitude – 'Bless His name'. How you show your gratitude to a doctor, coach or teacher, whom you want to thank, is to tell other people about him or her. That is what we are to do for God, 'for the Lord is good, his steadfast love endures forever'.*

**Help me, Lord, so to live and speak for You, that others may come to be joyful in You for themselves. Amen.**

## "I will come again." (John 14:3)

And while they were gazing into heaven as he went, behold, two men stood by them in white robes, and said, "Men of Galilee, why do you stand looking into heaven? This Jesus, who was taken up from you into heaven, will come in the same way as you saw him go into heaven" (Acts 1:10–11). "For the Son of Man is going to come with his angels in the glory of his Father" (Matthew 16:27). For the Lord himself will descend from heaven with a cry of command, with the voice of an archangel, and with the sound of the trumpet of God. And the dead in Christ will rise first. Then we who are alive, who are left, will be caught up together with them in the clouds to meet the Lord in the air, and so we will always be with the Lord. Therefore encourage one another with these words (1 Thessalonians 4:16–18). "Surely I am coming soon." Amen. Come, Lord Jesus! (Revelation 22:20)

*Throughout the New Testament there are a number of references to the fact that Jesus Christ will return bodily to the earth He left on the first Ascension Day. His second coming, as it is called, will be very different from His first. Last time He came secretly and silently, a prince landing disguised in enemy-occupied territory to set up a resistance movement which He called His church. Next time it will be like a full-scale invasion. He will come as a King, with His army of angels, to claim that kingdom for Himself and to establish an eternal reign of justice and peace. This hope in His final solution to the world's problems should be a tremendous source of encouragement to Christians.*

Help me, Lord, to live in such a way that I shall not be ashamed to meet You when You come. Amen.

**"Not by might, nor by power, but by my Spirit, says the Lord of hosts." (Zechariah 4:6)**

The angel of the Lord appeared to Gideon and said to him, "The Lord is with you, O mighty man of valour." And Gideon said to him, "Please, sir, if the Lord is with us, why then has all this happened to us? . . . The Lord has forsaken us and given us into the hand of Midian." And the Lord turned to him and said, "Go in this might of yours and save Israel from the hand of Midian; do not I send you?" And he said to him, "Please, Lord, how can I save Israel? Behold, my clan is the weakest in Manasseh, and I am the least in my father's house." And the Lord said to him, "But I will be with you, and you shall strike the Midianites as one man." . . . The Spirit of the Lord clothed Gideon . . . God has given into his hand Midian and all the camp . . . and all the army ran. They cried out and fled . . . And the men of Israel . . . pursued after Midian (Judges 6:12–16, 34, 7:14, 21, 23).

*Read for yourself the full story of Gideon, 'The Reluctant General', and how God enabled him to conquer the Midianites. Gideon mobilized an army of thirty-two thousand men, and the first thing God did was to reduce it to three hundred, 'lest Israel boast over me, saying "My own hand has saved me."' And so Gideon learnt the lesson which runs all the way through the Bible – that in God's service weakness is not a liability, but an asset. What a feeble, flabby thing a boxing glove is by itself, but put the fist of some heavy-weight champion inside, and it is of almost lethal power. So we read that 'the Spirit of the Lord clothed himself [that is the literal meaning] with Gideon' and achieved His great purpose. He can use you in that way too.*

**Lord, clothe Yourself with me. Nerve my arm and stiffen my will to fight and fight and fight again for You. Amen.**

## Alienated from the life of God. (Ephesians 4:18)

For those who live according to the flesh set their minds on the things of the flesh, but those who live according to the Spirit set their minds on the things of the Spirit. To set the mind on the flesh is death, but to set the mind on the Spirit is life and peace. For the mind that is set on the flesh is hostile to God, for it does not submit to God's law; indeed, it cannot. Those who are in the flesh cannot please God (Romans 8:5–8). For I know that nothing good dwells in me, that is, in my flesh. For I have the desire to do what is right, but not the ability to carry it out (Romans 7:18). The natural person does not accept the things of the Spirit of God, for they are folly to him, and he is not able to understand them because they are spiritually discerned (1 Corinthians 2:14). That which is born of the flesh is flesh, and that which is born of the Spirit is spirit (John 3:6).

*The word 'flesh' in the New Testament does not refer to our bodies, but to the natural, sinful state in which we were born into this world. And so there are two kinds of people in the world, 'natural' ('born of the flesh') and 'spiritual' ('born of the Spirit' or 'born again' through faith in Christ). There are two things 'natural' people cannot do. They* cannot please God, *because they are in a state of rebellion ('hostile') to Him, and the only good thing a rebel can do is to surrender. Second, they* cannot know God. *Have you tried explaining the things of God to someone and seen a glazed, blank look come over their face? They are like a fish out of water. They lack the faculty of faith by which alone they can live in a spiritual environment.*

**Lord, give me the strength I need each day to resist the claims of the natural person. Help me to live always on a spiritual level. Amen.**

**Thanks be to God, who gives us the victory
through our Lord Jesus Christ.
(1 Corinthians 15:57)**

The reason the Son of God appeared was to destroy the works
of the devil (1 John 3:8). That through death he might destroy
the one who has the power of death, that is, the devil, and
deliver all those who through fear of death were subject to lifelong slavery (Hebrews 2:14–15). Our Saviour Christ Jesus, who
abolished death and brought life and immortality to light
through the gospel (2 Timothy 1:10). And you, who were dead
in your trespasses . . . God made alive together with him, having forgiven us all our trespasses, by cancelling the record of
debt that stood against us with its legal demands. This he set
aside, nailing it to the cross. He disarmed the rulers and
authorities and put them to open shame, by triumphing over
them in him (Colossians 2:13–15).

*June 18, 1815 was the date of the Battle of Waterloo. People waiting
anxiously in this country for news were horrified to receive the message 'Wellington defeated'. Could that really be so? Was this the
end? A little later came the correction. One word was added:
'Wellington defeated* Napoleon'. *Good Friday, to those who
watched, must have seemed like an awful defeat: 'Jesus defeated'. But
two days later came the news that Christ was risen and victorious
from the grave. Jesus the conqueror had finally defeated, and mortally wounded, that great enemy of humankind, Satan. Jesus
destroyed the power of sin and death. 'The war is won, but it is not
yet over'. That was true in January 1945, and it is true in the
Christian life today. The enemy is defeated, but he has not yet surrendered.*

**Thank You, Lord, for the price You paid to win the victory.
Amen.**

## Declared to be the Son of God. (Romans 1:4)

Now when Jesus came into the district of Caesarea Philippi, he asked his disciples, "Who do people say that the Son of Man is?" And they said, "Some say John the Baptist, others say Elijah, and others Jeremiah or one of the prophets." He said to them, "But who do you say that I am?" Simon Peter replied, "You are the Christ, the Son of the living God." And Jesus answered him, "Blessed are you, Simon Bar-Jonah! For flesh and blood has not revealed this to you, but my Father who is in heaven. And I tell you, you are Peter, and on this rock I will build my church, and the gates of hell shall not prevail against it. I will give you the keys of the kingdom of heaven, and whatever you bind on earth shall be bound in heaven, and whatever you loose on earth shall be loosed in heaven" (Matthew 16:13–19).

*It has been said that Jesus was either mad, bad, or God. If He thought Himself to be the Son of God when He was not, then He must have been mad. If He pretended to be the Son of God when He was not, misleading and deceiving the people, then He was bad. If the stupendous claims He made for Himself were true, then He was God. Many people, wanting to avoid these conclusions, think of Jesus as a great prophet like Elijah or Jeremiah. But this choice is simply not open to us. Either He was very much more – or very much less. 'Aut deus, aut homo non bonus' – 'Either God, or not a good man'. Simon Peter, in his blunt, direct way, got it right the first time. He had heard the authority with which Jesus spoke, watched His life in which no one could find a trace of sin, and seen the marvellous miracles He performed. 'You are the Son of the living God', he said. This truth is the foundation stone of the Christian faith. All who know this can introduce others to the kingdom of God because they themselves have been given the 'members' key'.*

**Thank You, Lord, for revealing to Peter who You are. I ask that I may share his faith and his conviction. Amen.**

## "By this my Father is glorified, that you bear much fruit." (John 15:8)

My beloved had a vineyard on a very fertile hill. He dug it and cleared it of stones, and planted it with choice vines; he built a watchtower in the midst of it, and hewed out a wine vat in it; and he looked for it to yield grapes, but it yielded wild grapes . . . What more was there to do for my vineyard, that I have not done in it? (Isaiah 5:1–2, 4). We . . . pray . . . that you may . . . walk in a manner worthy of the Lord, fully pleasing to him, bearing fruit in every good work (Colossians 1:9–10). The fruit of the Spirit is love, joy, peace, patience, kindness, goodness, faithfulness, gentleness, self-control (Galatians 5:22–23). "Abide in me, and I in you. As the branch cannot bear fruit by itself, unless it abides in the vine, neither can you, unless you abide in me" (John 15:4). From me comes your fruit (Hosea 14:8).

*How sad it is when, after much care and attention, and perhaps some early promise, a fruit tree proves completely barren. God feels that sort of disappointment, I am afraid, when He looks at the lives of some Christians and sees no fruit. What is the secret of producing the kind of fruit He expects to find? The key word is 'abide'. An electric light bulb taken from its socket can give no light. It must abide, or keep in contact, with the source of power. A branch cut from a tree quickly withers and fades. A Christian who fails to keep in constant touch with Christ through prayer, Bible reading and meditation will soon run out of power and will have nothing to show. For 'without Him we can do nothing'.*

**Lord, save me from a barren, empty Christian life, and make me fruitful and pleasing to You. Amen.**

## Strengthened with power through his Spirit in your inner being. (Ephesians 3:16)

I rejoiced in the Lord greatly that now at length you have revived your concern for me. You were indeed concerned for me, but you had no opportunity. Not that I am speaking of being in need, for I have learned in whatever situation I am to be content. I know how to be brought low, and I know how to abound. In any and every circumstance, I have learned the secret of facing plenty and hunger, abundance and need. I can do all things through him who strengthens me. Yet it was kind of you to share my trouble . . . And my God will supply every need of yours according to his riches in glory in Christ Jesus. To our God and Father be glory forever and ever (Philippians 4:10–14, 19–20).

*How easily and how often we grumble! The food, the weather and the government are perhaps our favourite targets for complaint. And yet here we find Paul, deprived of many of the things which we consider essential for a full life, perfectly content. What was his secret? Surely it was the fact that Paul's source of happiness lay within himself and not outside. For the person who has Christ in his heart, and is drawing deeply and daily from His wells of love and power, 'stone walls do not a prison make, nor iron bars a cage'. Many, many modern Christian prisoners like Bonhoeffer and Wurmbrand have proved this and, in the most appalling conditions, have retained their confidence in God and their concern for others.*

**Lord, help me not to be so wedded to, and dependent upon, earthly things that their loss would leave me desperate and forlorn. Amen.**

## We are not ignorant of Satan's designs.
## (2 Corinthians 2:11)

That ancient serpent, who is called the devil and Satan, the deceiver of the whole world (Revelation 12:9). Now the serpent was more crafty than any other beast of the field that the Lord God had made. He said to the woman, "Did God actually say, 'You shall not eat of any tree in the garden'?" And the woman said to the serpent, "We may eat of the fruit of the trees in the garden, but God said, 'You shall not eat of the fruit of the tree that is in the midst of the garden, neither shall you touch it, lest you die.'" But the serpent said to the woman, "You will not surely die" (Genesis 3:1–4). "The devil . . . has nothing to do with the truth, because there is no truth in him. When he lies, he speaks out of his own character, for he is a liar and the father of lies" (John 8:44). Give no opportunity to the devil (Ephesians 4:27). Resist the devil, and he will flee from you (James 4:7).

*Notice how very cleverly Satan set to work upon Eve. He began by sowing a* doubt *in her mind ('Did God say?') and, after giving doubt a little time to mature, he faced her with an outright* denial *('You will not die'). With such a glaring example before us, we have no excuse for being 'ignorant of his devices'. He starts with a question: 'Wouldn't it be rather fun?' 'Isn't it grey rather than black?' 'Won't it add to your experience?' And then, if we are silly enough to listen to him, he will come with a statement: 'It's all right', 'Just this once', 'No one will know'. How do we deal with him? First, we must give him no opportunity and turn a deaf ear to his enticing suggestions; then, if he does gain a foothold, we must resist him for all we are worth.*

**Lord, help me to learn from Eve's mistake and to give the devil no encouragement whatsoever. Amen.**

## Conduct yourselves wisely. (Colossians 4:5)

Trust in the Lord with all your heart, and do not lean on your own understanding. In all your ways acknowledge him, and he will make straight your paths. Be not wise in your own eyes; fear the Lord, and turn away from evil. It will be healing to your flesh and refreshment to your bones . . . Then you will walk on your way securely, and your foot will not stumble. If you lie down, you will not be afraid; when you lie down, your sleep will be sweet. Do not be afraid of sudden terror or of the ruin of the wicked, when it comes, for the Lord will be your confidence and will keep your foot from being caught (Proverbs 3:5–8, 23–26).

*'Trust and obey, for there's no other way to be happy in Jesus, but to trust and obey.' That would be the New Testament summary of this passage. True wisdom is a spiritual, and not a natural, gift, and the secret of making right decisions and finding the correct path through life is depending upon God's judgment and having confidence in His power – in other words, 'trust and obey'. Notice how the writer seems to link all this with physical health and good sleep. Is there anything in this? Many physical disorders are due to worry, anxiety, jealousy, impatience and so on – just the very things, in fact, which the Lord can deal with in our lives. But we must make it possible for Him to do so by trusting and obeying. Physically, therefore, and spiritually, we can 'walk on our way securely'.*

**Lord, please save me from the mistakes and blunders which come from relying on my own imperfect judgment and insight, and help me to trust and obey You. Amen.**

### There was a man sent from God, whose name was John. (John 1:6)

The Jews sent priests . . . to ask John, "Who are you?" He confessed . . . "I am not the Christ." And they asked him, "What then? Are you Elijah?" He said, "I am not." "Are you the Prophet?" And he answered, "No." So they said to him, "Who are you?" . . . He said, "I am the voice of one crying out in the wilderness, 'Make straight the way of the Lord'" (John 1:19–23). And John looked at Jesus as he walked by and said, "Behold, the Lamb of God!" (John 1:36). "The one who has the bride is the bridegroom. The friend of the bridegroom, who stands and hears him, rejoices greatly at the bridegroom's voice. Therefore this joy of mine is now complete. He must increase, but I must decrease" (John 3:29–30). "There has arisen no one greater than John the Baptist" (Matthew 11:11). "He was a burning and shining lamp" (John 5:35).

*We notice two things particularly about John the Baptist. First, we see* his authority. *His voice rang through the hills and valleys, turning people back to God and preparing the way for Christ. They flocked to hear him, and even Herod was moved by his preaching. Second, we note* his humility. *Notice how his answers to the priests got shorter and sharper as he turned their thoughts away from himself – 'I am not the Christ', 'I am not', 'No'. John was perfectly content to be the best man, the runner-up, the second string, the silver medallist. He wanted Jesus to have all the glory and the credit. John was the 'voice', but Jesus was the 'Word' which gave it meaning. John was the 'lamp', but Jesus was the 'Light' which shone through it. Authority and humility don't often go together. Most people have one or the other. John the Baptist had both.*

**Lord, I thank You for the life of John the Baptist. Give me something of his humility and, when I have to speak in Your name, his authority as well. Amen.**

## The Lord ... said ... "Where are you?"
## (Genesis 3:9)

And Adam said, "I heard the sound of you in the garden, and I was afraid, because I was naked, and I hid myself" (Genesis 3:10). Jonah rose to flee to Tarshish from the presence of the Lord. He went down to Joppa and found a ship going to Tarshish. So he paid the fare and went on board, to go with them to Tarshish, away from the presence of the Lord (Jonah 1:3). "The younger son gathered all he had and took a journey into a far country, and there he squandered his property in reckless living" (Luke 15:13). Where shall I go from your Spirit? Or where shall I flee from your presence? If I ascend to heaven, you are there! If I make my bed in Sheol, you are there! (Psalm 139:7–8) At that time separated from Christ, alienated ... and strangers ... but now in Christ Jesus you who once were far off have been brought near by the blood of Christ (Ephesians 2:12–13). You were straying like sheep, but have now returned to the Shepherd ... of your souls (1 Peter 2:25).

*We are familiar with the idea of human beings searching for God, but it is also true that God is searching for us. The question 'Where are you?' is an eternal refrain because we are always trying to flee from the presence of the Lord – out of fear, perhaps, or because we are looking for pleasure and excitement somewhere else. But we can never get out of God's sight or reach. He knows the answer to His own question, and He only asks it so that we will admit our need. With Him it is never a case of someone being 'last heard of six months ago touring in Scotland', as we hear so often on the radio. But He will never force us back. He calls us firmly and gently. Be sure to read sometime Francis Thompson's famous poem 'The Hound of Heaven'. 'I fled Him down the nights and down the days, I fled Him down the arches of the years . . .'*

**I thank You, dear Lord, that I cannot get beyond Your reach, but I ask that I may never try to flee from You. Amen.**

**He interpreted to them in all the Scriptures the things concerning himself. (Luke 24:27)**

Behold, the virgin shall conceive and bear a son, and shall call his name Immanuel (Isaiah 7:14). For to us a child is born, to us a son is given . . . and his name shall be called Wonderful Counsellor, Mighty God, Everlasting Father, Prince of Peace (Isaiah 9:6). Each will be like a hiding place from the wind, a shelter from the storm, like streams of water in a dry place, like the shade of a great rock in a weary land (Isaiah 32:2). The Spirit of the Lord God is upon me, because the Lord has anointed me to bring good news to the poor; he has sent me to bind up the brokenhearted, to proclaim liberty to the captives, and the opening of the prison to those who are bound (Isaiah 61:1). Surely he has borne our griefs and carried our sorrows; yet we esteemed him stricken, smitten by God, and afflicted. But he was wounded for our transgressions; he was crushed for our iniquities . . . and with his stripes we are healed (Isaiah 53:4–5).

*These remarkable passages in the book of Isaiah, written hundreds of years before the birth of Christ, must have puzzled the prophet because he knew that he was dealing with matters which did not refer to his own time, but to ours (1 Peter 1:10–12). For us the meaning is marvellously plain. A child. As Christians look at the babe in the manger at Bethlehem, they see much more than an ordinary child. They see 'the Mighty God, the Everlasting Father' revealed in human form. A man. And in the man Christ Jesus we see one who was 'wounded for our transgressions' on the cross and who rose again to offer His followers two things which everyone wants – security and liberty. But have you ever thought how seldom in ordinary life we can enjoy both those things together? In Christ we can do so.*

**Lord, I thank You today for what You are, for what You have done, and for what You can be to me. Amen.**

**The word of the Lord remains forever. (1 Peter 1:25)**

From childhood you have been acquainted with the sacred writings, which are able to make you wise for salvation through faith in Christ Jesus. All Scripture is breathed out by God and profitable for teaching, for reproof, for correction, and for training in righteousness, that the man of God may be competent, equipped for every good work (2 Timothy 3:15–17). Knowing this first of all, that no prophecy of Scripture comes from someone's own interpretation. For no prophecy was ever produced by the will of man, but men spoke from God as they were carried along by the Holy Spirit (2 Peter 1:20–21). He spoke by the mouth of his holy prophets from of old (Luke 1:70). Long ago, at many times and in many ways, God spoke to our fathers by the prophets, but in these last days he has spoken to us by his Son (Hebrews 1:1–2).

*It is nowhere suggested that God Himself actually wrote the Bible, but what is claimed is that He inspired and breathed into the minds of the writers what He wanted them to write. So the Scriptures do not contain merely human ideas. They express the will and purpose of God – like a conductor with his orchestra or like St Paul's Cathedral. Sir Christopher Wren probably did not build any of the structure himself, but as the architect he breathed his plan and purpose into the minds of the workmen. It is helpful to think of the Bible as a portrait. The central figure is Christ, who is portrayed for us in the Gospels. The Old Testament provides the background, giving meaning to the figure. The later books of the New Testament are like His robes and His armour. As we read, the figure steps out of the canvas and introduces Himself to us – out of literature into life, and out of history into experience.*

**Lord, I thank You for Your living Word, and for what it is able to do for me in guiding and instructing me. Amen.**

## Sorrow and sighing shall flee away. (Isaiah 35:10)

"When a woman is giving birth, she has sorrow because her hour has come, but when she has delivered the baby, she no longer remembers the anguish, for joy that a human being has been born into the world. So also you have sorrow now, but I will see you again and your hearts will rejoice, and no one will take your joy from you" (John 16:21–22). And when Paul had said these things, he knelt down and prayed with them all. And there was much weeping on the part of all; they embraced Paul and kissed him, being sorrowful most of all because of the word he had spoken, that they would not see his face again (Acts 20:36–38). But we do not want you to be uninformed, brothers, about those who are asleep, that you may not grieve as others do who have no hope (1 Thessalonians 4:13). "God . . . will wipe away every tear from their eyes, and death shall be no more, neither shall there be mourning nor crying nor pain" (Revelation 21:4).

*Saying goodbye is always a sad business, and when the time comes for us to take the long, last farewell of someone we love, it is only natural that our hearts should be full of sorrow. But, for the Christian, sorrow must never be the last and surviving emotion. Sorrow must give way in the end to joy. Why? Because for us death is not the end of the journey, but only where we 'change' en route. It's not a precipice over which we fall, to be seen no more, but a horizon beyond which we pass into a new and better world where tears will be unknown. Someone has said that for the Christian the opposite of joy is not sorrow, but sin. We can 'trace the rainbow through the rain, and feel the promise is not vain, that morn shall tearless be'.*

**Lord, give me the faith and hope that brighten sorrow and dispel tears. Amen.**

## "You are Simon . . . You shall be called Peter." (John 1:42)

Jesus said to Simon, "Put out into the deep and let down your nets for a catch." And Simon answered, "Master, we toiled all night and took nothing! But at your word I will let down the nets." And when they had done this, they enclosed a large number of fish . . . When Simon Peter saw it, he fell down at Jesus' knees, saying, "Depart from me, for I am a sinful man, O Lord" (Luke 5:4–6, 8). Jesus said to them, "But who do you say that I am?" Simon Peter replied, "You are the Christ, the Son of the living God" (Matthew 16:15–16). Jesus said to him . . . "Simon . . . do you love me?" Peter was grieved because he said to him the third time, "Do you love me?" and he said to him, "Lord, you know everything; you know that I love you" (John 21:17).

*Jesus had been a carpenter, and no doubt they had often brought great lengths of rough timber into the workshop from which He had produced tables, chairs or cabinets. 'You are . . . you shall be' is what He may have said to it. And that was how He greeted Simon Peter. From the rough, unpromising Simon Jesus produced one of His great masterpieces – Peter the Apostle. Notice how He set to work. There were at least three critical moments in Peter's life. On the first occasion Jesus touched his conscience and showed him his need for forgiveness. On the second, it was Peter's mind that was awakened to see who Jesus really was. Finally, after his tragic denial, Jesus touched his heart and called out that love which was to inspire Peter for the rest of his life.*

**Forgive me, Lord, for my failures. Enlighten me to know You better. Enflame me with Your love. Amen.**

**And God said, "Let there be light," and there was light. (Genesis 1:3)**

Therefore, having this ministry by the mercy of God, we do not lose heart. But we have renounced disgraceful, underhanded ways. We refuse to practice cunning or to tamper with God's word, but by the open statement of the truth we would commend ourselves to everyone's conscience in the sight of God. And even if our gospel is veiled, it is veiled only to those who are perishing. In their case the god of this world has blinded the minds of the unbelievers, to keep them from seeing the light of the gospel of the glory of Christ, who is the image of God. For what we proclaim is not ourselves, but Jesus Christ as Lord, with ourselves as your servants for Jesus' sake. For God, who said, "Let light shine out of darkness," has shone in our hearts to give the light of the knowledge of the glory of God in the face of Jesus Christ (2 Corinthians 4:1-6).

*We notice again the three words we read yesterday – conscience, mind and heart. They refer to the moral, the intellectual and the emotional parts of our make-up. It is possible to be influenced towards Christ only horizontally, along one of these three levels. But the true Christian is someone who has responded to His call at all three levels. True 'conversion' is a vertical experience. Notice that in trying to win others for Christ it is we who do the* commending, *but God does the* commanding. *We can demonstrate our faith by our lives and explain it with our lips, but it is only God Himself who can bring light and understanding to heart and mind and conscience.*

**Help me, O Lord, to recommend the gospel to others by the way I live and the things I say. Amen.**

## Blessed is the man who remains steadfast under trial. (James 1:12)

The Lord knows how to rescue the godly from trials (2 Peter 2:9). For because he himself has suffered when tempted, he is able to help those who are being tempted (Hebrews 2:18). No temptation has overtaken you that is not common to man. God is faithful, and he will not let you be tempted beyond your ability, but with the temptation he will also provide the way of escape, that you may be able to endure it (1 Corinthians 10:13). "Watch and pray that you may not enter into temptation. The spirit indeed is willing, but the flesh is weak" (Matthew 26:41). Praying at all times in the Spirit, with all prayer and supplication. To that end keep alert with all perseverance (Ephesians 6:18). Be sober-minded; be watchful (1 Peter 5:8).

*A Frenchman who had become naturalized as an Englishman was asked what difference he found it had made. He thought for a moment and then said, 'Last year Waterloo was a defeat, but now it's a victory.' That ought to be the Christian's experience so far as temptation is concerned, because we are now on the winning side. We are linked to the One who conquered every temptation and so is able to help us to escape and to endure. But we must play our part. To watch means to keep an eye on our enemy, and to guard those places where he might try to land on the coastline of our lives. 'The price of freedom is eternal vigilance.' To pray means to keep an eye on our friend, Jesus Christ, and to call upon Him to help us whenever we feel the pressure and power of temptation.*

'Be my guardian and my guide, and hear me when I call; let not my slippery footsteps slide, and hold me lest I fall.' Amen.

### "Look at him! . . . A friend of tax collectors and sinners." (Matthew 11:19)

There is a friend who sticks closer than a brother (Proverbs 18:24). "Greater love has no one than this, that someone lay down his life for his friends. You are my friends if you do what I command you. No longer do I call you servants, for the servant does not know what his master is doing; but I have called you friends, for all that I have heard from my Father I have made known to you" (John 15:13–15). The friendship of the Lord is for those who fear him (Psalm 25:14). Thus the Lord used to speak to Moses face to face, as a man speaks to his friend (Exodus 33:11). And . . . Abraham . . . was called a friend of God (James 2:23).

*Charles Kingsley was once asked the secret of his happiness in life. 'I had a friend', was his reply. He did not say who that friend was, but no one will question the value of a really loyal human friend. How much more precious, therefore, is the friendship of the Lord, who sticks to us more closely than a brother? Two things distinguish this friendship. First, there must be* obedience on our part. *At first sight this is a curious equation: friendship = obedience. But it makes sense when we remember that it is the obedience which springs from respect ('fear') and even more from love for One who has died for us. Second, there must be* openness on His part. *'There are no secrets between friends' and, as we get to know Him better, He will begin to reveal to us some of the deep things of God.*

**Lord, make me grateful for Your friendship, make me worthy of it, and help me to benefit from it in every phase of my daily life. Amen.**

## The royal law. (James 2:8)

And God spoke all these words, saying, "I am the Lord your God, who brought you out of . . . the house of slavery. You shall have no other gods before me. You shall not make for yourself a carved image . . . You shall not bow down to them or serve them . . . You shall not take the name of the Lord your God in vain . . . Remember the Sabbath day, to keep it holy . . . Honour your father and your mother . . . You shall not murder. You shall not commit adultery. You shall not steal. You shall not bear false witness against your neighbour. You shall not covet your neighbour's house . . . or anything that is your neighbour's" (Exodus 20:1–17). "You shall love the Lord your God with all your heart and with all your soul and with all your strength and with all your mind, and your neighbour as yourself" (Luke 10:27). Love is the fulfilling of the law (Romans 13:10).

*If neighbouring countries are going to live in harmony and peace, it is important to clearly draw the frontiers between them. Today we read of the frontiers which God has set for us in our relations with Him, with our parents and with our neighbours. Notice that the Ten Commandments are concerned with every aspect of our lives – our deeds (murder, theft, adultery), our words (blasphemy and false witness) and our thoughts (covet). Jesus summed up all ten commandments in one word – love. It is the golden rule for fulfilling all the other rules, for if we love God and one another then we shall keep His Law without even thinking about it – just as by driving 'with due care' we automatically keep the highway code.*

**O Lord, may my love for You incline my heart to keep Your Law. Amen.**

## Love never ends. (1 Corinthians 13:8)

If I speak in the tongues of men and of angels, but have not love, I am a noisy gong or a clanging cymbal. And if I have prophetic powers, and understand all mysteries and all knowledge, and if I have all faith, so as to remove mountains, but have not love, I am nothing. If I give away all I have, and if I deliver up my body to be burned, but have not love, I gain nothing. Love is patient and kind; love does not envy or boast; it is not arrogant or rude. It does not insist on its own way; it is not irritable or resentful; it does not rejoice at wrongdoing, but rejoices with the truth. Love bears all things, believes all things, hopes all things, endures all things (1 Corinthians 13:1–7).

*In this famous passage Paul is contrasting the gifts of the Spirit with the fruit of the Spirit. He is not condemning the former, but he is anxious to show that even the most coveted gifts like prophecy, knowledge and faith – and even generosity and self-sacrifice – are useless unless they spring from, and are accompanied by, genuine love. Paul then takes this word love and, passing it, as it were, through a prism, he breaks it up into its component colours or virtues. Negatively, love is never jealous, proud, rude, selfish, touchy or malevolent. Positively, love has a passive side (for it is longsuffering and patient) and an active side (for it is kind and keen to believe and hope for the best).*

**Lord, You have taught us that all our doings without love are worth nothing. Pour into my heart this most excellent virtue, that I may love You with all my soul, and my neighbour as myself. Amen.**

## "Whoever comes to me I will never cast out." (John 6:37)

"Therefore go out from their midst, and be separate from them, says the Lord, and touch no unclean thing; then I will welcome you" (2 Corinthians 6:17). Jesus cried out with a loud voice, "Lazarus, come out." The man who had died came out, his hands and feet bound with linen strips . . . Jesus said . . . "Unbind him, and let him go" (John 11:43–44). Jesus looked up and said, "Zachchaeus, hurry and come down, for I must stay at your house today" (Luke 19:5). And Jesus . . . said to them, "If anyone would come after me, let him deny himself and take up his cross and follow me" (Mark 8:34). "Come to me, all who labour and are heavy laden, and I will give you rest" (Matthew 11:28). "A man once gave a great banquet and invited many. And at the time for the banquet he sent his servant to say to those who had been invited, 'Come, for everything is now ready.' But they all alike began to make excuses" (Luke 14:16–18).

*Becoming a Christian is like answering an invitation to come to Christ as the One who can give us true and lasting satisfaction in life. But it is an invitation that some people find hard to accept. It means coming out from all that is sinful and unworthy, for if we follow Christ we must forsake all that is wrong. It means coming down from the pedestal of pride, perhaps, or self-esteem, on which we have perched ourselves. It means coming after Him, bearing His cross, and perhaps sharing in the misunderstanding and ridicule which were heaped on Him. Some shrink from this and fear that friends will think they are becoming pious or are 'taking religion seriously'. Sin, pride and fear are the three most common excuses for being 'unable to accept the kind invitation . . .'*

**Lord, I thank You for Your invitation. Thank You that You offer all who accept it so much more than they ever have to give up. Amen.**

### "If only I may finish my course." (Acts 20:24)

For to me to live is Christ, and to die is gain. If I am to live in the flesh, that means fruitful labour for me. Yet which I shall choose I cannot tell. I am hard pressed between the two. My desire is to depart and be with Christ, for that is far better. But to remain in the flesh is more necessary on your account (Philippians 1:21–24). So I am eager to preach the gospel to you also who are in Rome. For I am not ashamed of the gospel, for it is the power of God for salvation (Romans 1:15–16). Then Paul answered, "What are you doing, weeping and breaking my heart? For I am ready not only to be imprisoned but even to die in Jerusalem for the name of the Lord Jesus" (Acts 21:13). For I am already being poured out as a drink offering, and the time of my departure has come. I have fought the good fight, I have finished the race, I have kept the faith (2 Timothy 4:6–7).

*'To be, or not to be, that is the question.' But it was a very different question for Paul than it was for Hamlet. Hamlet had no happiness in life and no hope in death; but life for Paul meant the joyful service of Christ and death the supreme privilege of meeting Him face-to-face. And so his motto was those three words – 'I am ready'. He was ready to spend his life travelling, writing, visiting, preaching the gospel – wherever he found himself and whatever the cost. And, when the time came (and it often looked like it was imminent), he was equally ready to answer the call of His Master to die for Him and move on into regions of activity beyond the grave.*

Lord, make me ready – ready for the demands of daily life and ready when the time comes to meet You face-to-face. Amen.

## "You have sinned against the Lord, and be sure your sin will find you out." (Numbers 32:23)

For we ourselves were once foolish, disobedient, led astray, slaves to various passions and pleasures (Titus 3:3). The fleeting pleasures of sin (Hebrews 11:25). But exhort one another every day, as long as it is called "today," that none of you may be hardened by the deceitfulness of sin (Hebrews 3:13). For sin . . . deceived me and . . . killed me (Romans 7:11). When you were slaves of sin, you were free in regard to righteousness. But what fruit were you getting at that time from the things of which you are now ashamed? The end of those things is death . . . For the wages of sin is death (Romans 6:20–21, 23). Desire when it has conceived gives birth to sin, and sin when it is fully grown brings forth death. Do not be deceived, my beloved brothers (James 1:15–16).

Sin delights. *If sin were not so pleasant in its early stages no one would indulge in it, and the world would be a much more righteous place. But many of the things which we know to be wrong are fun, and there is no denying that we get pleasure out of being selfish, lazy, angry, dishonest and proud when it suits our purpose.* Sin deceives. *But very quickly the taste of sin, so sweet to start with, becomes bitter and sour and we decide we would give almost anything to undo what we have done. 'My days are in the yellow leaf; the flowers and fruits of love are gone; the worm, the canker, and the grief are mine alone.' That is what Byron wrote on his thirty-seventh birthday.* Sin destroys. *Like a thick cloud or mist, sin sweeps between us and God – separating us from His presence and exposing us to His wrath.*

Lord, help me not to be deceived by the colour and taste of sin, but help me to detect its poison and leave the fruit unpicked. Amen.

## How great is his goodness. (Zechariah 9:17)

Bless the Lord, O my soul, and all that is within me, bless his holy name! Bless the Lord, O my soul, and forget not all his benefits, who forgives all your iniquity, who heals all your diseases, who redeems your life from the pit, who crowns you with steadfast love and mercy, who satisfies you with good so that your youth is renewed like the eagle's (Psalm 103:1–5). "He did not leave himself without witness, for he did good by giving you rains from heaven and fruitful seasons, satisfying your hearts with food and gladness" (Acts 14:17). God, who richly provides us with everything to enjoy (1 Timothy 6:17). Oh, how abundant is your goodness, which you have stored up for those who fear you (Psalm 31:19). The earth is full of the steadfast love of the Lord (Psalm 33:5).

*There is something very attractive about genuine goodness when we meet it – that selfless concern for the interests of others, regardless of the cost and trouble caused to oneself. The only perfect example of it is, of course, God Himself – and all human goodness stems from Him. As someone has said, 'You can't make 'Go(o)d' without 'God'.' Every day we enjoy God's goodness to us in some shape or form, whether in material benefits such as food and shelter or in those inner spiritual gifts of forgiveness, courage, wisdom and strength. But what about the victims of natural disasters – famine, fire and flood? Is God being good to them? This is a vast problem. Part of the answer must lie in the fact that there is a life to come in which God has 'prepared such good things as pass man's understanding'. But probably most readers have many present blessings which they can count and for which they can thank God today.*

I thank You today, O God, for my creation, preservation and all the blessings of this life. Amen.

## Wash me thoroughly from my iniquity, and cleanse me from my sin! (Psalm 51:2)

Naaman, commander of the army of the king of Syria, was a great man with his master and in high favour, because by him the Lord had given victory to Syria. He was a mighty man of valour, but he was a leper . . . when Elisha . . . heard . . . he sent to the king, saying . . . "Let him come now to me, that he may know that there is a prophet in Israel." So Naaman came . . . And Elisha sent a messenger to him, saying, "Go and wash in the Jordan seven times . . . and you shall be clean." But Naaman was angry and went away, saying, "Behold, I thought that he would surely come out to me and stand and call upon the name of the Lord his God, and wave his hand over the place and cure the leper." . . . So he turned and went away in a rage. But his servants . . . said to him, ". . . It is a great word the prophet has spoken to you; will you not do it? Has he actually said to you, 'Wash, and be clean'?" So he went down and dipped himself seven times in the Jordan . . . and his flesh was restored like the flesh of a little child, and he was clean (2 Kings 5:1, 8–14).

*Leprosy in the Bible is often taken as an illustration of sin, because it spoils a person's life, spreads throughout the body, and separates the sufferer from others. For Naaman, pride very nearly proved his undoing. He was a great man, and he expected a dramatic and spectacular cure. Instead he was told to go and wash in the Jordan, a stream which compared miserably with the sparkling rivers in his own country. Happily he had some wise advisors who persuaded him to pocket his pride and find the remedy. Neither is there any 'great thing' or good deed that will earn us forgiveness. The cure for sin lies not at the top of the ladder, as so many suppose, but at the foot of the cross.*

**Cleanse me from my sin, O Lord, and create a new heart within me. Amen.**

**The prayer of a righteous person has great power as it is working. (James 5:16)**

The Lord's hand is not shortened, that it cannot save, or his ear dull, that it cannot hear; but your iniquities have made a separation between you and your God, and your sins have hidden his face from you so that he does not hear (Isaiah 59:1–2). If I had cherished iniquity in my heart, the Lord would not have listened (Psalm 66:18). You ask and do not receive, because you ask wrongly, to spend it on your passions (James 4:3). If we ask anything according to his will he hears us. And if we know that he hears us in whatever we ask, we know that we have the requests that we have asked of him (1 John 5:14–15). But let him ask in faith, with no doubting, for the one who doubts is like a wave of the sea that is driven and tossed by the wind. For that person must not suppose that he will receive anything from the Lord (James 1:6–7).

*Prayer is perhaps the most important weapon that God has put into our hands, and 'more things are wrought by prayer than this world dreams of'. But it doesn't always seem to work. We ask, and we receive not. Why? We must remember, of course, that God knows best and may withhold certain things from us for our own good. Having said that, there are three conditions that must be met if we want God to answer our prayer.* The man (or woman) must be right *before God. God cannot give us what we ask for if we are secretly cherishing some sin in our hearts.* The motive must be right *– not our own personal satisfaction, but His will and glory.* The method must be right. *It does no good for us to ask if all the time we seriously doubt whether God is able to grant our requests. Faith is as essential to prayer as flour is to bread.*

**Lord, I thank You for what prayer can achieve, but I ask for Your help always to pray aright. Amen.**

**"I always do the things that are pleasing to him."
(John 8:29)**

I have set the Lord always before me; because he is at my right hand, I shall not be shaken (Psalm 16:8). Always carrying in the body the death of Jesus, so that the life of Jesus may also be manifested in our bodies (2 Corinthians 4:10). Praying at all times in the Spirit, with all prayer and supplication. To that end keep alert with all perseverance, making supplication (Ephesians 6:18). As sorrowful, yet always rejoicing (2 Corinthians 6:10). Rejoice in the Lord always; again I will say, Rejoice (Philippians 4:4). Always being prepared to make a defence to anyone who asks you for a reason for the hope that is in you; yet do it with gentleness and respect (1 Peter 3:15–16). "And behold, I am with you always, to the end of the age" (Matthew 28:20).

*Some people get the idea that Christianity is 'for Sundays only', but verses like these make it very clear that this is not so. For the true Christian there is no five-day week. We are never off duty, and we never go on leave. In our own secret life we continually keep up our habits of prayer and obedience to Christ, and we allow nothing to interfere with them. We drink from the hidden wells of joy within ourselves. In our public life before others we seek to display the beauty and the goodness of Christ; and we are always ready to take opportunities to explain our faith to others. But the Lord also never takes the day off. He promises to be with us all the time to give us the strength and help we need to always do what is pleasing to Him.*

**Lord, help me not to be an occasional Christian, when the mood suits me. Make me a Christian for all seasons. Amen.**

## Their heart is false. (Hosea 10:2)

They should not be like their fathers . . . a generation whose heart was not steadfast, whose spirit was not faithful to God (Psalm 78:8). Solomon loved the Lord, walking in the statutes of David his father, only he sacrificed and made offerings at the high places (1 Kings 3:3). Joash did what was right in the eyes of the Lord, yet not like David his father (2 Kings 14:3). "Of whom he . . . said, 'I have found in David . . . a man after my heart, who will do all my will'" (Acts 13:22). "They have not wholly followed me" (Numbers 32:11). "No one can serve two masters" (Matthew 6:24). "To the angel of the church in Laodicea write: . . . 'I know your works: you are neither cold nor hot. Would that you were either cold or hot! So, because you are lukewarm, and neither hot nor cold, I will spit you out of my mouth'" (Revelation 3:14–16).

*What an unpleasant thing a cup of coffee is when it is lukewarm! You wish it were one or the other – either really hot or iced. I am afraid it is fatally easy for Christians to get into this condition, to want to follow the Lord, but . . . all sorts of things can dilute the warmth of their love for Christ – an unhelpful friendship, the love of money, obsession with some game or other interest. If Satan cannot stop us from becoming Christians, then he will do his best to make us half-hearted and lukewarm. 'It's all right,' he'll whisper, 'of course you can serve two masters and have the best of both worlds.' 'Luke Warm' is a very unsatisfactory and unhappy Christian. Before long he will assume one of his other aliases – 'Mark Time' or 'Peter Out'.*

**'Lord, it is my chief complaint that my love is weak and faint; yet I love You and adore, O for grace to love You more.' Amen.**

**Do not be anxious about anything, but in everything by prayer . . . (Philippians 4:6)**

Fret not yourself because of evildoers; be not envious of wrongdoers! For they will soon fade like the grass and wither like the green herb. Trust in the Lord, and do good; dwell in the land and befriend faithfulness. Delight yourself in the Lord, and he will give you the desires of your heart. Commit your way to the Lord; trust in him, and he will act. He will bring forth your righteousness as the light, and your justice as the noonday. Be still before the Lord and wait patiently for him; fret not yourself over the one who prospers in his way, over the man who carries out evil devices! Refrain from anger, and forsake wrath! Fret not yourself; it tends only to evil (Psalm 37:1–8).

*There are two ways of going through life – rusting or trusting. Rusting. Three times in this passage we are told to 'fret not'. In other words, we are not to allow our lives to become frayed or rusted so that we grow irritable, resentful and angry. Perhaps nothing can have this damaging effect more than the sight of people 'getting away with' practices which we know to be evil – cheating the tax authorities, shoplifting, travelling without a ticket and so on. Such people won't get away with it (not in the long run, and not in God's sight), so there is no point in fretting. Instead, we must practice* trusting *– learning to commit our way to Him each day, resting in His power and love, delighting in His presence and doing His will.*

**'Drop Your still dews of quietness, till all our striving cease: take from our souls the strain and stress: and let our ordered lives confess the beauty of Your peace.' Amen.**

## The free gift of God is eternal life in Christ Jesus our Lord. (Romans 6:23)

For God so loved the world, that he gave his only Son, that whoever believes in him should not perish but have eternal life (John 3:16). "My sheep hear my voice, and I know them, and they follow me. I give them eternal life, and they will never perish, and no one will snatch them out of my hand" (John 10:27–28). God gave us eternal life, and this life is in his Son. Whoever has the Son has life; whoever does not have the Son of God does not have life (1 John 5:11–12). "And this is eternal life, that they know you the only true God, and Jesus Christ whom you have sent" (John 17:3). "Lord, to whom shall we go? You have the words of eternal life, and we have believed, and have come to know, that you are the Holy One of God" (John 6:68–69). I write these things to you who believe in the name of the Son of God that you may know that you have eternal life (1 John 5:13).

*When we are born into this world of human parents we start natural life which ends in death. But when we receive Christ we are 'born again' and begin a spiritual, or eternal, life that will never end. 'Eternal life', therefore, is not just a form of endless existence waiting for us beyond the grave – it is life on a new plane, with a new dimension, which we can begin here and now. Imagine a bird which had never discovered that it could fly. It would have life of a sort, but not the real, full life for which it was intended. It would be earthbound when it was made to be air-borne. It is that kind of difference which Christ can make to those who receive Him – endless, yes, but also boundless.*

**Lord, I thank You for the wonderful gift of eternal life, and I ask for strength to live it to the full. Amen.**

## "'Be faithful unto death, and I will give you the crown of life.'" (Revelation 2:10)

For I am already being poured out as a drink offering, and the time of my departure has come. I have fought the good fight, I have finished the race, I have kept the faith. Henceforth there is laid up for me the crown of righteousness, which the Lord, the righteous judge, will award to me on that Day . . . Do your best to come to me soon. For Demas, in love with this present world, has deserted me . . . Luke alone is with me . . . At my first defence no one came to stand by me, but all deserted me. May it not be charged against them! But the Lord stood by me and strengthened me, so that through me the message might be fully proclaimed and all the Gentiles might hear it. So I was rescued from the lion's mouth. The Lord will rescue me from every evil deed and bring me safely into his heavenly kingdom. To him be the glory forever and ever. Amen (2 Timothy 4:6–11, 16–18).

*This was the last of Paul's letters, written not long before his final trial and execution. It is our final glimpse of this great warrior, and we notice his great spiritual strength as well as his sensitivity. He was grateful to his friends and yet terribly hurt by the failure of some whom he had trusted.* The backward look. *Just for once Paul allowed himself to look back, and he could honestly do so without any self-reproach.* The forward look. *Paul never feared death. For him it was just the tunnel through which he must travel to reach the immediate presence of Christ. Already he could see the light at the other end.* The upward look. *Meanwhile he faced injustice, cruelty and death, quietly confident in the Lord who stood by him.*

Help me, O Lord, to live in such a way that I may always be able to look back without regret and forward without fear. Amen.

### "For this purpose I have come into the world." (John 18:37)

"Do not think that I have come to abolish the Law or the Prophets; I have not come to abolish them but to fulfil them" (Matthew 5:17). "I came not to call the righteous, but sinners" (Matthew 9:13). The saying is trustworthy and deserving of full acceptance, that Christ Jesus came into the world to save sinners (1 Timothy 1:15). "For even the Son of Man came not to be served but to serve, and to give his life as a ransom for many" (Mark 10:45). "Now is my soul troubled. And what shall I say? 'Father, save me from this hour'? But for this purpose I have come to this hour. Father, glorify your name" (John 12:27–28). "The thief comes only to steal and kill and destroy. I came that they may have life and have it abundantly" (John 10:10).

*If you are lucky enough to be able to choose what you want to be in life, you are able from quite an early age to bend all your hopes and ambitions in that direction. So it was with Jesus. Even as a child He told His parents that He must be 'about his Father's business'. And what was this 'family business' to which He felt called so young and so strongly? It was nothing less than the salvation of humankind in fulfilment of the Scriptures. Most people come to live, but Jesus came to die. Most people are remembered for what they do, but Jesus is remembered for what He suffered. We remember His passion rather than His action, and yet that passion brought forgiveness and life to imprisoned humanity.*

Lord, I thank You that You did not leave humankind to its fate, but that You mounted the most wonderful rescue operation in history. Amen.

## "Seek the welfare of the city where I have sent you." (Jeremiah 29:7)

First of all, then, I urge that supplications, prayers, intercessions, and thanksgivings be made for all people, for kings and all who are in high positions, that we may lead a peaceful and quiet life, godly and dignified in every way. This is good, and it is pleasing in the sight of God our Saviour (1 Timothy 2:1–3). Let every person be subject to the governing authorities. For there is no authority except from God, and those that exist have been instituted by God (Romans 13:1). Remind them to be submissive to rulers and authorities, to be obedient, to be ready for every good work, to speak evil of no one, to avoid quarrelling, to be gentle, and to show perfect courtesy toward all people (Titus 3:1–2). Be subject for the Lord's sake to every human institution . . . Honour everyone. Love the brotherhood. Fear God. Honour the emperor (1 Peter 2:13, 17).

*Perhaps you don't live in a city but in a country town or village, or maybe you're at college. But whichever it is, these rules apply. And what wonderfully happy places they would be if everyone lived in this way!* The Church. *Do we make a point of going every Sunday, amongst other things to pray for the leaders in our country and commonwealth? They need our prayers very badly.* The Town Hall. *Are we careful to observe the rules that are made, living as responsible and law-abiding members of the community? It honours God if we do.* The Supermarket. *Are we friendly, gentle, honest and courteous in our personal relationships with people we meet in everyday life, in the shops and on the streets? By doing this we commend the gospel to others, even without speaking a word.*

**Lord, I pray today for the place where I live and work. Make me a worthy member, and may I seek the welfare of all those among whom I live. Amen.**

**Fervent in spirit, serve the Lord. (Romans 12:11)**

Share in suffering as a good soldier of Christ Jesus (2 Timothy 2:3). For we do not wrestle against flesh and blood, but against . . . the spiritual forces of evil in the heavenly places (Ephesians 6:12). Fight the good fight of the faith (1 Timothy 6:12). We are ambassadors for Christ, God making his appeal through us. We implore you on behalf of Christ, be reconciled to God (2 Corinthians 5:20). Pray . . . for me, that words may be given to me in opening my mouth boldly to proclaim the mystery of the gospel, for which I am an ambassador in chains (Ephesians 6:18–20). "Now therefore, O our God, listen to the prayer of your servant and to his pleas for mercy, and for your own sake, O Lord, make your face to shine upon your sanctuary, which is desolate. O my God, incline your ear and hear . . . O Lord, hear; O Lord, forgive. O Lord, pay attention and act" (Daniel 9:17–20).

*There are at least three ways in which we are called to serve Christ. Active service. The Christian is a soldier, engaged in a lifelong war against evil in every shape and form. Every temptation we conquer is a battle won, and in the end total victory is assured. Diplomatic service. We are ambassadors for Christ, taking His place in the town, home, college or school where we happen to live. We are the channel through which His message of the gospel can reach others. Secret service. This is perhaps the hardest area of all, and the most important. Prayer is a mysterious force which somehow loosens Satan's grip on people and situations and releases God's power to work in the world. We don't have to choose which form of service to enter – every Christian is called into all three.*

**Lord, may You find me to be a faithful, fervent servant, fighting, living and praying according to Your will. Amen.**

## "He is Lord of lords and King of kings. (Revelation 17:14)

Who is this King of glory? The Lord, strong and mighty, the Lord, mighty in battle . . . The Lord of hosts, he is the King of glory! (Psalm 24:8, 10) Behold, wise men from the east came to Jerusalem, saying, "Where is he who has been born king of the Jews? For we saw his star when it rose and have come to worship him" (Matthew 2:1–2). "Say to the daughter of Zion, 'Behold, your King is coming to you, humble, and mounted on a donkey, and on a colt, the foal of a beast of burden'" (Matthew 21:5). And over his head they put the charge against him, which read, "This is Jesus, the King of the Jews" (Matthew 27:37). "The kingdom of the world has become the kingdom of our Lord and of his Christ, and he shall reign forever and ever" (Revelation 11:15). To the King of ages, immortal, invisible, the only God, be honour and glory forever and ever. Amen (1 Timothy 1:17).

*For centuries the Jews had been looking forward to the arrival of a king who would set up a great earthly kingdom. But when Jesus came His kingdom was of a very different sort – spiritual and eternal. By what right does Jesus claim to be King? By conquest, because through His death and resurrection He defeated 'the prince of this world', Satan. By birth. He was the man 'born to be king' – not just an ordinary human being, but God manifested in the flesh. By invitation. He does not force Himself on people. If they want they can say, 'We will not have this man to reign over us.' But if we receive Him then He makes our hearts His palace and His royal throne. It is interesting that our own history illustrates these three ways of becoming king – William I by conquest, William II by birth, William III by invitation.*

'Oh, come and reign, Lord Jesus; rule over everything! and keep me always loyal, and true to You, my King.' Amen.

**The fear of man lays a snare. (Proverbs 29:25)**

Saul said to Samuel, "I have sinned, for I have transgressed the commandment of the Lord and your words, because I feared the people and obeyed their voice" (1 Samuel 15:24). Many even of the authorities believed in him, but for fear of the Pharisees they did not confess it, so that they would not be put out of the synagogue; for they loved the glory that comes from man more than the glory that comes from God (John 12:42–43). Then a servant girl, seeing Peter as he sat in the light . . . said, "This man also was with him." But he denied it, saying, "Woman, I do not know him" (Luke 22:56–57). Joseph of Arimathea . . . was a disciple of Jesus, but secretly for fear of the Jews (John 19:38). "Do not be afraid of them, for I am with you to deliver you, declares the Lord" (Jeremiah 1:8). So we can confidently say, "The Lord is my helper; I will not fear; what can man do to me?" (Hebrews 13:6).

*I shouldn't think there is a single Christian who has not at some time or other failed the Master as Peter did because we have been afraid of what others might think or say or do. Someone we know is being slandered maliciously behind his back and we do nothing to stand up for him or to contradict what is being said. A particularly unpleasant joke gets a general laugh and weakly we join in because we don't want to be thought pious or prudish. Some malpractice is suggested, and instead of dissociating ourselves from it at the start we spinelessly adopt a stance of benevolent neutrality. We are afraid of those scornful, hostile looks we shall get if we take an unpopular line. But more than ever in these days Christians need to stand up and be counted. It will encourage us greatly if we remember that we do not stand alone. It will give us that boldness we may feel we lack.*

**Lord, You know how easily and how often I fall into the trap of fearing what others will think. Please give me courage to stand firmly for what I know to be right. Amen.**

### The hand of the Lord was on Elijah.
### (1 Kings 18:46)

Elijah was a man with a nature like ours, and he prayed fervently that it might not rain, and for three years and six months it did not rain on the earth. Then he prayed again, and heaven gave rain (James 5:17–18). Then he . . . cried to the Lord . . . "Let this child's life come into him again." And the Lord listened to the voice of Elijah. And . . . the child . . . revived (1 Kings 17:21–22). Then Elijah said to the people . . . "you call upon the name of your god, and I will call upon the name of the Lord, and the God who answers by fire, he is God." And . . . Elijah . . . said . . . "Answer me, O Lord, answer me, that this people may know that you, O Lord, are God" . . . Then the fire of the Lord fell (1 Kings 18:22–24, 36–38). "I know that you can do all things, and that no purpose of yours can be thwarted" (Job 42:2). The prayer of a righteous person has great power as it is working (James 5:16).

*All the Old Testament characters have something to teach us, and perhaps the greatest thing about Elijah was that he was a man of prayer. Whatever the crisis – whether domestic, as in the case of the dead child, or national – he met it head-on in prayer. Just as someone can throw a switch in a generating station and light up a whole city perhaps miles away, so the prayer of a righteous person has great power in its effects. How can you exercise that power today? Is there someone you are trying to influence towards Christ? Some problem that needs to be resolved at home? Someone who is lonely, sick or troubled? Some missionary facing a crisis? 'The sad had joy that day, the sick had ease, because a friend took time to pray, Lord help them, please.'*

**Lord, I am ashamed when I think how cold my prayers are. Please give me something of Elijah's faith and fervour. Amen.**

### You who love the Lord, hate evil! (Psalm 97:10)

I will not set before my eyes anything that is worthless. I hate the work of those who fall away; it shall not cling to me. A perverse heart shall be far from me; I will know nothing of evil . . . No one who practices deceit shall dwell in my house; no one who utters lies shall continue before my eyes (Psalm 101:3–4, 7). I would rather be a doorkeeper in the house of my God than dwell in the tents of wickedness (Psalm 84:10). I hate every false way (Psalm 119:104). Abhor what is evil; hold fast to what is good (Romans 12:9). Hate evil, and love good (Amos 5:15). Turn away from evil and do good (Psalm 34:14). Joseph said . . . "How then can I do this great wickedness and sin against God?" (Genesis 39:9). There was a man . . . whose name was Job, and that man was blameless and upright, one who feared God and turned away from evil (Job 1:1). The fear of the Lord is hatred of evil (Proverbs 8:13). No one born of God makes a practice of sinning, for God's seed abides in him, and he cannot keep on sinning because he has been born of God (1 John 3:9).

*The Christian is rather like a footballer who has been transferred to a new club, for an immense fee, from its most deadly rival. Not only has he changed sides, but his outlook and attitude have changed as well. In future, when the two teams meet, he must check any hankering affection he still has for the old club and strenuously resist any suggestion or bribe to play below his best for his new club. He must now devote all his talents, strength and experience to serving his new captain and ensuring continual victory and success. If we are to be victorious Christians, we must develop a great hatred towards everything that is base, sinful, unworthy and unjust. We may be tempted to be 'soft' towards sin 'for old times' sake'. We must resist that temptation and regard it with relentless hostility.*

**Lord, develop within me a perfect hatred for sin, because of the way it can spoil my life, and because of what it cost You to redeem me from it. Amen.**

**Eager to maintain the unity of the Spirit in the bond of peace. (Ephesians 4:3)**

Wives, submit to your husbands, as is fitting in the Lord. Husbands, love your wives, and do not be harsh with them. Children, obey your parents in everything, for this pleases the Lord. Fathers, do not provoke your children, lest they become discouraged. Slaves, obey in everything those who are your earthly masters, not by way of eye-service, as people-pleasers, but with sincerity of heart, fearing the Lord. Whatever you do, work heartily, as for the Lord and not for men, knowing that from the Lord you will receive the inheritance as your reward. You are serving the Lord Christ. For the wrongdoer will be paid back for the wrong he has done, and there is no partiality (Colossians 3:18–25).

*These words come rather strangely to modern ears. 'Elders' are no longer regarded as 'betters'. But two things are perhaps worth saying. First, family or social life which lacks any sort of firm structure very quickly begins to fall apart and disintegrate. For their own happiness and security, people, and especially children, need to know where they fit into that structure. Second, this structure will only work in peace and love and harmony if we accept the Lord as the ultimate Head and authority. He is mentioned five times in this passage, and without Him as the central reference point in a family or a firm, strife – whether domestic or industrial – is almost inevitable.*

**Help me, O Lord, to live with others in a relationship of affection and respect, cemented by a mutual love for You. Amen.**

### He has granted to us his precious and very great promises. (2 Peter 1:4)

"Blessed be the Lord who has given rest to his people Israel, according to all that he promised. Not one word has failed of all his good promise, which he spoke by Moses his servant" (1 Kings 8:56). Not one word of all the good promises that the Lord had made to the house of Israel had failed; all came to pass (Joshua 21:45). No distrust made Abraham waver concerning the promise of God, but he grew strong in his faith as he gave glory to God, fully convinced that God was able to do what he had promised (Romans 4:20–21). For he who promised is faithful (Hebrews 10:23). The Lord is not slow to fulfil his promise as some count slowness (2 Peter 3:9). Since we have these promises, beloved, let us cleanse ourselves from every defilement of body and spirit, bringing holiness to completion in the fear of God (2 Corinthians 7:1). And we desire each one of you to . . . be . . . imitators of those who through faith and patience inherit the promises (Hebrews 6:11–12). For all the promises of God find their Yes in him [Christ] (2 Corinthians 1:20).

*When someone makes you a promise, you need to exercise two qualities – faith and patience. You must believe that the person who made the promise is a person of his or her word and will fulfil it; and you must allow that person to do so in their own time and way. That is how God expects us to treat Him. Nothing that He has promised will fail to come to pass but some of the promises, such as His promise to come again, may take a long time to fulfil. It is quite a good practice to go through the Bible and put a mark against some of the most outstanding promises of God (for example, His promise to forgive, to come into our hearts, to strengthen and accompany us), and to see how they have been fulfilled in our own lives.*

Lord, help me to mark, to believe and to enjoy Your promises. Amen.

## God made man in his own image. (Genesis 9:6)

For those whom he foreknew he also predestined to be conformed to the image of his Son, in order that he might be the
firstborn among many brothers (Romans 8:29). And we all,
with unveiled face, beholding the glory of the Lord, are being
transformed into the same image from one degree of glory to
another. For this comes from the Lord who is the Spirit (2 Corinthians 3:18). Until we all attain to the unity of the faith and
of the knowledge of the Son of God, to mature manhood, to
the measure of the stature of the fullness of Christ (Ephesians
4:13). And have put on the new self, which is being renewed in
knowledge after the image of its creator (Colossians 3:10). We
know that when he appears we shall be like him, because we
shall see him as he is. And everyone who thus hopes in him
purifies himself as he is pure (1 John 3:2–3).

*Have you ever possessed a very old coin – a Victorian penny, perhaps
– on which the image of the sovereign's head is only just discernable?
That is like us. We were made with the bright, clear image of God
stamped upon us but sin has slowly and surely marred, and often
obliterated, that image altogether. When we become Christians, God
sets to work upon us to restore that image to its original beauty. It is
a long, slow and sometimes painful process, but one day it will be
complete and we shall be 'like Him'. How does He do it? One way is
by keeping the perfection of Christ constantly in front of us so that
gradually we are 'changed by beholding'. This truth is beautifully
illustrated in a short story by Nathaniel Hawthorne called 'The
Great Stone Face'. Read it if you have time one day.*

**Grant, O Lord, that increasingly the beauty of Jesus may be
seen in me. Amen.**

**Jesus stood up and cried out, "If anyone thirsts, let him come to me and drink." (John 7:37)**

There came a woman of Samaria to draw water. Jesus said to her, "Give me a drink." . . . The . . . woman said to him, "How is it that you, a Jew, ask for a drink from me, a woman of Samaria?" . . . Jesus answered her, "If you knew the gift of God, and who it is that is saying to you, 'Give me a drink,' you would have asked him, and he would have given you living water." The woman said to him, "Sir, you have nothing to draw water with, and the well is deep. Where do you get that living water?" . . . Jesus said to her, "Everyone who drinks of this water will be thirsty again, but whoever drinks of the water that I will give him will never be thirsty again. The water that I will give him will become in him a spring of water welling up to eternal life." The woman said to him, "Sir, give me this water, so that I will not be thirsty or have to come here to draw water" (John 4:7, 9–11, 13–15).

*In John 3 we read of the talk which Jesus had with Nicodemus. That interview was with a good man who was a Jew. This conversation in John 4 was with a bad woman who was a Samaritan. It is worth noting how Jesus refused to recognize the usual frontiers of social intercourse: sex, nationality and reputation. His love flowed out to all who were in need, regardless of their background. And this woman had a great need – not for ordinary water, but for the water of life, the presence and power of Jesus Himself which alone can quench the deepest longings of the human heart for peace and satisfaction. Friends of mine have a mountain stream running by their garden, and their water supply is always fresh and always free. So it is with the Christian, and we need never thirst again.*

**I came to You, Lord, and I drank of that life-giving stream; thank You for quenching my thirst and reviving my soul. Amen.**

## Preach the word. (2 Timothy 4:2)

How are they to call on him in whom they have not believed? And how are they to believe in him of whom they have never heard? And how are they to hear without someone preaching? And how are they to preach unless they are sent? (Romans 10:14–15). And Jesus said to them, "Go into all the world and proclaim the gospel to the whole creation" (Mark 16:15). And every day, in the temple and from house to house, they did not cease teaching and preaching Jesus as the Christ (Acts 5:42). To me, though I am the very least of all the saints, this grace was given, to preach to the Gentiles the unsearchable riches of Christ (Ephesians 3:8). For necessity is laid upon me. Woe to me if I do not preach the gospel! (1 Corinthians 9:16) I am under obligation both to Greeks and to barbarians, both to the wise and to the foolish. So I am eager to preach the gospel to you also who are in Rome (Romans 1:14–15).

*Christians must regard themselves as debtors to their fellow human beings, not as benefactors. By preaching the gospel to others we are not bestowing a favour upon them, but discharging a debt. We owe people the gospel, and the principal way which God has ordained for conveying it to them is preaching. This does not mean that we can only use a pulpit or platform, because perhaps the most effective sermons are those which are 'preached' to one person on his or her own. Could you explain simply and clearly why we need Christ, how He can meet our needs and what we have to do to commit ourselves to Him? You ought to be able to do so, and to know just where to turn in the Bible for the answers to this sort of question.*

**Strengthen, O Lord, all those who try to pass on the gospel to others, and give them sincerity, clarity and simplicity. Amen.**

**"I will never leave you nor forsake you."
(Hebrews 13:5)**

There Elijah came to a cave and lodged in it. And behold, the
word of the Lord came to him, and he said to him, "What are
you doing here, Elijah?" He said, "I have been very jealous for
the Lord, the God of hosts. For the people of Israel have forsaken your covenant, thrown down your altars, and killed
your prophets with the sword, and I, even I only, am left, and
they seek my life, to take it away" (1 Kings 19:9–10). And the
Lord said to Paul one night in a vision, "Do not be afraid, but
go on speaking and do not be silent, for I am with you, and no
one will attack you to harm you, for I have many in this city
who are my people" (Acts 18:9–10). I, John, your brother and
partner in the tribulation and the kingdom and the patient
endurance that are in Jesus, was on the island called Patmos
on account of the word of God and the testimony of Jesus . . .
But he laid his right hand on me, saying, "Fear not, I am the
first and the last, and the living one. I died, and behold I am
alive for evermore" (Revelation 1:9, 17–18).

*Every Christian knows what it is to have periods of depression and
loneliness, and here we read of three great men who needed encouragement at a critical moment.* Elijah the fugitive *had incurred the
fury of Ahab and Jezebel and did not know where to turn for help. At
that moment God met him and put new heart and life into him.* Paul
the stranger, *wandering round the streets of Corinth (perhaps the
most corrupt city in the ancient world), felt overwhelmed by the hostile sinfulness of the people until the Lord visited him with strong
words of encouragement.* John the exile, *now a very old man and
suffering his share of persecution, was greatly heartened by the
Lord's reminder that He was the author and finisher of John's faith.*

**Lord, I thank You for that promise to be with me always,
even to the end of the world. Amen.**

## "All authority in heaven and on earth has been given to me." (Matthew 28:18)

A centurion came . . . to him, appealing . . . "Lord, my servant is lying paralyzed at home, suffering terribly." And he said to him, "I will come and heal him." But the centurion replied, "Lord, I am not worthy to have you come under my roof, but only say the word, and my servant will be healed. For I too am a man under authority, with soldiers under me. And I say to one, 'Go,' and he goes, and to another, 'Come,' and he comes . . ." When Jesus heard this, he marvelled and said . . . "Truly, I tell you, with no one in Israel have I found such faith" (Matthew 8:5–10). The crowds werer astonished at Jesus' teaching, for he was teaching them as one who had authority) (Matthew 7:28–29). "He commands even the unclean spirits, and they obey him" (Mark 1:27). And they marvelled, saying to one another, "Who then is this, that he commands even winds and water, and they obey him?" (Luke 8:25). "The Son of Man has authority on earth to forgive sins" (Mark 2:10). "I do nothing on my own authority, but speak just as the Father taught me" (John 8:28).

*This Roman centurion knew what it was to exercise authority in a limited way, and he recognized at once in Jesus someone who had infinite authority, 'in heaven and on earth'. This also struck everyone who came into contact with Jesus. Notice two things about Jesus' authority. First, it was* derived from God. *An ambassador's authority is derived from his government, and Jesus never claimed to be the source of authority but to have received it from God Himself. Second, it was* exercised for humankind. *'On earth' He brought relief from suffering and subdued the forces of nature, while 'in heaven' He opened the gate of everlasting life by doing what none but God could do – forgive the sins of people.*

**Lord, grant that, like the centurion, my faith may match Your authority. Amen.**

**"There is no rock like our God." (1 Samuel 2:2)**

For God alone my soul waits in silence; from him comes my salvation. He only is my rock and my salvation, my fortress; I shall not be greatly shaken. How long will all of you attack a man to batter him, like a leaning wall, a tottering fence? . . . For God alone, O my soul, wait in silence, for my hope is from him. He only is my rock and my salvation, my fortress; I shall not be shaken. On God rests my salvation and my glory; my mighty rock, my refuge is God. Trust in him at all times, O people; pour out your heart before him; God is a refuge for us . . . Once God has spoken; twice have I heard this: that power belongs to God, and that to you, O Lord, belongs steadfast love. For you will render to a man according to his work (Psalm 62:1–3, 5–8, 11–12).

*In a desert or wilderness there was something so steadfast and permanent about a large rock that it was natural for people to compare it with the everlasting presence of God. Such rocks served several purposes. They were* landmarks, *so that travellers could find their way through otherwise featureless countryside. They also provided shelter (Isaiah 32:2) – from the heat of the midday sun, perhaps, or from rain and from enemy attacks. They were* vantage points, *too, because standing on top of it the traveller could see for miles around and get a wide and distant view. Translating this into terms of Christian living, you can see how it adds up to the word 'salvation'. 'Salvation' is not just something that comes from the Lord, for He Himself is our salvation. When we have Him we have all we need. We shall not be 'greatly moved' and, in fact, need not even be 'moved' at all.*

I thank You, O Lord, that You are not a tottering wall in which I can place no confidence but the 'Rock of Ages'. Amen.

## "Behold, the Lamb of God, who takes away the sin of the world!" (John 1:29)

Now from the sixth hour there was darkness over all the land until the ninth hour. And about the ninth hour Jesus cried out with a loud voice . . . "My God, my God, why have you forsaken me?" (Matthew 27:45–46) Smitten by God, and afflicted . . . he was wounded for our transgressions; he was crushed for our iniquities; upon him was the chastisement that brought us peace, and with his stripes we are healed (Isaiah 53:4–5). For our sake God made him to be sin who knew no sin (2 Corinthians 5:21). Christ . . . becoming a curse for us (Galatians 3:13). When Jesus had received the sour wine, he said, "It is finished," and he bowed his head and gave up his spirit (John 19:30). And the curtain of the temple was torn in two, from top to bottom (Mark 15:38). "Having accomplished the work that you gave me to do" (John 17:4). He has appeared once for all at the end of the ages to put away sin by the sacrifice of himself (Hebrews 9:26).

*As Jesus hung upon the cross He spoke seven times, His words are like windows into His mind – showing us the love, patience and courage that lay within. Today we learn two very important things. First, we glimpse what our sins did to Him. All His life Jesus had enjoyed unbroken friendship with His Father. But now, during these hours of darkness, the great cloud of human sin swept between them and God, who is 'of purer eyes than to see evil', had to turn His face away from His only beloved Son. Second, we learn what He did to our sins. He took that great burden of debt which was against us, and He settled it once and for all. Nothing now stands between us and God, and the torn curtain in the temple was a sign to all who saw it that Jesus had made a way back into God's presence. The kingdom of heaven was open to all believers.*

**Thank You, Lord, for what You suffered for me upon the cross. Thank You, too, for what You achieved. Amen.**

**Fruit in every good work. (Colossians 1:10)**

"I am the true vine, and my Father is the vinedresser. Every branch of mine that does not bear fruit he takes away, and every branch that does bear fruit he prunes, that it may bear more fruit . . . Abide in me, and I in you. As the branch cannot bear fruit by itself, unless it abides in the vine, neither can you, unless you abide in me. I am the vine; you are the branches. Whoever abides in me and I in him, he it is that bears much fruit, for apart from me you can do nothing . . . If you abide in me, and my words abide in you, ask whatever you wish, and it will be done for you. By this my Father is glorified, that you bear much fruit and so prove to be my disciples . . . If you keep my commandments, you will abide in my love" (John 15:1–2, 4–5, 7–8, 10).

Abiding. *A true Christian is someone who has been attached to Christ just as a branch is grafted into a tree, or as an electric light bulb is fastened into the socket. As we trust Him and obey, this relationship is maintained and the strength we need to live the Christian life will flow from Him into us.* Abounding. *The Bible calls the fruit that will result from this close link 'The fruit of the Spirit', and it consists of things like love, joy, peace, patience, kindness, humility and self-control (Galatians 5:22–23). When people see this fruit they will know that we are disciples of Jesus, because you can always tell a tree by its fruit. They won't congratulate the branch, but the hope is that they will praise the vinedresser and want to know the secret of abundant life for themselves.*

**Lord, prune my life of unworthy things so that I may bring forth much fruit and so that others may see it and praise You. Amen.**

### "The Lord God is my strength." (Isaiah 12:2)

A young lion came toward him [Samson] roaring. Then the Spirit of the Lord rushed upon him, and . . . he tore the lion in pieces as one tears a young goat (Judges 14:5–6). Delilah said to Samson, "Please tell me where your great strength lies." . . . And he . . . said to her, ". . . If my head is shaved, then my strength will leave me, and I shall become weak and be like any other man" . . . She made him sleep on her knees. And she called a man and had him shave off the seven locks of his head . . . And the Philistines seized him . . . Then Samson called to the Lord and said, "O Lord God, please remember me and please strengthen me only this once" . . . And Samson grasped the two middle pillars on which the house rested, and he leaned his weight against them . . . Then he bowed with all his strength, and the house fell upon the lords and upon all the people who were in it (Judges 16:6, 17, 19, 21, 28–30).

The sunrise. *That is what the name 'Samson' means, and it must have seemed like that to the oppressed Israelites when this fabulous young man emerged to lead a resistance movement against the hated Philistines who occupied their country. For a while, so long as he trusted the Lord, all went well.* The power cut. *But sadly he grew overconfident and disobedient. He made a disastrous marriage, and it was his wife who finally betrayed him to the enemy. 'Eyeless in Gaza, at the mill with slaves', this pathetic, blinded giant ground corn for his captors and entertained them with feats of his still-considerable strength.* The comeback. *But, in his distress, he turned again to the Lord who gave him the power for one final, mighty act of heroism for his country. Read the whole story if you have time.*

Lord, help me always to remember that apart from You I can do nothing. Amen.

**"This is my blood of the covenant, which is poured out for many for the forgiveness of sins."
(Matthew 26:28)**

I received from the Lord what I also delivered to you, that the Lord Jesus on the night when he was betrayed took bread, and when he had given thanks, he broke it, and said, "This is my body which is for you. Do this in remembrance of me." In the same way also he took the cup, after supper, saying, "This cup is the new covenant in my blood. Do this, as often as you drink it, in remembrance of me." For as often as you eat this bread and drink the cup, you proclaim the Lord's death until he comes. Whoever, therefore, eats the bread or drinks the cup of the Lord in an unworthy manner will be guilty of profaning the body and blood of the Lord. Let a person examine himself, then, and so eat of the bread and drink of the cup (1 Corinthians 11:23–28).

*The Lord's Supper, or Holy Communion, is the service which Jesus asked His disciples to continue as a perpetual memorial of His death and passion. But it is more than a memorial, for it is what we call a sacrament – the bread and the wine being symbols of His body broken upon the cross and His blood shed for us. Moreover, symbols can often strengthen the things they symbolize, just as a handshake can deepen a friendship or a kiss can deepen love. They can also proclaim to others the feelings of our heart and mind. These are all reasons why Christians should attend Holy Communion. Looking back, we remember His great love with gratitude. Looking up, we draw nearer to Him in devotion and faith. Looking out, we proclaim to others by our attendance that we are not ashamed to be known as His soldiers and followers.*

**Lord, help me always to attend this service in the right frame of mind – humble and grateful. Amen.**

## Glorify God in your body. (1 Corinthians 6:20)

You formed my inward parts; you knitted me together in my mother's womb. I praise you, for I am fearfully and wonderfully made. Wonderful are your works; my soul knows it very well. My frame was not hidden from you, when I was being made in secret, intricately woven in the depths of the earth. Your eyes saw my unformed substance; in your book were written, every one of them, the days that were formed for me, when as yet there were none of them (Psalm 139:13–16). "Your hands fashioned and made me" (Job 10:8). Do you not know that your bodies are members of Christ? . . . Do you not know that your body is a temple of the Holy Spirit within you, whom you have from God? (1 Corinthians 6:15, 19). I discipline my body and keep it under control, lest after preaching to others I myself should be disqualified (1 Corinthians 9:27).

*What a marvellous thing the human body is! We congratulate ourselves on our modern inventions – the internal combustion engine, our central heating and telecommunications systems – but all these existed in the human body long before we adapted them to these uses. Some people have thought that because certain temptations (greed, lust, sloth) reach us through our bodies, the body itself is evil and so they have maltreated and neglected it. The Bible will have nothing to do with such an idea. The body is like a dog or a horse – well controlled and wisely disciplined it can become the means of giving pleasure and doing endless good. It can be a 'limb' though which Christ works in the world and the dwelling place of the Holy Spirit.*

**Lord, make me grateful for the body You have given me and help me to train it to be of continual use to You. Amen.**

**You were . . . but now you are . . . (1 Peter 2:10)**

And you were dead in the trespasses and sins in which you once walked, following the course of this world, following the prince of the power of the air, the spirit that is now at work in the sons of disobedience – among whom we all once lived in the passions of our flesh, carrying out the desires of the body and the mind, and were by nature children of wrath, like the rest of mankind. But God, being rich in mercy, because of the great love with which he loved us, even when we were dead in our trespasses, made us alive together with Christ – by grace you have been saved – and raised us up with him and seated us with him in the heavenly places in Christ Jesus, so that in the coming ages he might show the immeasurable riches of his grace in kindness toward us in Christ Jesus (Ephesians 2:1–7).

*Have you seen those advertisements that show you someone 'before' and then 'after' taking some medicine or using some lotion? We get that kind of contrast in today's passage.* By nature. *The natural, easy thing to do is to conform to the pattern of life dictated by Satan, described here as 'the prince of the power of the air', and to give way to every temptation and to become the slaves of our bodily desires and passions. Such a life brings us under the wrath of God.* By grace. *But while we are in this condition, Jesus Christ comes to us with the offer of His transforming grace. He wants to forgive us our sins, to make us alive spiritually and responsive to Himself. He wants then to share with us the immeasurable riches of His friendship, now and in the life to come. Is it 'before' or 'after' for you?*

**Lord, thank You again for the amazing grace which found me when I was lost and revived me when I was dead. Amen.**

## "I have loved you," says the Lord. (Malachi 1:2)

"I have loved you with an everlasting love; therefore I have continued my faithfulness to you" (Jeremiah 31:3). "It was not because you were more in number than any other people that the Lord set his love on you and chose you . . . it is because the Lord loves you" (Deuteronomy 7:7–8). "For God so loved the world, that he gave his only Son, that whoever believes in him should not perish but have eternal life" (John 3:16). God shows his love for us in that while we were still sinners, Christ died for us (Romans 5:8). God is love. In this the love of God was made manifest among us, that God sent his only Son into the world, so that we might live through him. In this is love, not that we have loved God but that he loved us and sent his Son to be the propitiation for our sins (1 John 4:8–10). See what kind of love the Father has given to us, that we should be called children of God (1 John 3:1).

*Just as you cannot think of wind that does not blow, or fire that does not burn, so we cannot think of a God who does not love. It is in His very nature to do so, because 'God is love'. There are three things to say about His love. First, it is* unlimited. *We cannot escape it or exhaust it, 'for the love of God is broader than the measures of man's mind, and the heart of the eternal is most wonderfully kind'. Second, it is* undeserved. *There is nothing lovable in us – rather the reverse, for we have turned from God and disobeyed Him. But in spite of our sins He loves us, and He proves it by His wonderful plan to cancel the debts we've incurred and adopt us into His family as His children. Third, God's love is* unanswered. *Not always, of course, but it is a sad fact that so few people in the world can truthfully say, 'We love Him because He first loved us.'*

**Lord, I thank You for Your great love to me, and I ask that it may stir my cold heart into an answering love for You. Amen.**

### "God . . . commands all people everywhere to repent." (Acts 17:30)

"Have I any pleasure in the death of the wicked, declares the Lord God, and not rather that he should turn from his way and live?" (Ezekiel 18:23). "The Lord persistently sent to you all his servants the prophets, saying, 'Turn now, every one of you, from his evil way and evil deeds . . . Then I will do you no harm'" (Jeremiah 25:4–6). Return . . . to the Lord your God, for you have stumbled because of your iniquity. Take with you words and return to the Lord; say to him, "Take away all iniquity" (Hosea 14:1–2). "Yet even now," declares the Lord, "return to me with all your heart . . . and rend your hearts and not your garments." Return to the Lord, your God, for he is gracious and merciful, slow to anger, and abounding in steadfast love (Joel 2:12–13). "Repent therefore, and turn again, that your sins may be blotted out" (Acts 3:19).

*I can remember an occasion when I had to choose between taking a lot of luggage in a very small car I had and giving a friend a lift. It is rather like that in the Christian life. Christ invites Himself to come with us on the journey, but we can only receive Him if we make room for Him by discarding the luggage of sin which so often clutters our lives. This is what the Bible means by 'repentance' – a willingness to abandon sin as a condition of accepting Christ and enjoying His friendship and help. It can be a difficult and painful process, but there is no other way. It is only by saying 'No' to sin that we are in a position to say 'Yes' to Christ.*

**Help me, O Lord, to turn my back upon all that is wrong, so that I may enjoy Your friendship face-to-face. Amen.**

## Keep me as the apple of your eye. (Psalm 17:8)

Jesus . . . said, "Father . . . I do not ask that you take them out of the world, but that you keep them from the evil one" (John 17:1, 15). He who keeps you will not slumber . . . The Lord will keep you from all evil (Psalm 121:3, 7). Who by God's power are being guarded through faith for a salvation ready to be revealed in the last time (1 Peter 1:5). Oh, guard my soul, and deliver me! Let me not be put to shame, for I take refuge in you (Psalm 25:20). Now to him who is able to keep you from stumbling and to present you blameless before the presence of his glory with great joy, to the only God, our Saviour, through Jesus Christ our Lord, be glory, majesty, dominion, and authority, before all time and now and forever (Jude 24–25). I am convinced that he is able to guard until that Day what has been entrusted to me (2 Timothy 1:12).

*We have all seen the sort of film or read the sort of book in which the hero is given something very precious – a letter, perhaps, or a jewel – which he has promised to 'guard with his life'. And we have watched him as he tries never to allow the treasure out of sight or out of reach. God promises, in a similar way, to keep those who have committed their lives to His safe custody. We have to make our way through a dangerous, sinful world. Like children, we can easily be knocked over; like an eye, we can easily be damaged; like a jewel, we can easily be stolen. But we may have complete confidence in the One who has promised to keep us.*

Thank You, Lord, for Your promise to keep me from all evil, and to guard me with Your life. Amen.

## I will uphold you with my righteous right hand. (Isaiah 41:10)

And in the fourth watch of the night Jesus came to them, walking on the sea. But when the disciples saw him walking on the sea, they were terrified, and said, "It is a ghost!" and they cried out in fear. But immediately Jesus spoke to them, saying, "Take heart; it is I. Do not be afraid." And Peter answered him, "Lord, if it is you, command me to come to you on the water." He said, "Come." So Peter got out of the boat and walked on the water and came to Jesus. But when he saw the wind, he was afraid, and beginning to sink he cried out, "Lord, save me." Jesus immediately reached out his hand and took hold of him, saying to him, "O you of little faith, why did you doubt?" And when they got into the boat, the wind ceased. And those in the boat worshiped him, saying, "Truly you are the Son of God" (Matthew 14:25–33).

*Fear and doubt are like twin golf bunkers – one on either side of the green guarding the approach. It is sad but interesting to notice how often Christians, like the disciples on this occasion, are caught in one or other of the two. Fear says, 'I can't.' It shrinks back from the challenge to do something difficult, to stand alone for Christ, to speak to someone else about Him, or perhaps to give up something that is sinful. Doubt says, 'He can't.' It fails to see that God, who has called us to do something hard, will give us the strength to see it through to a finish. God's commands are His enablings, and He does not ask us to do something without also supplying the necessary tools for the job.*

**Help me, O Lord, neither to fear the size of the problem nor to doubt the sufficiency of Your strength. Amen.**

## Living as servants of God. (1 Peter 2:16)

Do you not know that if you present yourselves to anyone as obedient slaves, you are slaves of the one whom you obey? . . . But now that you have been set free from sin and have become slaves of God (Romans 6:16, 22). Servants of Christ, doing the will of God from the heart, rendering service with a good will as to the Lord and not to man (Ephesians 6:6–7). And the Lord's servant must not be quarrelsome but kind to everyone, able to teach, patiently enduring evil, correcting his opponents with gentleness (2 Timothy 2:24–25). "His master said to him, 'Well done, good and faithful servant. You have been faithful over a little; I will set you over much. Enter into the joy of your master'" (Matthew 25:21). "'We are unworthy servants; we have only done what was our duty'" (Luke 17:10). Great is the Lord, who delights in the welfare of his servant! (Psalm 35:27)

*William Barclay points out that the same architect who made Liverpool Cathedral also designed an ordinary, everyday, common-or-garden telephone kiosk – the lofty and the lowly. So it is that God calls some Christians to occupy places of great responsibility and others to do hidden, humble jobs which never attract much attention. But He judges both servants alike – not by the size or success of their work, but by the faithful, humble efficiency with which they have carried it out. And both kinds of servant are equally the object of their Master's carefulness and concern. Can you work in the limelight without getting proud, and in the shadows without becoming resentful?*

**Help me, O Lord, to serve You as You deserve – humbly, faithfully and from the heart. Amen.**

### He has covered me with the robe of righteousness. (Isaiah 61:10)

When the goodness and loving kindness of God our Saviour appeared, he saved us, not because of works done by us in righteousness, but according to his own mercy (Titus 3:4–5). Not because of our works but because of his own purpose and grace, which he gave us in Christ Jesus before the ages began (2 Timothy 1:9). We have all become like one who is unclean, and all our righteous deeds are like a polluted garment. We all fade like a leaf, and our iniquities, like the wind, take us away (Isaiah 64:6). For our sake God made him to be sin who knew no sin, so that in him we might become the righteousness of God (2 Corinthians 5:21). And be found in him, not having a righteousness of my own that comes from the law, but that which comes through faith in Christ, the righteousness from God that depends on faith (Philippians 3:9). Abraham believed God, and it was counted to him as righteousness . . . just as David also speaks of the blessing of the one to whom God counts righteousness apart from works (Romans 4:3, 6).

*'I would love to go, but I have nothing suitable to wear.' Sometimes we hear people say that as they look wistfully at an invitation to a party or a dinner. We are a bit like that as we consider God's invitation to present ourselves in His presence. He expects perfect righteousness, and our own righteousness is like filthy rags. What can we do? No patching and mending will do but, because Jesus has borne our sins, He is able to offer us His righteousness like a robe – or like the 'wedding garment' in the story Jesus told (Matthew 22:11). Our sins were put down to Christ, and His righteousness is put down to us. By faith therefore we can be accepted by God, for there is never a moment when He sees the believer in Christ to be otherwise than perfectly righteous.*

**Thank You, Lord, for providing me with the robe of righteousness and enabling me to accept Your Father's invitation. Amen.**

**"Hold fast what you have, so that no one may seize your crown." (Revelation 3:11)**

As for you, O man of God, flee these things. Pursue righteousness, godliness, faith, love, steadfastness, gentleness. Fight the good fight of the faith. Take hold of the eternal life to which you were called and about which you made the good confession in the presence of many witnesses. I charge you . . . to keep the commandment unstained and free from reproach until the appearing of our Lord Jesus Christ . . . O Timothy, guard the deposit entrusted to you. Avoid the irreverent babble and contradictions of what is falsely called "knowledge," for by professing it some have swerved from the faith. Grace be with you (1 Timothy 6:11–14, 20–21).

*The other day we thought of how the Lord keeps us in the often adventurous journey through life, and today we consider ourselves, and the things which have been committed to us as Christian servants. God wants us to present all these things and ourselves to Him, intact, at the end of our lives. The message is the gospel of Jesus Christ, which we must preserve from all forms of false or empty teaching that pollute its purity or weaken its effects. The treasure is a life which has consistently 'shunned' all that is sinful and unworthy and 'aimed' at what is good and pure and right. 'A king's (or queen's) messenger' is someone entrusted with government documents which are too important to be sent by ordinary mail. It is quite a good description of a Christian, but it sets a very high standard to live up to. Look out for thieves!*

**Lord, help me to preserve intact that which has been committed to me, and give me strength to resist every attack made upon me to surrender it. Amen.**

## "I will extend peace to her like a river."
## (Isaiah 66:12)

"Peace I leave with you; my peace I give to you. Not as the world gives do I give to you. Let not your hearts be troubled, neither let them be afraid" (John 14:27). "I have said these things to you, that in me you may have peace. In the world you will have tribulation. But take heart; I have overcome the world" (John 16:33). "You keep him in perfect peace whose mind is stayed on you, because he trusts in you" (Isaiah 26:3). Great peace have those who love your law; nothing can make them stumble (Psalm 119:165). The effect of righteousness will be peace, and the result of righteousness, quietness and trust forever (Isaiah 32:17). Do not be anxious about anything, but in everything by prayer and supplication with thanksgiving let your requests be made known to God. And the peace of God, which surpasses all understanding, will guard your hearts and your minds in Christ Jesus (Philippians 4:6–7).

*What is peace? Two artists once tried to paint a picture to illustrate the word. One painting showed a calm sunset over a tranquil sea and the other a robin, perched happily on a twig overhanging a rushing mountain stream. The latter won the prize, because peace is not the tranquillity of unruffled seas but calm in storm. It is not isolation, but insulation – not being taken out of the world with all its troubles, but being kept calm and steady in the world. What is the secret of peace? This passage seems to suggest three things. First, a quiet trust in the presence and power of Christ, for 'in Him' there is peace. Second, peace is the result of obedience to God's law. Righteous, upright living results in a clear conscience. Third, peace comes through prayer as we bring our needs to a heavenly Father who knows and cares and understands.*

**Save me, O Lord, from seeking peace by escaping life's problems. May I find peace instead in facing the storm with You. Amen.**

**He shall divide the spoil with the strong, because he poured out his soul to death and . . . bore the sin of many. (Isaiah 53:12)**

"I am the good shepherd. The good shepherd lays down his life for the sheep . . . For this reason the Father loves me, because I lay down my life that I may take it up again. No one takes it from me, but I lay it down of my own accord. I have authority to lay it down, and I have authority to take it up again. This charge I have received from my Father" (John 10:11, 17–18). "The Son of Man came . . . to give his life as a ransom for many" (Mark 10:45). For there is one God, and there is one mediator between God and men, the man Christ Jesus, who gave himself as a ransom for all (1 Timothy 2:5–6). He himself bore our sins in his body on the tree . . . By his wounds you have been healed (1 Peter 2:24). He disarmed the rulers and authorities and put them to open shame, by triumphing over them in him (Colossians 2:15). "This Jesus . . . you crucified . . . God raised him up, loosing the pangs of death, because it was not possible for him to be held by it" (Acts 2:23–24).

*Three things make the death of Jesus different from other deaths. First, it was* voluntary. *To the very end, even when He hung upon the cross, He could have escaped. But He refused to do so and drained to the dregs the cup which His Father gave Him. Why? Jesus' death was also* vicarious. *This means that He died in our place, instead of us. 'He knew how wicked men had been; He knew that God must punish sin; but out of pity Jesus said, I'll bear the punishment instead.' By His wounds we have been ransomed, reconciled and restored. Finally, His death was* victorious. *The cross was the great encounter between Jesus and Satan. Satan could not stop it and thereby prevent the salvation of humankind from taking place. Jesus won that battle and demonstrated the fact by His great victory parade on the first Easter Day.*

**Grant, O Lord, that I may show my gratitude for Your death by living in the power of Your resurrection. Amen.**

**"Whoever believes has eternal life." (John 6:47)**

About midnight Paul and Silas were praying and singing hymns to God, and the prisoners were listening to them, and suddenly there was a great earthquake, so that ... all the doors were opened, and everyone's bonds were unfastened. When the jailer woke ... he drew his sword and was about to kill himself, supposing that the prisoners had escaped. But Paul cried ... "Do not harm yourself, for we are all here." And the jailer ... rushed in, and ... fell down before Paul and Silas ... and said, "Sirs, what must I do to be saved?" And they said, "Believe in the Lord Jesus, and you will be saved, you and your household." And they spoke the word of the Lord to him and to all who were in his house. And he took them ... and washed their wounds; and he was baptized at once, he and all his family. Then he brought them up into his house and set food before them. And he rejoiced along with his entire household that he had believed in God (Acts 16:25–34).

*What extraordinary prisoners Paul and Silas were! Instead of cursing and complaining, they sang and prayed. Instead of escaping as fast as they could, they quietly stayed put. No wonder the jailer was impressed by such courage, kindness and faith and wanted to know how he, too, could be saved! He wasted no time and listened eagerly as they explained what it meant to know Christ. Notice too how his faith, like that of Paul and Silas, immediately showed itself in action. His prisoners became his friends, and he did everything he could to show kindness and sympathy to them. Behaviour is always the blossom of belief.*

**Help me to remember, O Lord, that (often when I least expect it) others are watching, listening and wondering. Amen.**

## And we know that for those who love God all things work together for good. (Romans 8:28)

"As for me, I would seek God, and to God would I commit my cause, who does great things and unsearchable, marvellous things without number . . . He frustrates the devices of the crafty, so that their hands achieve no success" (Job 5:8–9, 12). But Joseph said to them . . . "As for you, you meant evil against me, but God meant it for good, to bring it about that many people should be kept alive, as they are today" (Genesis 50:19–20). The king's heart is a stream of water in the hand of the Lord; he turns it wherever he will (Proverbs 21:1). When a man's ways please the Lord, he makes even his enemies to be at peace with him (Proverbs 16:7). "No weapon that is fashioned against you shall succeed" (Isaiah 54:17). Surely the wrath of man shall praise you (Psalm 76:10). The lot is cast into the lap, but its every decision is from the Lord (Proverbs 16:33).

*It often looks, doesn't it, as if things happen by chance? But really for the Christian there is no such thing as chance, and it is simply the 'nickname' we give to Providence – that is, to the goodness of God working through nature, history and circumstances. So often when we look back upon some apparent disappointment or even disaster we can trace the rainbow through the rain and realize that 'God meant it for good'. Always remember three things: God is never taken by surprise; God knows what is best for us; God never loses control of events. Holding on to these truths will be a great help in times of difficulty and distress.*

**Lord, I thank You that nothing is too big for You to control, and nothing is too small for You to care about. Amen.**

## God's Spirit dwells in you. (1 Corinthians 3:16)

Because you are sons, God has sent the Spirit of his Son into our hearts, crying, "Abba! Father!" (Galatians 4:6). The Spirit himself bears witness with our spirit that we are children of God (Romans 8:16). Likewise the Spirit helps us in our weakness. For we do not know what to pray for as we ought, but the Spirit himself intercedes for us with groanings too deep for words (Romans 8:26). Praying at all times in the Spirit (Ephesians 6:18). And . . . God's love has been poured into our hearts through the Holy Spirit who has been given to us (Romans 5:5). Now concerning spiritual gifts, brothers, I do not want you to be uninformed . . . Now there are varieties of gifts . . . All these are empowered by one and the same Spirit, who apportions to each one individually as he wills (1 Corinthians 1, 4, 11). But the fruit of the Spirit is love, joy, peace, patience, kindness, goodness, faithfulness, gentleness, self-control (Galatians 5:22–23).

*When we believe on the Lord Jesus Christ and receive Him into our hearts it is the Holy Spirit who takes up residence there. As we know, when anyone comes to live with us permanently it makes a difference – sometimes a radical one – to our way of life. The house. His presence brings a new atmosphere of confidence and love. Doubts are dispelled, prayer becomes more meaningful and His loving influence prevails. The garden. Plants begin to be seen in the Christian's life which were never there before, and others begin to enjoy the fruit that is grown there and find in a true Christian a centre of helpfulness and happiness.*

I thank You, O Lord, for the gift of Your Holy Spirit, and I ask that He may enjoy unhindered control of my life. Amen.

## That I may know him and the power of his resurrection. (Philippians 3:10)

"This is eternal life, that they know you the only true God, and Jesus Christ whom you have sent" (John 17:3). "Let us know; let us press on to know the Lord; his going out is sure as the dawn; he will come to us as the showers, as the spring rains that water the earth" (Hosea 6:3). I know whom I have believed, and I am convinced that he is able to guard until that Day what has been entrusted to me (2 Timothy 1:12). "No longer shall each one teach his neighbour and each his brother, saying, 'Know the Lord,' for they shall all know me, from the least of them to the greatest, declares the Lord. For I will forgive their iniquity, and I will remember their sin no more" (Jeremiah 31:34). And by this we know that we have come to know him, if we keep his commandments (1 John 2:3).

*When we talk about knowing someone, there are perhaps three stages, or degrees, of knowledge.* By name. *There are many people whom we may never meet, but we know all about them – because they are famous and their names are household words. There must be millions of people who have that sort of knowledge of God.* By sight. *Other people we recognize at once because we have seen their picture or because they live near us – even though we have never been introduced. So it is that there are many who have a form of knowledge of God. Perhaps they go to church regularly but the relationship stops at that point.* By heart. *Yet again there are others whom we have come to know personally, and whose friendship we enjoy. That is how God wants us to know Him, so that He can refresh our lives, guard us from evil and forgive our sins. We in turn, then, will want to keep His commandments.*

**Lord, let me not be content with having been introduced to You, but help me to press on to know You more and more. Amen.**

## Competent in the Scriptures. (Acts 18:24)

Now these Jews were more noble than those in Thessalonica; they received the word with all eagerness, examining the Scriptures daily to see if these things were so (Acts 17:11). From childhood you have been acquainted with the sacred writings, which are able to make you wise for salvation through faith in Christ Jesus (2 Timothy 3:15). Jesus answered them, "You are wrong, because you know neither the Scriptures nor the power of God" (Matthew 22:29). And beginning with Moses and all the Prophets, he interpreted to them in all the Scriptures the things concerning himself (Luke 24:27). And Paul went in, as was his custom, and on three Sabbath days he reasoned with them from the Scriptures, explaining and proving that it was necessary for the Christ to suffer and to rise from the dead (Acts 17:2–3).

*During the last war Winston Churchill used to write in the margins of very urgent documents, 'Action this day'. And that is the sort of challenge with which the Bible presents us. We can't just read it and then put it back on the shelf like any ordinary book. It demands action.* We must examine it. *Christians ought to know their Bibles well. Some of the equipment we should have to help us to do this includes a concordance, a good modern translation and a commentary.* We must explain it. *Sometimes we meet an expert economist or scientist who cannot explain what he or she knows to others. We must not be like that. Start by explaining the truths of the Bible to yourself – as you lie awake, or go for a walk, or take a bath. Then, as your confidence grows, you will be able to explain it, as Jesus did and as Paul did, to those who want to share your faith in Christ.*

**Lord, help me to be competent in the Scriptures, understanding deeply and explaining clearly. Amen.**

## "Blessed are the dead who die in the Lord" . . . "that they may rest from their labours, for their deeds follow them!" (Revelation 14:13)

Then one of the elders addressed me, saying, "Who are these, clothed in white robes, and from where have they come?" I said to him, "Sir, you know." And he said to me, "These are the ones coming out of the great tribulation. They have washed their robes and made them white in the blood of the Lamb. Therefore they are before the throne of God, and serve him day and night in his temple; and he who sits on the throne will shelter them with his presence. They shall hunger no more, neither thirst anymore; the sun shall not strike them, nor any scorching heat. For the Lamb in the midst of the throne will be their shepherd, and he will guide them to springs of living water, and God will wipe away every tear from their eyes" (Revelation 7:13–17).

*This passage seems to refer to those Christians who have come through some particular time of persecution and suffering, but it also gives us a glimpse of what we may expect in heaven.* We shall be occupied. *The Victorians had a quaint phrase to describe the death of a Christian. They used to say that he or she had been 'called to higher service'. You will still see it on tombstones. It expressed a very real truth, for it is clear from many parts of the Bible that we are being prepared down here for greater responsibility when we go to be with Christ.* We shall be satisfied. *Do you know that feeling of utter contentment and peace when you finally reach shelter after a long, thirsty and scorching walk or march? That is one of the good things which passes our understanding which God has prepared for those who love Him.*

Lord, thank You for going to prepare a place for me. Help me to prepare myself for Your service. Amen.

### "If anyone would come after me, let him deny himself." (Luke 9:23)

As they were going along the road, someone said to him, "I will follow you wherever you go." And Jesus said to him, "Foxes have holes, and birds of the air have nests, but the Son of Man has nowhere to lay his head." To another he said, "Follow me." But he said, "Lord, let me first go and bury my father." And Jesus said to him, "Leave the dead to bury their own dead. But as for you, go and proclaim the kingdom of God." Yet another said, "I will follow you, Lord, but let me first say farewell to those at my home." Jesus said to him, "No one who puts his hand to the plough and looks back is fit for the kingdom of God" (Luke 9:57–62).

*Jesus never made it easy for people to follow Him. He always made it clear to them that the road ahead was hard and steep. 'Narrow road ahead!' 'Don't follow me,' He said, 'if you want an easy, comfortable life. You must be prepared for tears and toil and sweat and blood.' 'Give way!' 'If your motto in life is "me first",' said Jesus, 'you won't make the sort of disciple I want.' (To 'bury' someone meant, as we might say, 'to see him out' – a process which could last for years.) 'No U-turns!' 'You'll never make a wholehearted follower,' He said, 'if you are looking over your shoulder all the time and wishing that you were back again in the old life. You must sever every tie.'*

**Lord, You have suffered so much for me. Make me willing for the small sacrifices You ask of me. Amen.**

## Love does not envy. (1 Corinthians 13:4)

"For from within, out of the heart of man, come evil thoughts ... coveting ... envy ... All these evil things come from within, and they defile a person" (Mark 7:21–23). Now the works of the flesh are evident: ... strife ... envy ... and things like these. I warn you, as I warned you before, that those who do such things will not inherit the kingdom of God (Galatians 5:19–21). "The patriarchs, jealous of Joseph, sold him into Egypt" (Acts 7:9). Pilate knew that it was out of envy that they had delivered Jesus up (Matthew 27:18). But the Jews were jealous ... set the city in an uproar, and attacked the house of Jason (Acts 17:5). Envy makes the bones rot (Proverbs 14:30). Wrath is cruel, anger is overwhelming, but who can stand before jealousy? (Proverbs 27:4).

*To envy someone is to think resentfully of the advantages that he or she enjoys over us or to allow ourselves to be jealous of the fact that someone else has succeeded where we have failed, or that they have a better job, a bigger income or a larger house than we have. Envy is a particularly unpleasant sin for two reasons. First, it can embitter us to the very depths of our being, acting like rust or cancer – rotting, so to speak, our bones. Those who give way to it have said goodbye to happiness and peace of mind. Second, envy so often leads to other sins. Joseph was kidnapped, Jesus was slain, Jason was assaulted – all because people who in other ways may have been quite respectable allowed themselves to become the victims of envy.*

**From envy, hatred and malice and all uncharitableness, good Lord, deliver me. Amen.**

### Doing the will of God from the heart.
### (Ephesians 6:6)

"Not everyone who says to me, 'Lord, Lord,' will enter the kingdom of heaven, but the one who does the will of my Father who is in heaven" (Matthew 7:21). And a crowd was sitting around him, and they said to him, "Your mother and your brothers are outside, seeking you." And he answered them, "Who are my mother and my brothers?" And looking about at those who sat around him, he said, "Here are my mother and my brothers! Whoever does the will of God, he is my brother and sister and mother" (Mark 3:32–35). "Now therefore . . . observe and seek out all the commandments of the Lord your God, that you may possess this good land" (1 Chronicles 28:8). For you have need of endurance, so that when you have done the will of God you may receive what is promised (Hebrews 10:36). "'A man after my heart, who will do all my will'" (Acts 13:22).

*Obedience to the will of God is perhaps the single most important secret of a successful Christian life. Outside His will we are like trains that have come off the tracks – there is no peace and no progress. There are three stages, or steps, in obeying God's will. First,* we must desire it. *Obedience must be our primary aim and purpose. Like the psalmist we must say, 'I delight to do your will, O my God.' Second,* we must discover it. *The most important part of God's will for us is found in the Bible, and we must 'seek out all his commandments', perhaps even marking them as we find them. Finally,* we must do it. *This is perhaps the hardest part, because it requires courage and endurance to follow His will against the tide of popular opinion. But just look at the 'special relationship' which obedience brings!*

**'Jesus, supreme in my heart, bid every rival depart, teach me I pray, with joy to obey, Jesus supreme in my heart.' Amen.**

### "Do not disbelieve, but believe." (John 20:27)

Philip found Nathanael and said to him, "We have found him of whom Moses . . . and also the prophets wrote, Jesus of Nazareth . . ." Nathanael said to him, "Can anything good come out of Nazareth?" Philip said to him, "Come and see." Jesus saw Nathanael coming toward him and said of him, "Behold, an Israelite indeed, in whom there is no deceit!" Nathanael said to him, "How do you know me?" Jesus answered him, "Before Philip called you, when you were under the fig tree, I saw you." Nathanael answered him, "Rabbi, you are the Son of God! You are the King of Israel!" Jesus answered him, "Because I said to you, 'I saw you under the fig tree,' do you believe? You will see greater things than these . . . You will see heaven opened, and the angels of God ascending and descending on the Son of Man" (John 1:45–51).

*Nathanael (whom many people identify with Bartholomew) was not unlike the many people we meet today whose first reaction, when we talk to them about Christ, is slightly sceptical and even cynical. 'Is it really relevant today?' they ask, or 'Hasn't Christianity been tried and found wanting?' Philip behaved so sensibly. He didn't allow himself to be drawn into a long argument. He just said, 'Come and see.' Nathanael was impressed and interested enough to do so, and he only needed one word from Jesus to be convinced and won over for life. 'Taste and see that the Lord is good', says the psalmist in answer to today's sceptics. 'Oh make but trial of His love, experience will decide', adds the hymn writer.*

**Lord, give me the attractiveness that Philip must have had, that when I speak to others they may come and see. Amen.**

**"Pray then like this." (Matthew 6:9)**

*Search me*, O God, and know my heart! Try me and know my thoughts! And see if there be any grievous way in me, and lead me in the way everlasting! (Psalm 139:23–24). Peter . . . walked on the water and came to Jesus. But when he saw the wind, he was afraid, and beginning to sink he cried out, "Lord, *save me*." Jesus immediately reached out his hand and took hold of him (Matthew 14:29–31). Moses said to the Lord, ". . . Now therefore, if I have found favour in your sight, please *show me* now your ways, that I may know you" (Exodus 33:12–13). Then Samson called to the Lord and said, "O Lord God, please remember me and please *strengthen me*" (Judges 16:28). And I heard the voice of the Lord saying, "Whom shall I send, and who will go for us?" Then I said, "Here am I! *Send me*" (Isaiah 6:8).

*Here are just a few examples (italics mine) of the many prayers we find in the Bible. They may be a help to us when we talk to God in prayer on our own. I have chosen them because they are appropriate for different situations in which we may find ourselves: when we are conscious of our sin; when we are attacked by temptation; when we feel the need to know God better; when we are faced with some difficulty or challenge; and when God calls us to some particular piece of work for Him. There is a time for formal prayer, and that can be very helpful, but on our own we want to be natural and simple and to speak from the heart – as you can see that these people did in their particular crises.*

'Lord Jesus, teach me how to pray, and help me in a natural way to bring my needs and my requests before You day by day.' Amen.

## God's varied grace. (1 Peter 4:10)

I will bless the Lord at all times; his praise shall continually be in my mouth. My soul makes its boast in the Lord; let the humble hear and be glad. Oh, magnify the Lord with me, and let us exalt his name together! I sought the Lord, and he answered me and delivered me from all my fears. Those who look to him are radiant, and their faces shall never be ashamed. This poor man cried, and the Lord heard him and saved him out of all his troubles. The angel of the Lord encamps around those who fear him, and delivers them. Oh, taste and see that the Lord is good! Blessed is the man who takes refuge in him! Oh, fear the Lord, you his saints, for those who fear him have no lack! The young lions suffer want and hunger; but those who seek the Lord lack no good thing (Psalm 34:1–10).

*This lovely psalm follows the pattern of so many others, for it is a record of human beings praising and God providing.* Humans praise. *A magnifying glass does not alter the stamp or print you are looking at, but it does bring it closer and make it clearer. And that is the way in which we praise God – not only with our lips, but also in our lives, so that as others watch us they get an altogether better view of God's greatness and goodness.* God provides. *'No good thing' will He withhold from us. It doesn't follow from this that we shall get everything we want in life because not everything, in God's opinion, is good for us. But we can be sure of this: if we seek Him then we shall lack nothing that will contribute to our spiritual happiness and welfare.*

**Grant, O Lord, that through me others may come to see You more clearly, to follow You more nearly and to love You more dearly. Amen.**

## A prisoner for Christ Jesus. (Ephesians 3:1)

"I myself was convinced that I ought to do many things in opposing the name of Jesus of Nazareth" (Acts 26:9). For you have heard of my former life in Judaism, how I persecuted the church of God violently and tried to destroy it (Galatians 1:13). "As I . . . drew near to Damascus, about noon a great light from heaven suddenly shone around me. And I fell to the ground and heard a voice saying to me, 'Saul, Saul, why are you persecuting me?' And I answered, 'Who are you, Lord?' And he said to me, 'I am Jesus of Nazareth, whom you are persecuting'" (Acts 22:6–8). For I am the least of the apostles, unworthy to be called an apostle, because I persecuted the church of God. But by the grace of God I am what I am, and his grace toward me was not in vain. On the contrary, I worked harder than any of them, though it was not I, but the grace of God that is with me (1 Corinthians 15:9–10). I press on to make it my own, because Christ Jesus has made me his own (Philippians 3:12).

*Paul was a prisoner of the Roman Empire, but there was a very real sense in which he regarded himself as a prisoner of Jesus Christ as well.* His crime. *Paul never forgave himself (though he rejoiced in God's forgiveness) for the havoc he wrought in the church, and to the end of his life he thought of himself as 'the chief among sinners'.* His arrest. *'In evil long he took delight, unawed by shame or fear, till a new object struck his sight, and stopped his wild career.' That is what the hymn writer John Newton wrote about his former, wicked life as captain of a slave ship, and it is what Paul might have said when brought face-to-face with Jesus.* His sentence. *'Hard labour for life' is what Paul gladly accepted in an attempt to do something to repay the love of Christ for him.*

**Lord, help me to labour for life out of love for You. Amen.**

## "Is anything too hard for the Lord?"
## (Genesis 18:14)

Then came one of the rulers of the synagogue, Jairus by name
. . . and implored Jesus earnestly, saying, "My little daughter is
at the point of death. Come and lay your hands on her, so that
she may be made well and live." And he went with him . . .
There came from the ruler's house some who said, "Your
daughter is dead. Why trouble the Teacher any further?" But
. . . Jesus said . . . "Do not fear, only believe." . . . When he had
entered, he said to them, "Why are you . . . weeping? The child
is not dead but sleeping." And they laughed at him. But he put
them all outside . . . and went in where the child was. Taking
her by the hand he said to her . . . "Little girl, I say to you,
arise." And immediately the girl got up and began walking
(for she was twelve years of age), and they were immediately
overcome with amazement (Mark 5:22–24, 35–36, 39–42).

The miracle. *Of all the many miracles performed by Jesus, none was
greater than the raising of dead people to life. It happened on three
occasions. There was this little girl who had been dead for only a few
minutes; the young man from Nain on his way to his own funeral
who had been dead presumably for a few hours; and Lazarus of
Bethany who had been in the grave for four days. It is miracles such
as these that convinced many people, and that help to convince us,
that Jesus was indeed the Son of God.* The mystery. *Almost as an
aside, Jesus threw light on the mystery of death by comparing it with
sleep. Just as you go to sleep in full and hopeful expectation of waking up to a new day, so one day we must approach death in sure and
certain hope of the resurrection to everlasting life.*

**Lord, I thank You that with You nothing is impossible.
Amen.**

**The blood of Jesus . . . cleanses us from all sin. (1 John 1:7)**

Have mercy on me, O God, according to your steadfast love; according to your abundant mercy blot out my transgressions. Wash me thoroughly from my iniquity, and cleanse me from my sin! (Psalm 51:1–2) "Come now, let us reason together, says the Lord: though your sins are like scarlet, they shall be as white as snow; though they are red like crimson, they shall become like wool" (Isaiah 1:18). "I will cleanse them from all the guilt of their sin against me" (Jeremiah 33:8). "I will sprinkle clean water on you, and you shall be clean from all your uncleannesses, and from all your idols I will cleanse you" (Ezekiel 36:25). If we say we have no sin, we deceive ourselves, and the truth is not in us. If we confess our sins, he is faithful and just to forgive us our sins and to cleanse us from all unrighteousness (1 John 1:8–9).

*Have you sometimes looked with dismay at a stain which has appeared on some otherwise spotless carpet or tablecloth? It spoils the appearance of the carpet and spreads over too wide an area for you to be able to conceal it. You try everything possible, and then at last someone produces a detergent which does the trick – and as if by magic the thing becomes as new. Sin has that staining effect on our lives, making us totally unworthy to present ourselves to God. People have tried every sort of 'detergent' – doing good, going to church, prayers, fasting and so on, but the stain remains as stubbornly fixed as ever. There is only one thing that can remove the stain of sin and cleanse our hearts and lives, and that is the blood of Jesus Christ shed for us upon the cross.*

**I thank You, Lord, that just as the lepers found cleansing from their disease from You, so Your blood can cleanse me from all sin. Amen.**

## The Lord has set apart the godly for himself. (Psalm 4:3)

But we ought always to give thanks to God for you, brothers beloved by the Lord, because God chose you as the firstfruits to be saved, through sanctification by the Spirit and belief in the truth (2 Thessalonians 2:13). Blessed be the God and Father of our Lord Jesus Christ, who . . . chose us in him before the foundation of the world, that we should be holy and blameless before him (Ephesians 1:3–4). "You did not choose me, but I chose you and appointed you that you should go and bear fruit and that your fruit should abide . . . If you were of the world, the world would love you as its own; but because you are not of the world, but I chose you out of the world, therefore the world hates you" (John 15:16, 19).

*When we become Christians and start to follow Christ it seems, doesn't it, as if it is our own choice and decision? That is how the disciples felt when they left their fishing and threw in their lot with Jesus. But in fact it is not so at all. Our choice is only a response to His. We choose Him because, from the very beginning, He has marked us out to belong to Him – like a dog following its new master from the kennels. Someone sees you walking towards the football field and says, 'I see you've decided to play football today.' 'Yes,' you reply, 'but only because I was chosen to play.' The fact that God has chosen us should give us great joy and confidence, but let us remember what He has chosen us for – to be forgiven, to be faultless and to be fruitful.*

**Lord, You have graciously chosen me to belong to You, but please grant that You may never be disappointed that You did so. Amen.**

## "For the Son of Man came to seek and to save the lost." (Luke 19:10)

There was a man named Zacchaeus. He was a chief tax collector and was rich. And he was seeking to see who Jesus was, but on account of the crowd he could not, because he was small of stature. So he ran on ahead and climbed up into a sycamore tree . . . And when Jesus came to the place, he looked up and said to him, "Zacchaeus, hurry and come down, for I must stay at your house today." So he hurried and came down and received him joyfully. And . . . they all grumbled, "He has gone in to be the guest of a man who is a sinner." And Zacchaeus stood and said to the Lord, "Behold, Lord, the half of my goods I give to the poor. And if I have defrauded anyone of anything, I restore it fourfold." And Jesus said to him, "Today salvation has come to this house" (Luke 19: 2–9).

A desire. *Zacchaeus was wealthy and apparently lacked nothing that money could buy, but he wanted to see Jesus – not just out of curiosity, but because he felt Jesus could help him to find the secret of true happiness.* A difficulty. *But like so many who seek Jesus, he ran into difficulty. For some it is a sceptical friend, a bad habit or a secret ambition. For Zacchaeus it was a very practical problem he quickly overcame.* A decision. *Jesus' invitation to come and stay was answered 'by return', and he did not lose a moment in welcoming his guest.* A difference. *Whenever Jesus comes into a person's life He makes a difference for good. In Zacchaeus' case cheating gave way to honesty, and greed to generosity. Which stage of his experience have you reached?*

**Lord, if I have wronged anybody help me to put it right as generously and quickly as possible. Amen.**

## Love does not insist on its own way.
## (1 Corinthians 13:5)

Let each of you look not only to his own interests, but also to the interests of others. Have this mind among yourselves, which is yours in Christ Jesus (Philippians 2:4–5). I hope . . . to send Timothy to you soon . . . I have no one like him, who will be genuinely concerned for your welfare. They all seek their own interests, not those of Jesus Christ (Philippians 2:19–21). Let no one seek his own good, but the good of his neighbour . . . I try to please everyone in everything I do, not seeking my own advantage, but that of many, that they may be saved . . . Be imitators of me, as I am of Christ (1 Corinthians 10:24, 33; 11:1). For Christ did not please himself (Romans 15:3).

*How easily and how often we catch ourselves out being selfish – putting our own interests and wishes before those of other people! It begins when we are very young, when I want the best cake or the last chocolate. It continues as we get older when it is my favourite television programme that must be switched on, or when others must give way to me over the holiday plans or are expected to keep the meal hot because I want to stay in bed or come home late. It ends when, as old men and women, we can't bear to see someone sitting in my favourite chair or disturbing the punctilious routine I have worked out for myself. True joy comes when it is Jesus, then Others, then Yourself – in that order. 'Yoj' must be as unpleasant as it sounds.*

**Save me, O Lord, from becoming the sort of person whose life is governed by the phrase 'me first'. Amen.**

## Persecuted, but not forsaken. (2 Corinthians 4:9)

Beloved, do not be surprised at the fiery trial when it comes upon you to test you, as though something strange were happening to you. But rejoice insofar as you share Christ's sufferings, that you may also rejoice and be glad when his glory is revealed. If you are insulted for the name of Christ, you are blessed (1 Peter 4:12–14). "Remember the word that I said to you: 'A servant is not greater than his master.' If they persecuted me, they will also persecute you" (John 15:20). Indeed, all who desire to live a godly life in Christ Jesus will be persecuted (2 Timothy 3:12). "Indeed, the hour is coming when whoever kills you will think he is offering service to God" (John 16:2). Do not be surprised, brothers, that the world hates you (1 John 3:13). "Do not fear what you are about to suffer ... Be faithful unto death, and I will give you the crown of life" (Revelation 2:10).

Do not wonder. *We must not be surprised if, as Christians, we meet with misunderstanding, mockery and even more active persecution. The world that crucified Jesus still hates Him, because He challenges so much of what the world stands for – selfishness, materialism and sin. His followers must not expect to escape unscathed. Should we not rather see it as a privilege to be allowed to share His sufferings?* Do not fear. *If you have read the stories of Christians who have suffered for their faith – in historical times, perhaps, or more recently under Nazi Germany or behind the Iron or Bamboo Curtain – you may wonder, as I often do, whether you would ever be able to stand up to it. People have been amazed by how God does help them in the hour of trial, and we must try to trust Him like that and not be afraid.*

**Lord, make me ready and willing to suffer for You, who suffered so much ridicule and shame for me. Amen.**

## The One who is high and lifted up . . . whose name is Holy. (Isaiah 57:15)

"Who is like you, O Lord, among the gods? Who is like you, majestic in holiness?" (Exodus 15:11). "Holy, holy, holy is the Lord of hosts" (Isaiah 6:3). Holy and awesome is his name! (Psalm 111:9). You who are of purer eyes than to see evil (Habakkuk 1:13). Your righteousness is righteous forever (Psalm 119:142). "There is none holy like the Lord" (1 Samuel 2:2). "Who is able to stand before the Lord, this holy God?" (1 Samuel 6:20). Our God is a consuming fire (Hebrews 12:29). Who among us can dwell with the consuming fire? "Who among us can dwell with everlasting burnings?" (Isaiah 33:14). Who shall ascend the hill of the Lord? And who shall stand in his holy place? He who has clean hands and a pure heart (Psalm 24:3–4). For the Lord is righteous; he loves righteous deeds; the upright shall behold his face (Psalm 11:7).

*In the early days of space travel, the great problem was that of re-entry into the earth's atmosphere. If the angle was not just right the space craft would either bounce off and go into permanent orbit or be burnt to a cinder. Our problem is rather like that. How can we stand in the presence of a God whose holiness is white-hot and like a devouring fire? There is only one 'angle' of approach – a 'right angle', or uprightness of heart. In other words, it is only those who have been cleansed from sin who can be accepted into His presence, because sin cannot survive even for an instant in the blazing heat of His holiness.*

**Lord Jesus, I thank You that it is Your righteousness which can cover my sinfulness and enable me to stand before God in His holiness. Amen.**

## "'For those who honour me I will honour'" (1 Samuel 2:30)

Daniel resolved that he would not defile himself with the king's food, or with the wine that he drank. Therefore he asked . . . not to defile himself (Daniel 1:8). When Daniel knew that the document had been signed, he went to his house . . . He got down on his knees three times a day and prayed and gave thanks before his God, as he had done previously . . . Daniel was brought and cast into the den of lions . . . Then, at break of day, the king arose and . . . cried out . . . "O Daniel, servant of the living God, has your God, whom you serve continually, been able to deliver you from the lions?" Then Daniel said to the king, ". . . My God sent his angel and shut the lions' mouths, and they have not harmed me . . ." So this Daniel prospered during the reign of Darius (Daniel 6:10, 16, 19–22, 28).

In danger from the king. *As a good Jew, Daniel could not eat the meat which came from the king's table because it had been offered to idols. Happily he was allowed a simpler diet which kept him perfectly fit, and all was well. But what courage! He was not going to sacrifice a* principle *for the sake of personal comfort or popularity.* In danger from the lions. *The death penalty was introduced for all caught praying to any God except the king, but Daniel was not going to abandon a lifelong* practice *to save his own skin. Once again God honoured His servant. God rendered the lions harmless and saved Daniel. Daniel had too much 'backbone' for their liking – not merely 'wish bone'! Sound principles and good practices are worth fighting for. They are the secret, as Daniel found in the end, of true prosperity.*

**Lord, give me Daniel's courage, and may I prove, as he did, Your power to help in times of crisis. Amen.**

## You were straying like sheep . . . (1 Peter 2:25)

And Jesus said, "There was a man who had two sons. And the younger of them said to his father, 'Father, give me the share of property that is coming to me.' And he divided his property between them. Not many days later, the younger son . . . took a journey into a far country, and there he squandered his property in reckless living. And when he had spent everything, a severe famine arose in that country, and he began to be in need. So he went and hired himself out to one of the citizens of that country, who sent him into his fields to feed pigs. And he was longing to be fed with the pods that the pigs ate, and no one gave him anything. But when he came to himself, he said, 'How many of my father's hired servants have more than enough bread, but I perish here with hunger! I will arise and go to my father, and I will say to him, "Father, I have sinned against heaven and before you. I am no longer worthy to be called your son. Treat me as one of your hired servants"'" (Luke 15:11–19).

*'Give me . . .' What was it, do you think, that caused this young man to 'drop out'? Perhaps it was boredom with his home life, or a desire to get rich quickly. Regardless of the reason, he found, as people always do, that the attraction of selfishness and sin quickly wears off and gives way to sorrow and degradation. No one can teach Satan anything about 'cosmetics'. He knows how to make evil look delightful, but he never tells you how quickly the paint wears off. 'Make me . . .' But however far we may wander from God, memory and conscience are inescapable. So when at last he paused to think, this young man 'came to himself' (repentance) and he came to his father (faith).*

**Lord, let me not be distracted by the sights that dazzle and the tempting sounds I hear. Amen.**

**. . . but have now returned to the Shepherd and Overseer of your souls. (1 Peter 2:25)**

"And he arose and came to his father. But while he was still a long way off, his father saw him and felt compassion, and ran and embraced him and kissed him. And the son said to him, 'Father, I have sinned against heaven and before you. I am no longer worthy to be called your son.' But the father said to his servants, 'Bring quickly the best robe, and put it on him, and put a ring on his hand, and shoes on his feet. And bring the fattened calf and kill it, and let us eat and celebrate. For this my son was dead, and is alive again; he was lost, and is found.' And they began to celebrate" (Luke 15:20–24).

The waiting father. *The father seems to have been on the lookout for his son, and perhaps every day he went to some point from which he could get a distant view of the road, hoping he might see a familiar figure making his way home. What a lovely picture of God's love for us! He 'desires not the death of a sinner, but rather that he may turn from his wickedness and live'. He is always eagerly on the lookout for our return.* The welcoming father. *Did you notice how the young man wasn't allowed to finish his prepared speech? His father's love gave him no chance. He was not just received back as a servant. He was restored to his place as a son with the best robe to cover his rags, the ring as a mark of sonship, the shoes so that he could work and the fatted calf – because there is joy in heaven over even one sinner who repents.*

**Thank You, Lord, for waiting up for me for so long. Amen.**

**Be kind to one another . . . forgiving one another. (Ephesians 4:32)**

"Now his older son was in the field, and as he came . . . to the house, he heard music and dancing. And he called one of the servants and asked what these things meant. And he said . . . 'Your brother has come, and your father has killed the fattened calf, because he has received him back safe and sound.' But he was angry and refused to go in. His father came out and entreated him, but he answered . . . 'Look, these many years I have served you, and I never disobeyed your command, yet you never gave me a young goat, that I might celebrate with my friends. But when this son of yours came, who has devoured your property with prostitutes, you killed the fattened calf for him!' And he said to him, 'Son, you are always with me, and all that is mine is yours. It was fitting to celebrate and be glad, for this your brother was dead, and is alive; he was lost, and is found'" (Luke 15:25–32).

*It is sad that this otherwise beautiful story of repentance and forgiveness should have been spoiled by the churlish, bad-tempered behaviour of the elder brother. It was like the Pharisee and the publican all over again. The father said, 'How marvellous to have you back!' But the brother said, 'How disgraceful of you to go away!' In Jesus' view the younger brother's sins of the body (things like drink, sex and gambling) were really less corrosive than the elder brother's sins of the mind (envy, uncharitablesness and pride), and that is why He once scandalized people by saying that the prostitutes had a better chance of getting to heaven than some of the priests. Certainly in this case the younger brother ended up inside and the elder one outside his father's house. There is truth in the saying that more people are kept from God by their righteousness than by their sin.*

**Help me, Lord, to rejoice with them that rejoice and to weep with them that weep. Amen.**

## "The Father is in me and I am in the Father." (John 10:38)

The Word became flesh and dwelt among us (John 1:14). Great indeed, we confess, is the mystery of godliness: He was manifested in the flesh (1 Timothy 3:16). No one has ever seen God; the only God, who is at the Father's side, he has made him known (John 1:18). He is the radiance of the glory of God and the exact imprint of his nature (Hebrews 1:3). He is the image of the invisible God (Colossians 1:15). For in him the whole fullness of deity dwells bodily (Colossians 2:9). Philip said to him, "Lord, show us the Father, and it is enough for us." Jesus said to him, "Have I been with you so long, and you still do not know me, Philip? Whoever has seen me has seen the Father. How can you say, 'Show us the Father'? Do you not believe that I am in the Father and the Father is in me?" (John 14:8–10). "I and the Father are one" (John 10:30). The glory of God in the face of Jesus Christ (2 Corinthians 4:6).

*What is God like? All our lives, I suppose, we have asked that question. It is answered for us today, because in Jesus Christ we see all of God that it is possible or necessary for human beings to know. Looking at the Son, we see the love, wisdom, holiness and power of the Father. You can have salt in solution (in the sea, for example) or in crystal form. In one case it is visible and in the other case not. So it is that Jesus makes God visible and tangible for us (1 John 1:1). In Rome there is a picture by Guido Reni painted on a very high ceiling. To help people to see it, a table has been placed immediately underneath with a highly polished mirror as its top. The mirror brings the painting down to earth for them. So it is that in the face of Jesus Christ we can see the glory of God.*

**O immortal, invisible God, I thank You that You have revealed Yourself to us in Jesus Christ. Amen.**

## The Lord said, "Do you do well to be angry?" (Jonah 4:4)

Let every person be quick to hear, slow to speak, slow to anger; for the anger of man does not produce the righteousness that God requires (James 1:19–20). Good sense makes one slow to anger, and it is his glory to overlook an offence (Proverbs 19:11). Cain was very angry, and . . . The Lord said to Cain, "Why are you angry, and why has your face fallen?" (Genesis 4:5–6). A man of wrath stirs up strife, and one given to anger causes much transgression (Proverbs 29:22). Put on . . . patience, bearing with one another (Colossians 3:12–13). Love . . . is not irritable or resentful (1 Corinthians 13:5). Whoever restrains his words has knowledge, and he who has a cool spirit is a man of understanding (Proverbs 17:27). Be angry and do not sin; do not let the sun go down on your anger, and give no opportunity to the devil (Ephesians 4:26–27).

*There are occasions when 'we do well to be angry'. The person who is left unmoved by cruelty or injustice must be a very cold sort of fish. Anger should be rather like a good police dog – unleashed now and then to do a special job, as Jesus Himself unleashed it when they turned the temple into a market-place, but very quickly brought under perfect control again. But the Christian should not be easily provoked into anger. Our 'thermostats' and 'flashpoints' must be set pretty high. And as Christians we should not allow our anger to go grumbling on after the event, breeding resentment and bitterness. It should cool down at sunset.*

Lord, help me never to lose my temper but give me a cool and calm spirit which is not easily provoked. Amen.

**May your whole spirit and soul and body be kept blameless at the coming of our Lord Jesus Christ. (1 Thessalonians 5:23)**

I appeal to you therefore, brothers, by the mercies of God, to present your bodies as a living sacrifice, holy and acceptable to God, which is your spiritual worship. Do not be conformed to this world, but be transformed by the renewal of your mind, that by testing you may discern what is the will of God, what is good and acceptable and perfect (Romans 12:1–2). You . . . were taught . . . to put off your old self, which belongs to your former manner of life and is corrupt through deceitful desires, and to be renewed in the spirit of your minds, and to put on the new self, created after the likeness of God in true righteousness and holiness (Ephesians 4:20–24). So glorify God in your body (1 Corinthians 6:20).

*It would be convenient if we could think of human beings as being like three-storey houses – body, mind and spirit. But the New Testament view is not quite as neat as that. We are more like rambling country houses where one room leads to another and where you are never quite sure which floor you are on. What we can say is that life is very largely made up of activities and attitudes, and in both these spheres the Christian is someone who has undergone a complete restoration. We put the* physical *part of ourselves, with our strength and energy, at the disposal of Christ – 'presented', as a soldier 'presents arms'. The* spiritual *part of us begins to look at life from God's point of view, wanting to do His will and wanting to be righteous and holy.*

**'Take my life, and let it be, consecrated, Lord to You; Take myself and I will be ever, only, all for You.' Amen.**

## "These men . . . proclaim . . . the way of salvation." (Acts 16:17)

For the grace of God has appeared, bringing salvation for all people (Titus 2:11). "Brothers . . . to us has been sent the message of this salvation" (Acts 13:26). God our Saviour, who desires all people to be saved and to come to the knowledge of the truth. For there is one God, and there is one mediator between God and men, the man Christ Jesus (1 Timothy 2:3–5). "And there is salvation in no one else, for there is no other name under heaven given among men by which we must be saved" (Acts 4:12). I am not ashamed of the gospel, for it is the power of God for salvation to everyone who believes (Romans 1:16). You also, when you heard the word of truth, the gospel of your salvation . . . believed in him (Ephesians 1:13). How shall we escape if we neglect such a great salvation? (Hebrews 2:3). Behold, now is the day of salvation (2 Corinthians 6:2).

*'Salvation' is one of those technical New Testament words used to describe our deliverance from the guilt and power of sin. It is a 'portmanteau' word and includes forgiveness, cleansing, redemption and justification. This salvation comes to us from the grace of God, through the death of Christ upon the cross and by faith on our part in Him. Think of how electric light comes into a room at night. It starts in the power station and comes through the cable, but it is only enjoyed and experienced when individual people 'switch on' and receive it for themselves. So it is that God's love is wasted, and Christ died in vain, unless we benefit by faith in the salvation that has been provided. We must be 'switched on' to Christ.*

**Thank You, Lord, for providing such a great salvation. May I benefit from it to the full. Amen.**

**"I have this against you, that you have abandoned the love you had at first." (Revelation 2:4)**

What shall I do with you, O Ephraim? What shall I do with you, O Judah? Your love is like a morning cloud, like the dew that goes early away (Hosea 6:4). "You did not call upon me, O Jacob; but you have been weary of me, O Israel!" (Isaiah 43:22) You were running well. Who hindered you from obeying the truth? (Galatians 5:7). "You are the salt of the earth, but if salt has lost its taste, how shall its saltiness be restored? It is no longer good for anything except to be thrown out and trampled under people's feet" (Matthew 5:13). You therefore, beloved, knowing this beforehand, take care that you are not carried away with the error of lawless people and lose your own stability. But grow in the grace and knowledge of our Lord and Saviour Jesus Christ (2 Peter 3:17–18).

*Few things are more disappointing than unfulfilled promise. It is something which the gardener, the doctor, the teacher and the coach all experience at times. For a while everything seemed to be going well. The plant was progressing, the patient recovering and the pupil advancing – and then everything seemed to go into reverse. God must often feel that sense of disappointment as He watches some Christians and sees the love cooling, the pace slowing down and the zeal disappearing. What causes this backsliding? Sometimes it is the love of other things – money, hobbies, unhelpful friends. Sometimes it is laziness over prayer, Bible reading and church. Sometimes it is fear of what others may think of us if we try to live wholeheartedly for Christ. 'Beware . . .'*

**Grant, O Lord, that I may not be a disappointment to You but rather that Your hopes for me may be abundantly fulfilled. Amen.**

## Wake up . . . and do not go on sinning.
## (1 Corinthians 15:34)

Now concerning the times and the seasons, brothers, you have
no need to have anything written to you. For you yourselves
are fully aware that the day of the Lord will come like a thief
in the night . . . But you are not in darkness, brothers, for that
day to surprise you like a thief. For you are all children of
light, children of the day. We are not of the night or of the darkness. So then let us not sleep, as others do, but let us keep
awake and be sober. For those who sleep, sleep at night, and
those who get drunk, are drunk at night. But since we belong
to the day, let us be sober, having put on the breastplate of faith
and love, and for a helmet the hope of salvation (1 Thessalonians 5:1–2, 4–8).

*In this passage Paul pictures the Lord's second coming as being like
a thief in the night. The Christian is like a sentry post to watch for
Him. There are three absolutely vital things about a sentry of which
Paul reminds us here. The sentry* must be awake. *Have you ever
been woken up by someone calling you and knocking at the door?
That is how Christ awakens us from selfishness and sin. The sentry*
must be alert. *A sentry who is drunk or distracted is worse than
useless, and we too must not allow ourselves to be drawn away from
following Christ by the world, the flesh or the devil. The sentry* must
be armed. *Perhaps the two most vital pieces of armour were those
that protected the head (the helmet) and the heart (the breastplate). In
other words, our faith and our love must be guarded and strengthened.*

**Lord, help me to be all ready and ever ready for Your com-
ing, whenever it may be. Amen.**

**Now in Christ Jesus you who once were far off have been brought near. (Ephesians 2:13)**

They are darkened in their understanding, *alienated* from the life of God because of the ignorance that is in them, due to their hardness of heart (Ephesians 4:18). And you, who once were alienated and hostile in mind, doing evil deeds, he has now reconciled in his body of flesh by his death (Colossians 1:21–22). While we were enemies we were reconciled to God (Romans 5:10). I appeal to you therefore, brothers, by the mercies of God, to present your bodies as a living sacrifice, holy and *acceptable* to God, which is your spiritual worship (Romans 12:1). Do your best to present yourself to God as one *approved*, a worker who has no need to be ashamed, rightly handling the word of truth (2 Timothy 2:15).

*Alienated, accepted, approved (italics mine) – that in a nutshell is the story of the Christian's experience. In 1945 there was a British soldier in Germany, in the army of occupation. He met and fell in love with a German girl – an alien – and after some difficulty and sacrifice he married her and brought her back to England. Had she come on her own she might not have been allowed to enter and would not have been welcome. But when introduced by him as his wife she was perfectly acceptable. Time passed, and because of her kindness, cheerfulness and charm, even the most suspicious were won over and she gained the approval of everyone. Can you see how that story illustrates the reading from the Bible and how you fit into that picture?*

**Thank You, Lord, for loving me when I was still Your enemy. Please help me to live a life which is pleasing to You. Amen.**

## In full assurance of faith. (Hebrews 10:22)

"Behold, I stand at the door and knock. If anyone hears my voice and opens the door, I will come in" (Revelation 3:20). He has said, "I will never leave you nor forsake you" (Hebrews 13:5). "Behold, I am with you always, to the end of the age" (Matthew 28:20). "Come to me, all who labour and are heavy laden, and I will give you rest" (Matthew 11:28). "All that the Father gives me will come to me, and whoever comes to me I will never cast out" (John 6:37). "My sheep hear my voice, and I know them, and they follow me. I give them eternal life, and they will never perish, and no one will snatch them out of my hand. My Father, who has given them to me, is greater than all, and no one is able to snatch them out of the Father's hand" (John 10:27–29).

*We have here three metaphors for starting the Christian life – 'receiving', 'coming' and 'following'. They all come to the same thing, because they all imply the start of a personal friendship and relationship with Jesus Christ. But what happens if we fall into sin? Will Christ give us up? These verses make the answer quite clear – No! No! No! I am fond of chess and so much prefer it to the sort of table game where one mistake sends you right back to the start. There is one piece in chess that cannot be taken – the king. He can be cornered and checked, 'cabined, cribbed, confined', but he cannot be removed. Sin may reduce Christ's influence in my life, but it can never remove His presence.*

**Thank You, Lord, that once You have come into my heart and life You are there to stay and have locked Yourself in. Amen.**

### "Seek first the kingdom of God." (Matthew 6:33)

And Jesus told them a parable, saying, "The land of a rich man produced plentifully, and he thought to himself, 'What shall I do, for I have nowhere to store my crops?' And he said, 'I will do this: I will tear down my barns and build larger ones, and there I will store all my grain and my goods. And I will say to my soul, Soul, you have ample goods laid up for many years; relax, eat, drink, be merry.' But God said to him, 'Fool! This night your soul is required of you, and the things you have prepared, whose will they be?' So is the one who lays up treasure for himself and is not rich toward God" (Luke 12:16–21).

*This little story has a very powerful message for our materialistic world today. The wealthy and successful farmer made three very grave mistakes.* He thought he was being wise, but God called him a fool. *The world regards God's wisdom as foolishness. God says, 'Give, if you want to possess; lose, if you want to find; die, if you want to live.' Like Alice trying to meet the Red Queen through the looking glass, we have to walk in the opposite direction to the world in our search for true joy.* He thought of his body, but God thought of his soul. *We cannot take material things with us when we die, only spiritual. 'Fame and pleasure and glittering gold, and all the treasures that life can hold; say, are they worth what the soul will be all through the years of eternity?'* He thought he had 'many years', but God required him 'this night'. *Poor man! He wasn't anywhere near ready, but I wonder whether I would be if God called me today?*

**Lord, detach me from too great a dependence upon, and love for, earthly things so that I may more easily 'take off' when the time comes. Amen.**

## The cross of Christ. (Galatians 6:12)

For the word of the cross is folly to those who are perishing, but to us who are being saved it is the power of God (1 Corinthians 1:18). For in him all the fullness of God was pleased to dwell, and through him to reconcile to himself all things, whether on earth or in heaven, making peace by the blood of his cross (Colossians 1:19–20). And Jesus called to him the crowd with his disciples and said to them, "If anyone would come after me, let him deny himself and take up his cross and follow me" (Mark 8:34). And as they led Jesus away, they seized one Simon of Cyrene, who was coming in from the country, and laid on him the cross, to carry it behind Jesus (Luke 23:26). But far be it from me to boast except in the cross of our Lord Jesus Christ, by which the world has been crucified to me, and I to the world (Galatians 6:14). I have been crucified with Christ (Galatians 2:20). Consider yourselves dead to sin (Romans 6:11).

*There are three things that we are told to do with the cross. We must look at it. Just as the children of Israel, plagued with poisonous snakes, were told to look at the brass serpent in order to be cured (Numbers 21), so we must look in faith at the cross of Christ. 'There is life for a look at the crucified One, there is life at that moment for me.' Second, we must take it up – metaphorically, just as Simon did literally. In other words, we must not be ashamed (as Simon was not ashamed) to be identified with Jesus and to be known as His associates. Lastly, we must get on it. Because Christ died it is as though we died – and our old nature, with its passions and lusts, has been crucified. We must treat it as if it were dead.*

**Lord, give me the faith to look to Your cross, the courage to take it up, and the determination to get on it. Amen.**

**Thus says the Lord, your Redeemer, "I am . . . the Creator." (Isaiah 43:14–15)**

Thus says the Lord, he who created you, O Jacob, he who formed you, O Israel: "Fear not, for I have redeemed you; I have called you by name, you are mine. When you pass through the waters, I will be with you; and through the rivers, they shall not overwhelm you; when you walk through fire you shall not be burned, and the flame shall not consume you. For I am the Lord your God, the Holy One of Israel, your Saviour. I give Egypt as your ransom, Cush and Seba in exchange for you . . . Fear not, for I am with you; I will bring your offspring from the east, and from the west I will gather you. I will say to the north, Give up, and to the south, Do not withhold; bring my sons from afar and my daughters from the end of the earth, everyone who is called by my name, whom I created for my glory, whom I formed and made" (Isaiah 43:1–3, 5–7).

*In this passage God reminds Israel that, whatever happens to them, God's loving purpose will finally be achieved. He will be with them in adversity and will restore them to prosperity. He is the Creator. God made humankind for Himself, first that we might enjoy fellowship with Him, and then that we might show Him forth to others. He has stamped His name, the 'Maker's name' upon us, but many people have rubbed it off and pretend that they owe Him nothing. He is the Redeemer. He sacrificed other countries to bring back Israel, because He loved her. In his war memoirs Churchill has a chapter called 'Africa Redeemed', and in it he tells at what tremendous cost the countries of northern Africa were bought back during 1940–43. Jesus had to pay an even greater price to redeem us from sin – His precious blood.*

**Lord, I am Yours because You made me and then bought me. Please take full possession of Your property. Amen.**

## They shall run and not be weary. (Isaiah 40:31)

Do you not know that in a race all the runners compete, but only one receives the prize? So run that you may obtain it. Every athlete exercises self-control in all things. They do it to receive a perishable wreath, but we an imperishable. So I do not run aimlessly . . . But I discipline my body and keep it under control (1 Corinthians 9:24–27). Therefore, since we are surrounded by so great a cloud of witnesses, let us also lay aside every weight, and sin which clings so closely, and let us run with endurance the race that is set before us, looking to Jesus (Hebrews 12:1–2). One thing I do: forgetting what lies behind and straining forward to what lies ahead, I press on toward the goal for the prize of the upward call of God in Christ Jesus (Philippians 3:13–14).

*We might compare the Christian life to two familiar kinds of races. The marathon. This is the most gruelling of all the Olympic running events, requiring great fitness, self-discipline and endurance. We shall need to equip ourselves in this way spiritually if we are to succeed. If you have recently begun the Christian life, don't start off with too great a rush. Pace yourself carefully, seek helpful advice and keep looking to Jesus. The obstacle race. We shall meet with all sorts of hazards and traps in the Christian life, and we must always be on the alert. But we shall be encouraged by the cloud of witnesses – fellow competitors past and present – and we must not be discouraged by failures and setbacks.*

'May I run the race before me, strong and brave to face the foe; looking only unto Jesus, as I onward go.' Amen.

## "I never knew you; depart from me."
## (Matthew 7:23)

"When the king came in . . . he saw there a man who had no wedding garment. And he said to him, 'Friend, how did you get in here without a wedding garment?' And he was speechless. Then the king said to the attendants, 'Bind him . . . and cast him into the outer darkness'" (Matthew 22:11–13). "The rich man . . . died . . . and in Hades, being in torment, he lifted up his eyes and saw Abraham far off . . . And he called out, 'Father Abraham, have mercy on me, and send Lazarus to dip the end of his finger in water and cool my tongue . . .' But Abraham said, '. . . Between us and you a great chasm has been fixed, in order that those who would pass from here to you may not be able, and none may cross from there to us'" (Luke 16:22–26). "The Son of Man will send his angels, and they will gather out of his kingdom all causes of sin and all law-breakers, and throw them into the fiery furnace. In that place there will be weeping and gnashing of teeth" (Matthew 13:41–42). They will suffer the punishment of eternal destruction, away from the presence of the Lord (2 Thessalonians 1:9).

*There is a popular myth that it was Paul, rather than Jesus, who had the stern things to say about the Christian life. But in fact Jesus has far more to say about hell than Paul. Who is it for? It is reserved for those who reject His offer of forgiveness and eternal life, like the man who thought his own clothes were good enough and so he didn't need the wedding garment always provided by the host. It is for those who, like the rich man, find no place for Him in their selfish, materialistic lives. What is it like? Jesus was probably using figurative language, but do you think He would have exaggerated? It is certainly a place from which people are separated by a great chasm from the presence of God – and a place of eternal misery.*

**Lord, help me never to underestimate the serious nature and consequences of sin. Amen.**

## Useful to the master. (2 Timothy 2:21)

After this Jesus went out and saw a tax collector named Levi, sitting at the tax booth. And he said to him, "Follow me." And leaving everything, he rose and followed him. And Levi made him a great feast in his house, and there was a large company of tax collectors and others reclining at table with them. And the Pharisees and their scribes grumbled at his disciples, saying, "Why do you eat and drink with tax collectors and sinners?" And Jesus answered them, "Those who are well have no need of a physician, but those who are sick. I have not come to call the righteous but sinners to repentance" (Luke 5:27–32).

*I wonder why Jesus chose Matthew (called Levi here) the tax collector to join His little circle of friends. He was very different from the others, and at first they may not have been very pleased to have him. I think Jesus chose him for three reasons. First,* his needs. *He saw right into Matthew, and 'His kind but searching glance can scan the very wounds that shame would hide.' Here was a man who needed forgiveness. Second,* his gifts. *Matthew must have been educated in order to be a tax collector, and perhaps Jesus saw how he could use his good memory and orderly mind in His service. He wasn't disappointed, for the result was 'The gospel according to Matthew'. Third,* his friends. *The first thing Matthew did was to hold a party for his many friends to introduce them to Jesus, whom they might otherwise never have met. Have you ever though that it is for these same three reasons that Jesus calls you and me into His service?*

**Lord Jesus, cleanse my sins, use my gifts and bless my friends. Amen.**

**Singing . . . in your hearts to God.
(Colossians 3:16)**

I waited patiently for the Lord; he inclined to me and heard my cry. He drew me up from the pit of destruction, out of the miry bog, and set my feet upon a rock, making my steps secure. He put a new song in my mouth, a song of praise to our God. Many will see and fear, and put their trust in the Lord. Blessed is the man who makes the Lord his trust, who does not turn to the proud, to those who go astray after a lie! You have multiplied, O Lord my God, your wondrous deeds and your thoughts toward us; none can compare with you! I will proclaim and tell of them, yet they are more than can be told (Psalm 40:1–5). You are my help and my deliverer; do not delay, O my God! (Psalm 40:17).

*We read today how David was cured from 'foot and mouth disease'. First, the Lord drew him out of the miry bog of sin and set him firmly and securely on a rock. Then He put a new song in his mouth, and we can be sure that David found plenty to sing about as he meditated upon God's loving thoughts towards him and His powerful deeds. Spiritual 'foot and mouth disease' is very common. Our feet slip into sin, and this seems to close our lips. But when we are re-established on solid ground we feel like singing again. Try to memorize some of the best Christian songs and sing them to yourself. They can be a great inspiration and a sure antidote to depression. Notice also in this psalm how God not only hears but also helps.*

**Keep my feet from falling, O Lord, and open my lips that my mouth may show forth Your praise. Amen.**

## Great is your faithfulness. (Lamentations 3:23)

If we confess our sins, God is faithful and just to forgive us our sins and to cleanse us from all unrighteousness (1 John 1:9). No temptation has overtaken you that is not common to man. God is faithful, and he will not let you be tempted beyond your ability, but with the temptation he will also provide the way of escape, that you may be able to endure it (1 Corinthians 10:13). Let us hold fast the confession of our hope without wavering, for he who promised is faithful (Hebrews 10:23). He who calls you is faithful; he will surely do it (1 Thessalonians 5:24). If we are faithless, he remains faithful (2 Timothy 2:13). Your steadfast love, O Lord, extends to the heavens, your faithfulness to the clouds (Psalm 36:5). Your faithfulness endures to all generations (Psalm 119:90). The heavens praise . . . your faithfulness (Psalm 89:5). I have spoken of your faithfulness (Psalm 40:10).

*A faithful person is one who can be relied upon completely. He or she never lets you down by breaking their promises or failing to stand by you in times of difficulty or need. We are very lucky if we have one or two friends who answer that description. But God's faithfulness is unlimited. It 'extends' everywhere and it 'endures' for ever. Someone has said that the verse 'Have faith in God' could be translated 'Hold the faithfulness of God'. That is what faith really is – not trying to work up a feeling of confidence in God ourselves, but relying on His complete trustworthiness. Faith comes not through perspiration on our part, but through inspiration on His part.*

I thank You, Lord, that nature, history and the Bible all proclaim Your faithfulness. I ask that I, too, may experience it and declare it to others. Amen.

**Let my prayer come before you; incline your ear to my cry! (Psalm 88:2)**

Jesus was praying in a certain place, and when he finished, one of his disciples said to him, "Lord, teach us to pray . . ." And he said to them, "When you pray, say: Father, hallowed be your name . . ." (Luke 11:1–2). "Your kingdom come, your will be done, on earth as it is in heaven" (Matthew 6:10). "Give us each day our daily bread, and forgive us our sins, for we ourselves forgive everyone who is indebted to us. And lead us not into temptation . . . And I tell you, ask, and it will be given to you; seek, and you will find; knock, and it will be opened to you. For everyone who asks receives, and the one who seeks finds, and to the one who knocks it will be opened. What father among you, if his son asks for a fish, will instead of a fish give him a serpent; or if he asks for an egg, will give him a scorpion? If you then, who are evil, know how to give good gifts to your children, how much more will the heavenly Father give the Holy Spirit to those who ask him!" (Luke 11:3–4, 9–13)

*Jesus taught His disciples in three different ways.* Demonstration. *It was watching Him in prayer that first whetted their appetites to know more about the subject themselves. They saw the link between His lonely times of prayer and His power among the people.* Explanation. *Prayer should begin with God, thinking about Him and thanking Him, and then move outwards to our own needs and the needs of others. 'Asking' suggests the simplicity of prayer, 'seeking' the earnestness, and 'knocking' the persistence – all of which are necessary.* Illustration. *Every earthly father has the good of his child at heart. How much more, therefore, will our heavenly Father be ready to hear and help us?*

**Lord, teach me to pray and give my prayers a new depth and warmth and strength. Amen.**

## The fool says in his heart, "There is no God." (Psalm 14:1)

They say to me continually, "Where is your God?" (Psalm 42:3). "The Almighty – we cannot find him" (Job 37:23). "Oh, that I knew where I might find him, that I might come even to his seat!" (Job 23:3) The heavens declare the glory of God, and the sky above proclaims his handiwork (Psalm 19:1). For his invisible attributes, namely, his eternal power and divine nature, have been clearly perceived, ever since the creation of the world, in the things that have been made. So they are without excuse (Romans 1:20). By faith we understand that the universe was created by the word of God (Hebrews 11:3). No one has ever seen God; the only God, who is at the Father's side, he has made him known (John 1:18). For in him the whole fullness of deity dwells bodily (Colossians 2:9). He is the radiance of the glory of God and the exact imprint of his nature (Hebrews 1:3).

*We cannot prove that God exists, in the same way that we can prove that 2 x 2 = 4, because then we should need something higher than God to which to refer Him. But (as in a court of law) the evidence for many people is so strong that it carried us 'beyond all reasonable doubt'. The evidence of our senses argues strongly in favour of a personal intelligence behind the universe in which we live. The evidence of the Scriptures shows that He is at work in the world and can enter into personal relationships with people. The evidence of the Son, with His tremendous claims to be equal to God, His miracles and His resurrection, provides the crowning proof. An atheist used to have a sort of anti-text over his fireplace which said, 'God is nowhere'. He pointed it out to his small grandson who, perhaps deliberately, misread it and said, 'God is now here'. That is the Christian's view of life.*

Thank You, Lord, that You have not left Yourself in the world without witnesses. Amen.

## Working together with him. (2 Corinthians 6:1)

The love of Christ controls us, because we have concluded this: that one has died for all, therefore all have died; and he died for all, that those who live might no longer live for themselves but for him who for their sake died and was raised . . . Therefore, if anyone is in Christ, he is a new creation. The old has passed away; behold, the new has come. All this is from God, who through Christ reconciled us to himself and gave us the ministry of reconciliation; that is, in Christ God was reconciling the world to himself, not counting their trespasses against them, and entrusting to us the message of reconciliation. Therefore, we are ambassadors for Christ, God making his appeal through us. We implore you on behalf of Christ, be reconciled to God (2 Corinthians 5:14–15, 17–20).

*God has called us to work for Him in this world as His representatives, or ambassadors. This passage tells us two important things about our work. First,* our message. *To 'reconcile' two people is to bring them together in peace and friendship after they have quarrelled. There were stories, after the last war, of people in remote parts not knowing for a long time that it was all over. Our task as Christians is to tell people that, because Christ died, the war between God and human beings is over and peace has been made. Second,* our motive. *We want to do this work – not for money or fame, but because we feel compelled to do so by the love of Christ. We should be like the Roman slave who, when he was set free by a wealthy benefactor, decided that he would not live for himself but for the one who had redeemed him and so became his faithful servant for life.*

**Thank You, Lord, for giving me the privilege of representing You as Your ambassador in the world. Amen.**

## The word of the Lord was rare in those days.
## (1 Samuel 3:1)

So Philip ran to him and heard him reading Isaiah the prophet and asked, "Do you understand what you are reading?" And he said, "How can I, unless someone guides me?" (Acts 8:30–31). Then he opened their minds to understand the Scriptures (Luke 24:45). Open my eyes, that I may behold wondrous things out of your law (Psalm 119:18). Oh how I love your law! It is my meditation all the day (Psalm 119:97). My eyes are awake before the watches of the night, that I may meditate on your promise (Psalm 119:148). "This Book of the Law shall not depart from your mouth, but you shall meditate on it day and night, so that you may be careful to do according to all that is written in it" (Joshua 1:8). Be doers of the word, and not hearers only (James 1:22).

Understanding. *To many people the Bible is very dull and meaningless. So is a stained glass window – until you come into the cathedral and see the light breaking through it. And so is a sundial – until the sun shines upon it. In other words, we must first enter God's kingdom and then ask Him to illuminate what we read if we want to understand it.* Meditating. *Meditation is a sort of mental digestion. It means pondering what we have read and applying it to ourselves. It is very helpful to try to learn by heart a little of what we read.* Doing. *We must translate understanding and meditation into positive action. We must obey the commands we read, heed the warnings, follow the examples and believe the promises.*

**Lord, help me to read, mark, learn and inwardly digest what You have to say to me from the Bible. Then help me to act upon it. Amen.**

## "This Jesus God raised up, and of that we all are witnesses." (Acts 2:32)

"Fear not, I am the first and the last, and the living one. I died, and behold I am alive for evermore, and I have the keys of Death and Hades" (Revelation 1:17–18). And was declared to be the Son of God in power according to the Spirit of holiness by his resurrection from the dead, Jesus Christ our Lord (Romans 1:4). We know that Christ being raised from the dead will never die again; death no longer has dominion over him (Romans 6:9). Knowing that he who raised the Lord Jesus will raise us also with Jesus (2 Corinthians 4:14). If in this life only we have hoped in Christ, we are of all people most to be pitied. But in fact Christ has been raised from the dead, the firstfruits of those who have fallen asleep. For as by a man came death, by a man has come also the resurrection of the dead. For as in Adam all die, so also in Christ shall all be made alive (1 Corinthians 15:19–22).

*What does the resurrection of Jesus prove? What difference would it make if it had never taken place?* The claims of Christ. *The resurrection was the crowning proof that Jesus was who He claimed to be, namely the Son of God, and that He had done what He came into the world to do – to make a full, perfect and sufficient sacrifice for the sins of the world. It was God's seal on Christ's divinity.* The chains of death. *Easter Day was a triumphant 'opening ceremony' performed by Jesus Himself. He opened the gate of everlasting life for us, turning the key and cutting the ribbon. He was the first to go through ('the firstfruits of those who have fallen asleep'), but all who believe in Him may follow. Because He lives, we shall live also.*

**Lord, I rejoice in the fact that You have risen from the dead and are alive for evermore. Amen.**

## The angels of God were ascending and descending on it! (Genesis 28:12)

Are they not all ministering spirits sent out to serve for the sake of those who are to inherit salvation? (Hebrews 1:14). And the angel said to them, "Fear not, for behold, I bring you good news of a great joy" (Luke 2:10). Then the devil left him, and behold, angels came and were ministering to him (Matthew 4:11). And there appeared to him an angel from heaven, strengthening him (Luke 22:43). An angel of the Lord descended from heaven and came and rolled back the stone and sat on it (Matthew 28:2). The angel of the Lord encamps around those who fear him, and delivers them (Psalm 34:7). For he will command his angels concerning you to guard you in all your ways (Psalm 91:11). Peter . . . said, "Now I am sure that the Lord has sent his angel and rescued me from the hand of Herod" (Acts 12:11).

*It seems from the Bible that angels are not promoted Christians who have been elevated, so to speak, to the 'House of Lords', but rather a distinct and separate order created by God for a special purpose. They are His attendants, who sing His praises and do His will, and, as we see today, they are associated with some of the most important events in the Bible. It isn't easy to know exactly what part they play in our own lives in these days, but it would appear that in unseen and unknown ways they do minister to our needs. We may owe far more to their intervention than we realize at present.*

**Grant, O Lord, that as Your holy angels always serve You in heaven, so at Your command they may help and defend us here on earth. Amen.**

### "I will not leave you as orphans." (John 14:18)

"Let not your hearts be troubled. Believe in God; believe also in me. In my Father's house are many rooms. If it were not so, would I have told you that I go to prepare a place for you? And if I go and prepare a place for you, I will come again and will take you to myself, that where I am you may be also . . . These things I have spoken to you while I am still with you. But the Helper, the Holy Spirit, whom the Father will send in my name, he will teach you all things and bring to your remembrance all that I have said to you. Peace I leave with you; my peace I give to you. Not as the world gives do I give to you. Let not your hearts be troubled, neither let them be afraid" (John 14:1–3, 25–27).

*Imagine a father saying goodbye to his children just before he sets off to a distant country to prepare a new home for them there at some future date. That is a picture of what Jesus was doing on this occasion. The home He has gone to get ready for us is in heaven, but meanwhile He gives us two most reassuring promises. First, He promises that He will come back again to take us to be with Him for ever. Second, He promises to send the Holy Spirit to take His place so that we won't be left 'desolate' (literally, 'orphans') and to act as our guardian. That is why He urges His disciples not to be troubled or afraid, because with these two promises they could have perfect peace.*

**Thank You, Lord, for Your promise to return to take me to be with You. Thank You that, meanwhile, I have Your Holy Spirit to guard me and to guide me. Amen.**

## "Lord, show us the Father, and it is enough for us." (John 14:8)

"*God is spirit*" (John 4:24). No one has ever seen God (John 1:18). The invisible God (Colossians 1:15). Who alone has immortality, who dwells in unapproachable light, whom no one has ever seen or can see (1 Timothy 6:16). Who inhabits eternity (Isaiah 57:15). *God is light*, and in him is no darkness at all (1 John 1:5). "Who is like you, O Lord, among the gods? Who is like you, majestic in holiness, awesome in glorious deeds, doing wonders?" (Exodus 15:11) "I the Lord your God am holy" (Leviticus 19:2). And day and night they never cease to say, "Holy, holy, holy, is the Lord God Almighty" (Revelation 4:8). *God is love* (1 John 4:8). "I have loved you with an everlasting love; therefore I have continued my faithfulness to you" (Jeremiah 31:3). "Can a woman forget her nursing child, that she should have no compassion on the son of her womb? Even these may forget, yet I will not forget you" (Isaiah 49:15). Neither death nor life . . . nor anything else in all creation, will be able to separate us from the love of God (Romans 8:38–39).

*A book was written some years ago with the title* Your God is Too Small. *Many people have a completely false picture of what God is like and think of Him as a kind of super fireman, spaceman or policeman. How, then, should we think of Him? We see three things above (italics mine). First,* He is a spiritual being. *He requires no physical form of existence but is able to be anywhere and everywhere at all times.* He is a moral being. *In one place He is described as 'a consuming fire' because nothing sinful can survive for a moment in the presence of His white-hot holiness.* He is personal. *He is able to enter into relationship with His creatures. They can come to know Him, to love Him and to commune with Him in prayer. Learn to 'think big' when you think about God.*

'Oh how I fear You, living God, with deepest, tenderest fears; and worship You with trembling hope, and penitential tears.' Amen.

**Oh come, let us worship and bow down; let us kneel before the Lord, our Maker! (Psalm 95:6)**

"You shall worship the Lord your God and him only shall you serve" (Matthew 4:10). "The true worshipers will worship the Father in spirit and truth, for the Father is seeking such people to worship him" (John 4:23). And Ezra blessed the Lord, the great God, and all the people answered, "Amen, Amen," lifting up their hands. And they bowed their heads and worshiped the Lord with their faces to the ground (Nehemiah 8:6). Worship the Lord in the splendour of holiness (Psalm 29:2). Let all God's angels worship him (Hebrews 1:6). The twenty-four elders fall down before him . . . and worship him who lives forever and ever. They cast their crowns before the throne, saying, "Worthy are you, our Lord and God, to receive glory and honour and power, for you created all things, and by your will they . . . were created" (Revelation 4:10–11).

*Charles Lamb and some dinner guests were discussing great people of the past and how interesting it would be if one of them could join them. Shakespeare's name was mentioned, and then someone spoke of Jesus Christ. There was a moment's silence, and then Charles Lamb said, 'If Shakespeare came into the room, we would all stand up; but if Jesus came in, we would fall at His feet.' That is the difference between mere admiration and adoration, or worship. God is the only One who deserves to be treated in that way. Worship is the homage we pay to Him in prayer, in song, and in the beauty of a holy life. It is our way of trying to show what He is really worth, for 'worship' originally meant 'worth-ship'.*

**Lord, please accept the humble homage of my lips and of my life. Amen.**

### "He has sent me to proclaim . . . recovering of sight to the blind." (Luke 4:18)

The god of this world has blinded the minds of the unbelievers, to keep them from seeing the light of the gospel of the glory of Christ, who is the image of God (2 Corinthians 4:4). The Lord opens the eyes of the blind (Psalm 146:8). Open my eyes, that I may behold wondrous things out of your law (Psalm 119:18). Having the eyes of your hearts enlightened, that you may know what is the hope to which he has called you (Ephesians 1:18). Then Elisha prayed and said, "O Lord, please open his eyes that he may see." So the Lord opened the eyes of the young man, and he saw, and behold, the mountain was full of horses and chariots of fire all around Elisha (2 Kings 6:17). Their eyes were opened, and they recognized him (Luke 24:31). "One thing I do know, that though I was blind, now I see" (John 9:25).

*Human beings are born blind – not physically, like kittens, of course, but spiritually blind. When people speak to us about the Bible, Jesus Christ, prayer and so on, it does not make sense and we cannot understand what they see in it all. But when we receive Christ as our Saviour and become true Christians it is just as though our eyes are opened for the first time. Everything looks different. Christ is no longer just a figure of history but a living Saviour and friend. The Bible ceases to be a mere textbook and becomes a guide book, full of 'wonderful things'. Temptation is an insuperable enemy no more, for we are surrounded by the overwhelming power of Christ. Even the world around us takes on brighter colours, and 'the station brook to my new eyes was babbling out of paradise'.*

Lord Jesus, open my eyes each day to new truths, new promises, new experiences of Your love and power. Amen.

## To please God . . . (1 Thessalonians 4:1)

Bless the Lord, O my soul, and *forget not* all his benefits (Psalm 103:2). "Take care lest . . . when you have eaten and are full and have built good houses and live in them . . . and your silver and gold is multiplied . . . then your heart be lifted up, and you forget the Lord your God" (Deuteronomy 8:11–14). *Fear not,* for I am with you; be not dismayed, for I am your God; I will strengthen you, I will help you, I will uphold you with my righteous right hand (Isaiah 41:10). Even though I walk through the valley of the shadow of death, I will fear no evil, for you are with me (Psalm 23:4). *Fret not* yourself because of evildoers; be not envious of wrongdoers! (Psalm 37:1) For the evil man has no future (Proverbs 24:20). They who wait for the Lord shall renew their strength. . . they shall run and not be weary; they shall walk and *not faint* (Isaiah 40:31). So we do not lose heart. Though our outer nature is wasting away, our inner nature is being renewed day by day (2 Corinthians 4:16).

*I can still remember the knots I learned as a Boy Scout over sixty years ago, and I often use them. Today, if you will forgive the pun, we are considering four (k)nots which we shall find of the greatest possible help in making successful progress in our Christian lives. There is a (k)not for all seasons – for when we are tempted to be self-satisfied and proud; for when we are under fire from temptation or in danger; for when we are irritated or frustrated by the apparently easy way people 'get away with' wicked practices and when wrongdoing seems to pay; and for when we feel low and discouraged. These (k)nots (italics mine, above) are well worth learning by heart. They will hold fast in every circumstance.*

**Lord, give me a faith that will not slip or loosen however great the strain that is placed upon it. Amen.**

## Long ago . . . God spoke to our fathers by the prophets. (Hebrews 1:1)

Concerning this salvation, the prophets who prophesied about the grace that was to be yours searched and inquired carefully, inquiring what person or time the Spirit of Christ in them was indicating when he predicted the sufferings of Christ and the subsequent glories. It was revealed to them that they were serving not themselves but you, in the things that have now been announced to you through those who preached the good news to you by the Holy Spirit sent from heaven, things into which angels long to look (1 Peter 1:10–12). No prophecy was ever produced by the will of man, but men spoke from God as they were carried along by the Holy Spirit (2 Peter 1:21).

The prophets. *The Old Testament prophets were rather like workmen producing different component parts of a car. They were working to a plan and knew exactly what they were doing, but they never lived to see how the different parts they were making fit together into the final product.* The preachers. *The New Testament preachers, and those who have lived since, are like the salesmen who offer the car to the public. They are the natural successors of the prophets and have taken over from them. 'Foretelling' has become 'forthtelling', and it is their task to explain and present the gospel to others. But notice how both prophets and preachers are dependent upon the presence and power of the Holy Spirit.*

I thank You, Lord, for all those marvellous pictures and shadows in the Old Testament which point to Your coming. Amen.

## The people whom I formed for myself.
## (Isaiah 43:21)

So I went down to the potter's house, and there he was working at his wheel. And the vessel he was making of clay was spoiled in the potter's hand, and he reworked it into another vessel, as it seemed good to the potter to do. Then the word of the Lord came to me: "O . . . Israel, can I not do with you as this potter has done? . . . Behold, like the clay in the potter's hand, so are you in my hand" (Jeremiah 18:3–6). "Does the clay say to him who forms it, 'What are you making?' or 'Your work has no handles?'" (Isaiah 45:9) If anyone cleanses himself from what is dishonourable, he will be a vessel for honourable use, set apart as holy, useful to the master of the house, ready for every good work (2 Timothy 2:21).

The Maker. *God has made us as we are, with our particular temperament and talents, and it is not for us to question His wisdom or to ask why He has not made us cleverer, or taller, or more handsome than we are. We must believe that He had a purpose in making us the way He did and gratefully accept what He has done. We must also come sensibly to terms with our own special characteristics, making the most of ourselves.* The Master. *Whatever we are, Christ can make very good use of us in His service. Of course, He has different work for different people, and some vessels have more important functions than others, but there is work for all and the only conditions for being used are that we should be cleansed from sin and filled with His Holy Spirit.*

Lord, I thank You for making me as You did, because You knew what You were doing. I ask that I may be useful to You, ready for every good work. Amen.

## Keep yourself pure. (1 Timothy 5:22)

Who shall ascend the hill of the Lord? And who shall stand in his holy place? He who has clean hands and a pure heart, who does not lift up his soul to what is false and does not swear deceitfully (Psalm 24:3–4). He who loves purity . . . will have the king as his friend (Proverbs 22:11). "Blessed are the pure in heart, for they shall see God" (Matthew 5:8). Whatever is pure . . . if there is anything worthy of praise, think about these things (Philippians 4:8). I thank God whom I serve . . . with a clear conscience (2 Timothy 1:3). We know that when he appears we shall be like him, because we shall see him as he is. And everyone who thus hopes in him purifies himself as he is pure (1 John 3:2–3). So that when he appears we may have confidence and not shrink from him in shame (1 John 2:28).

*To 'keep yourself pure' means to have a heart with unalloyed motives and intentions where God feels at home. It means having a mind that feeds on what is good and wholesome and that rejects what is evil and unworthy. It means having a conscience which is at rest and not stirring uneasily at something we have said or done that is wrong. Notice the results of a pure life: dwelling with God, seeing God, having Him as a friend. Notice the incentive for living such a life: the fact that He Himself is 'of purer eyes than to see evil' and that we must be like Him if we are not to be ashamed at His coming.*

**Purify me, O Lord, in heart and mind and conscience, so that I may be useful to You now and not ashamed to meet You face-to-face. Amen.**

**For the law was given through Moses; grace . . .
came through Jesus Christ. (John 1:17)**

Jesus said to him, "You shall love the Lord your God with all
your heart and with all your soul and with all your mind. This
is the great and first commandment. And a second is like it:
You shall love your neighbour as yourself. On these two commandments depend all the Law and the Prophets" (Matthew
22:37–40). The law is holy, and the commandment is holy and
righteous and good (Romans 7:12). I delight in the law of God,
in my inner being, but I see in my members another law wag-
ing war against the law of my mind (Romans 7:22–23). I have
the desire to do what is right, but not the ability to carry it out
(Romans 7:18). "Fear not, for behold, I bring you good news of
a great joy" (Luke 2:10). For the grace of God has appeared,
bringing salvation for all people (Titus 2:11). For by grace you
have been saved through faith. And this is not your own
doing; it is the gift of God, not a result of works, so that no one
may boast (Ephesians 2:8–9).

*'Standards'. The Old Testament sets the standard that God intend-
ed human beings to reach, but as it was a 100% pass mark nobody
reached it. For 'all have sinned and fall short of the glory of God'. We
know the standard to be good and right, but we utterly lack the
power to reach it. 'News'. The New Testament brings the wonderful
tidings that through Christ we can all become 'honorary members' of
God's kingdom. The entrance exam has been abolished, and the
entrance fee has been paid by Christ Himself. We are no longer under
the Law, but under grace. 'Run then, and work, the Law commands,
but gives you neither feet nor hands; it's better news the Gospel
brings: it bids you fly, and gives you wings.'*

**Thank You, Lord, for receiving me into Your kingdom when
I did not deserve a place. Please make me a worthy member
of it. Amen.**

## Casting all your anxieties on him, because he cares for you. (1 Peter 5:7)

Anxiety in a man's heart weighs him down (Proverbs 12:25). "Do not be anxious about your life, what you will eat or what you will drink, nor about your body, what you will put on" (Matthew 6:25). Do not be anxious about anything, but in everything by prayer and supplication with thanksgiving let your requests be made known to God. And the peace of God, which surpasses all understanding, will guard your hearts and your minds in Christ Jesus (Philippians 4:6–7). Cast your burden on the Lord, and he will sustain you (Psalm 55:22). "Blessed is the man who trusts in the Lord . . . He is like a tree planted by water, that sends out its roots by the stream, and does not fear when heat comes, for its leaves remain green, and is not anxious in the year of drought, for it does not cease to bear fruit" (Jeremiah 17:7–8).

*A farmer once gave a lift to a man who was carrying a heavy ruck-sack. After a mile or two he looked behind him to see how his passenger was and found him sitting in the back of the trailer – but he was still carrying his backpack. 'Why don't you put it down?' asked the farmer. 'You were kind enough to take me,' replied the man, 'but I didn't think I could ask you carry this rucksack as well.' A pretty silly story! I agree – except that many people treat God in that way. They claim Him as their guide and friend and then continue to fret and worry as if He were not even there. We ought to have faith enough to 'let go and let God'. As William Blake put it, 'Think not you can weep a tear, and your Maker is not near'.*

**Lord, in times of trouble and anxiety, please grant that I may not cease to trust You. Let me show the fruit of love, joy and peace. Amen.**

**He came to his own, and his own people did not receive him. (John 1:11)**

"There was a master of a house who planted a vineyard . . . and leased it to tenants, and went into another country. When the season for fruit drew near, he sent his servants to the tenants to get his fruit. And the tenants took his servants and beat one, killed another, and stoned another. Again he sent other servants . . . And they did the same to them. Finally he sent his son to them, saying, 'They will respect my son.' But when the tenants saw the son, they said . . . 'This is the heir. Come, let us kill him and have his inheritance.' And they took him and threw him out of the vineyard and killed him. When therefore the owner of the vineyard comes, what will he do to those tenants?" They said to him, "He will put those wretches to a miserable death and let out the vineyard to other tenants who will give him the fruits in their seasons" (Matthew 21:33–41).

*This parable, of course, was aimed in the first place at the Jewish nation. They had stoned and beaten the prophets whom God had sent to them, and now they threatened to kill His Son, Jesus Christ. But there is a wider application. Our lives are like vineyards, planted by God and lovingly cared for and protected by Him. We can adopt one of two attitudes. We can act like* tenants, *seeing our lives as something to be used for Him, bearing the fruit of goodness and bringing glory to His name. Or we can act like* owners, *dismissing His claims, usurping His position and giving Him no respect. We can, if we want, simply 'Live for ourselves, and think for ourselves, and none beside; just as if Jesus had never lived, and as if He had never died'. What a foolish, and fatal, mistake to make!*

**Lord, make me a good tenant whom You can trust to be both faithful and fruitful. Amen.**

## We were eyewitnesses of his majesty.
## (2 Peter 1:16)

Jesus took with him Peter and James, and John . . . and led them up a high mountain by themselves. And he was transfigured before them, and his face shone like the sun, and his clothes became white as light . . . A bright cloud overshadowed them, and a voice . . . said, "This is my beloved Son, with whom I am well pleased; listen to him." When the disciples heard this, they fell on their faces and were terrified (Matthew 17:1–2, 5–6). I saw seven golden lampstands, and in the midst of the lampstands one like a son of man, clothed with a long robe and with a golden sash around his chest. The hairs of his head were white like wool, as white as snow. His eyes were like a flame of fire, his feet were like burnished bronze, refined in a furnace, and his voice was like the roar of many waters . . . his face was like the sun shining in full strength. When I saw him, I fell at his feet as though dead (Revelation 1:12–17).

*Now and then the disciples were given a glimpse of the true majesty of Jesus. It was then that they realized their friend and leader was the King of kings. To John, the disciple who was closest to Jesus, was granted the further vision during his exile on the Isle of Patmos. Do you notice how everything about Jesus was bright? Even the cloud that overshadowed them on the mountain was 'a bright cloud'. The snow suggests Jesus' utter purity, for in Him there was not the faintest shadow of sin. The sun suggests His majestic power and strength. No wonder those who saw Him fell at His feet! For what could be brighter than the combination of snow and sun?*

'How wonderful, how beautiful, the sight of You must be,
Your endless wisdom, boundless power, and awful purity!'
Amen.

**We have the mind of Christ. (1 Corinthians 2:16)**

Have this mind among yourselves, which is yours in Christ Jesus (Philippians 2:5). Do not be conformed to this world, but be transformed by the renewal of your mind (Romans 12:2). Be renewed in the spirit of your minds (Ephesians 4:23). If then you have been raised with Christ, seek the things that are above, where Christ is, seated at the right hand of God. Set your minds on things that are above, not on things that are on earth (Colossians 3:1–2). For those who live according to the flesh set their minds on the things of the flesh, but those who live according to the Spirit set their minds on the things of the Spirit. To set the mind on the flesh is death, but to set the mind on the Spirit is life and peace (Romans 8:5–6). Prove me, O Lord, and try me; test my heart and my mind (Psalm 26:2).

*Broadly speaking, there are two ways of looking at life. 'To set the mind on the flesh' is to regard this life as an end in itself. The important things to go for, in that case, are material comforts and benefits. Because there is nothing to look forward to at the end, 'to set the mind on the flesh is death'. 'To set the mind on the Spirit', on the other hand, is to see this life here as the prelude to another one to come. In that case the all-important thing is the cultivation of the spirit in preparation. Because there is something to look forward to at the end, 'to set the mind on the Spirit is life and peace' is the goal. Of course, it is possible to be so heavenly-minded that we are no earthly good, and everyone must play his or her part as a citizen of this world. But it is a question of balance and of where my centre of gravity lies. If in doubt, why not get your mind tested? You can do it by reference to the Bible.*

**'May the mind of Christ my Saviour live in me from day to day, by His love and power controlling all I do and say.' Amen.**

### Having gifts that differ according to the grace given to us, let us use them. (Romans 12:6)

"A man going on a journey . . . called his servants and entrusted to them his property. To one he gave five talents, to another two, to another one, to each according to his ability" (Matthew 25:14–15). In a great house there are not only vessels of gold and silver but also of wood and clay (2 Timothy 2:20). "Now after a long time the master of those servants came and settled accounts with them. And he who had received the five talents came forward, bringing five talents more, saying, 'Master, you delivered to me five talents; here I have made five talents more.' His master said to him, 'Well done, good and faithful servant' (Matthew 25:19–21). Moreover, it is required of stewards that they be found trustworthy (1 Corinthians 4:2). I say to everyone . . . not to think of himself more highly than he ought to think, but to think with sober judgment (Romans 12:3). For who sees anything different in you? What do you have that you did not receive? If then you received it, why do you boast as if you did not receive it? (1 Corinthians 4:7).

*I wonder what your particular gifts or talents are. Perhaps you are artistic or musical or have a gift for languages or science. Or perhaps you have the gift of leadership, sympathy or friendliness. Look at yourself soberly and make a cool assessment of those things with which God has endowed you. When you have done that, determine to use those gifts in two ways. Faithfully. 'Fan into flame the gift of God which is in you', just as you would stir the sugar into a cup of tea so that it permeates the whole cup and doesn't just lie wasted, a little sticky puddle at the bottom. Make the very most of your talents. Humbly. But remember that you are a steward, or trustee. It is God who has bestowed the gifts on you, and there is nothing to be proud about.*

**Master, You delivered a talent to me. Help me to use it wisely and well. Amen.**

**God has made him both Lord and Christ, this Jesus whom you crucified. (Acts 2:36)**

Have this mind among yourselves, which is yours in Christ Jesus, who, though he was in the form of God, did not count equality with God a thing to be grasped, but made himself nothing, taking the form of a servant, being born in the likeness of men. And being found in human form, he humbled himself by becoming obedient to the point of death, even death on a cross. Therefore God has highly exalted him and bestowed on him the name that is above every name, so that at the name of Jesus every knee should bow, in heaven and on earth and under the earth, and every tongue confess that Jesus Christ is Lord, to the glory of God the Father (Philippians 2:5–11).

The shame. *It would have been very wonderful if God had come into this world as an angel, lived as a prince and died as a hero. But in fact He did something very much more wonderful. He came as a man, He lived as a worker and He died as a criminal, suffering the shameful death of crucifixion. He did not just visit the slums from some palatial residence – He became a slum-dweller. The fame. Just as there were three steps downwards, so there followed three upward steps. First, a new rank, for He was exalted to the right hand of God. Second, a new title, for though He had always been the Son of God, He was now 'Jesus', the Saviour of the world. Third, a new power, for in time every knee will bow to Him and every tongue confess His majesty and Lordship.*

**I thank You, Lord, for the great descent You made for me, and now I praise and worship You as Saviour and King. Amen.**

## "Be on your guard" Mark 13:9)

Examine yourselves, to see whether you are in the faith. Test yourselves. Or do you not realize this about yourselves, that Jesus Christ is in you? – unless indeed you fail to meet the test! (2 Corinthians 13:5) Do not present your members to sin as instruments for unrighteousness, but present yourselves to God as those who have been brought from death to life, and your members to God as instruments for righteousness (Romans 6:13). Build yourselves up in your most holy faith; pray in the Holy Spirit; keep yourselves in the love of God (Jude 20–21). Keep yourselves from idols (1 John 5:21). Since therefore Christ suffered in the flesh, arm yourselves with the same way of thinking . . . to live . . . no longer for human passions but for the will of God (1 Peter 4:1–2). Humble yourselves, therefore, under the mighty hand of God so that at the proper time he may exalt you (1 Peter 5:6).

*We are all familiar with the phrase 'God helps those who help themselves'. Rightly understood there is some truth in it, because there is a part we have to play in the Christian life in order to make it possible for God to play His part. Our role is that of the gardener. We dig and plant and water and thereby create the conditions in which God can produce the fruits and flowers He wants to see in our lives. In these verses we have a number of very important 'topical tips', which we must try to put into practice. We must not just sit back lazily and expect God to do what He is really expecting us to do for ourselves.*

**Lord, stir me to help You to make me what You want me to be: a spiritual garden which is a credit to You and a blessing to others. Amen.**

**If riches increase, set not your heart on them. (Psalm 62:10)**

See the man who would not make God his refuge, but trusted in the abundance of his riches and sought refuge in his own destruction! (Psalm 52:7) And as Jesus was setting out on his journey, a man ran up and knelt before him and asked him, "Good Teacher, what must I do to inherit eternal life?" And Jesus said to him, ". . . You know the commandments . . ." And he said to him, "Teacher, all these I have kept from my youth." And Jesus, looking at him, loved him, and said to him, "You lack one thing: go, sell all that you have and give to the poor, and you will have treasure in heaven; and come, follow me." Disheartened by the saying, he went away sorrowful, for he had great possessions (Mark 10:17–22). Keep your life free from love of money (Hebrews 13:5). For riches do not last forever (Proverbs 27:24). "Then the Almighty will be your gold and your precious silver . . . then you will delight yourself in the Almighty" (Job 22:25–26).

*Money is very like a drug. Wisely used and in the right hands it can do an enormous amount of good, but it is also terribly easy to get 'hooked' on it. For some strange reason, the more we have the more we seem to want – the millionaire always wants to become the multi-millionaire. Most people don't have a problem because they barely have enough money for their daily needs. But if you are one of the 'lucky' ones, then heed two words of advice. First, try not to set your heart upon money but live as loosely attached to it as you can. Second, think of ways you can be 'rich toward God' by using some of it to support Christian causes.*

**Lord, help me not to look upon my money as my own but as something You have lent to me and are trusting me to use wisely and well. Amen.**

## "I have come down from heaven, not to do my own will but the will of him who sent me." (John 6:38)

Jesus . . . lifted up his eyes to heaven, and said, "Father, the hour has come; glorify your Son that the Son may glorify you, since you have given him authority over all flesh, to give eternal life to all whom you have given him. And this is eternal life, that they know you the only true God, and Jesus Christ whom you have sent. I glorified you on earth, having accomplished the work that you gave me to do. And now, Father, glorify me in your own presence with the glory that I had with you before the world existed. I have manifested your name to the people whom you gave me out of the world . . . For I have given them the words that you gave me, and they have received them and have come to know in truth that I came from you; and they have believed that you sent me" (John 17:1–8).

'The work that you gave me.' *Jesus was about to return to heaven to his Father's presence, His great life-giving work of redemption accomplished. It was a work which none but He could do. Angels might be able to strengthen people, and prophets warn and teach, but the work of salvation could only be done by the sinless Son of God Himself. 'There was no other good enough . . .'* 'The words that you gave me.' *The redemption of humankind was Jesus' chief task while on earth, but He also came to show men and women what God was like, to 'manifest his name' and will and purpose to people. And what did Jesus Himself get? What was His reward? On earth it was that little band of disciples – 'the people whom you gave me out of the world', and in heaven it was to be the glory which He had 'before the world existed'.*

**Thank You, Lord, that I am able today to rejoice in the work You have done and read the words You have given. Amen.**

**There are varieties of service, but the same Lord.
(1 Corinthians 12:5)**

Epaphras, my fellow prisoner in Christ Jesus, sends greetings
to you, and so do Mark, Aristarchus, Demas, and Luke, my fellow workers (Philemon 23–24). Who have laboured side by
side with me in the gospel (Philippians 4:3). Do your best to
come to me soon. For Demas . . . has deserted me and gone to
Thessalonica. Crescens has gone to Galatia, Titus to Dalmatia.
Luke alone is with me (2 Timothy 4:9–11). Luke the beloved
physician (Colossians 4:14). It seemed good to me [Luke] also,
having followed all things closely for some time past, to write
an orderly account for you, most excellent Theophilus, that
you may have certainty concerning the things you have been
taught (Luke 1:3–4). That your faith might not rest in the wisdom of men but in the power of God (1 Corinthians 2:5).

Luke, the doctor. *By training Luke was a doctor, and he has become
the patron saint of the medical profession. But he gave up any sort of
general practice or consultancy in order to accompany Paul on his
arduous journeys as his medical adviser. We can be sure that,
humanly speaking, Paul owed much to the wise counsel of this man.
How grateful we should be for Christian doctors! Thank God today
for any you know.* Luke, the writer. *Perhaps he began by keeping a
diary of his travels, but Luke's gift as a writer quickly blossomed and
it is thanks to him that we have the gospel in his name and also the
book of Acts. Christians who can write clearly and simply about their
faith are needed in every generation. Why not try your hand at it?*

**Thank You, Lord, for the variety of gifts You bestow on Your
servants. Help me to discover my gifts and use them to the
full. Amen.**

## Tempted as we are, yet without sin.
## (Hebrews 4:15)

The tempter came and said to Jesus, "If you are the Son of God, command these stones to become loaves of bread." But he answered, "It is written, 'Man shall not live by bread alone, but by every word that comes from the mouth of God.'" Then the devil took him to the holy city and set him on the pinnacle of the temple and said to him, "If you are the Son of God, throw yourself down, for it is written, 'He will command his angels concerning you,'" . . . Jesus said to him, "Again it is written, 'You shall not put the Lord your God to the test.'" Again, the devil took him to a very high mountain and showed him all the kingdoms of the world and their glory. And he said to him, "All these I will give you, if you will fall down and worship me." Then Jesus said to him, "Be gone, Satan! For it is written, 'You shall worship the Lord your God and him only shall you serve'" (Matthew 4:3–10).

*'If . . .' That is Satan's favourite opening move on the chess board of temptation – a hint, a suggestion, an idea pushed gently forward like a pawn. It's never anything dramatic or too startling at first – just a polite and plausible proposal: 'Wouldn't it be a good idea if . . . ?' In the case of Jesus, Satan tried to make Him set up His kingdom in the wrong way, by appealing to the flesh (the loaves), the world (leap from the temple) and the devil. 'It is written . . .' Notice how Jesus dealt with each temptation – not with a question or an argument, but with a clear statement from Scripture. He was using the Word of God as 'the sword of the Spirit', and after the third thrust 'the devil left him'.*

**Lord, I am not ignorant of Satan's devices, but give me the will to resist his every approach. Amen.**

**"He has sent me to proclaim . . . recovering of sight to the blind." (Luke 4:18)**

And they came to Jericho. And as he was leaving Jericho . . . Bartimaeus, a blind beggar . . . was sitting by the roadside. And when he heard that it was Jesus of Nazareth, he began to cry out and say, "Jesus, Son of David, have mercy on me!" And many rebuked him, telling him to be silent. But he cried out all the more, "Son of David, have mercy on me!" And Jesus stopped and said, "Call him." And they called the blind man, saying to him, "Take heart. Get up; he is calling you." And throwing off his cloak, he sprang up and came to Jesus. And Jesus said to him, "What do you want me to do for you?" And the blind man said to him, "Rabbi, let me recover my sight." And Jesus said to him, "Go your way; your faith has made you well." And immediately he recovered his sight and followed him on the way (Mark 10:46–52).

*The other day it was a rich ruler who approached Jesus, and today it is a blind beggar. This is one of the wonderful things about the Lord – that you find people drawn to Him from every country, colour and class. Unlike some, Bartimaeus knew exactly why he needed Jesus and he refused to be silenced. 'O give me light! Rabbi, restore the blind man's sight. And Jesus answers, Go in peace, your faith from blindness gives release.' 'Go your way,' said Jesus, but for Bartimaeus that meant 'Come my way' and, instead of returning home, he joined the followers of Jesus. Like so many others who have come to Christ, Bartimaeus took those four familiar steps – he heard, he came, he received and he followed.*

**Lord, I thank You that I have no need, known or unknown to me, which You cannot reach and touch and heal. Amen.**

## The church, which is his body.
## (Ephesians 1:22–23)

For as in one body we have many members, and the members do not all have the same function, so we, though many, are one body in Christ, and individually members one of another (Romans 12:4–5). If one member suffers, all suffer together; if one member is honoured, all rejoice together (1 Corinthians 12:26). Having gifts that differ according to the grace given to us, let us use them: if prophecy, in proportion to our faith; if service, in our serving; the one who teaches, in his teaching; the one who exhorts, in his exhortation (Romans 12:6–8). For building up the body of Christ, until we all attain to the unity of the faith and of the knowledge of the Son of God, to mature manhood, to the measure of the stature of the fullness of Christ (Ephesians 4:12–13).

*The Christian church is likened to a body of which Christ is the Head and through which He works in the world. There are two things to notice about a body. Its variety. It is made up of all sorts of different organs and members, some more important than others. But, if the body is to function properly, each separate component part must do its share of work. Its unity. The sad thing is that often the individual members of the body get diseased or simply fall out with each other, and a healthy variety becomes disunity. That is the state of the church in many countries today, and the healing of these rifts calls for much sympathetic work and prayer. It is not that we want uniformity. If the church used its divisions as military rather than political divisions, it would increase its effectiveness in the world. What we need is variety of function and unity of Spirit.*

**Lord, make me a useful, and at the same time a unifying, influence in the church to which I belong. Amen.**

## He satisfies the longing soul. (Psalm 107:9)

O God, you are my God; earnestly I seek you; my soul thirsts for you; my flesh faints for you, as in a dry and weary land where there is no water. So I have looked upon you in the sanctuary, beholding your power and glory. Because your steadfast love is better than life, my lips will praise you. So I will bless you as long as I live; in your name I will lift up my hands. My soul will be satisfied as with fat and rich food, and my mouth will praise you with joyful lips, when I remember you upon my bed, and meditate on you in the watches of the night; for you have been my help, and in the shadow of your wings I will sing for joy. My soul clings to you; your right hand upholds me (Psalm 63:1–8).

*David probably wrote this psalm at a time when he was in the wilderness, a fugitive from the armies of Saul. There can have been very little in his circumstances to make him happy or hopeful, but almost every word of this psalm breathes confidence and contentment. Three things are very hard to find in a wilderness – water, food and shelter. But whatever the material supplies were like, David, as he says, found every spiritual need abundantly met by the Lord. Just as the needle of a compass will always automatically find its way to the magnetic north, so David's mind turned to the Lord. When he wasn't praying, he was praising and singing and, when he wasn't doing that, in the dark watches of the night he was feeding on the Lord in his heart by faith with thanksgiving.*

**Lord, wean me from such great dependence upon the things of the world and help me to lean more heavily upon You. Amen.**

## Having the appearance of godliness, but denying its power. (2 Timothy 3:5)

"This people draw near with their mouth and honour me with their lips, while their hearts are far from me, and their fear of me is a commandment taught by men" (Isaiah 29:13). "They hear what you say but they will not do it; for with lustful talk in their mouths they act; their heart is set on their gain" (Ezekiel 33:31). "And when you pray, you must not be like the hypocrites. For they love to stand and pray in the synagogues and at the street corners, that they may be seen by others" (Matthew 6:5). "And for a pretence make long prayers" (Mark 12:40). "Why do you call me 'Lord, Lord,' and not do what I tell you?" (Luke 6:46). "Not everyone who says to me, 'Lord, Lord,' will enter the kingdom of heaven, but the one who does the will of my Father who is in heaven" (Matthew 7:21). They profess to know God, but they deny him by their works (Titus 1:16).

*At my school there was a clock with two faces – one looking into the main court and the other down a drive. At one stage the two faces told different times, and you could be late or early according to which face you were going by. That clock was a hypocrite, a living liar. It was one thing in secret and another in public. There are two kinds of hypocrite.* Words without thoughts. *It is very easy to pray and even preach with the lips only while the heart is secretly occupied in other ways. Such prayers and sermons are like plastic flowers. They may look all right, but the living fragrance is missing.* Words without deeds. *Again, we need to guard against this. The man who writes a letter of righteous indignation to the local paper about the shoplifting in his town but fiddles with his income tax returns is a fraud and a sham.*

**Lord, make me sincere and help me always to mean what I pray and to do what I say. Amen.**

## "Look to the rock from which you were hewn, and to the quarry from which you were dug." (Isaiah 51:1)

Remember that you were at that time separated from Christ . . . having no hope and without God in the world. But now in Christ Jesus you who once were far off have been brought near by the blood of Christ (Ephesians 2:12–13). Once you were not a people, but now you are God's people; once you had not received mercy, but now you have received mercy . . . For you were straying like sheep, but have now returned to the Shepherd and Overseer of your souls (1 Peter 2:10, 25). The unrighteous will not inherit the kingdom of God . . . And such were some of you. But you were washed, you were sanctified, you were justified in the name of the Lord Jesus Christ and by the Spirit of our God (1 Corinthians 6:9, 11). My soul thirsts for God, for the living God. When shall I come and appear before God? (Psalm 42:2)

*Hewn from a rock. Michelangelo is said to have produced his statue of David from a huge, discarded block of marble. If it had been alive, that figure could have looked back with gratitude and amazement at what the sculptor had done. Peter must often have done that when he thought of what Jesus had made out of Simon – see John 1:42. Drawn from a bog. Perhaps you have had to rescue your dog from a miry bog and, if so, you will know that three things have to happen before the animal can really be 'received' by you. The dog must be lifted out, taken back and cleaned up. That is how God comes to the rescue of those who have strayed from Him. Like the dog, we too can look back to the bog from which He drew us and say, 'We were . . . but we are . . .'*

**Lord, I thank You that when I was lost You found me, and that when I was stained through sin You cleansed me. Amen.**

### The city . . . whose designer and builder is God. (Hebrews 11:10)

For here we have no lasting city, but we seek the city that is to come (Hebrews 13:14). But our citizenship is in heaven, and from it we await a Saviour, the Lord Jesus Christ (Philippians 3:20). "If the world hates you, know that it has hated me before it hated you. If you were of the world, the world would love you as its own; but because you are not of the world, but I chose you out of the world, therefore the world hates you" (John 15:18–19). Set your minds on things that are above, not on things that are on earth (Colossians 3:2). "Lay up for yourselves treasures in heaven . . . For where your treasure is, there your heart will be also" (Matthew 6:20–21). Storing up treasure for themselves as a good foundation for the future, so that they may take hold of that which is truly life (1 Timothy 6:19).

*Have you ever lived and worked overseas? If so you will know that strange feeling of 'belonging' to two places at once. Your work, we will suppose, keeps you in Hong Kong, but your real home, your heart, your possessions and perhaps most of your family are in the United Kingdom. You* live *in Hong Kong, but you* belong *to the U.K. We Christians are in that position. We have dual nationality. We live and work in this world, but we belong to heaven and we are really only colonists here. It must not surprise us if we are sometimes looked upon as foreigners who talk a different language and have different habits. Of course we shall enjoy our life here enormously, but we must not forget that our real home is with Christ – and that is where our fortune should be kept. When our work is done, we shall retire to be with Christ.*

**Lord, in the busy hectic life I spend here, help me not to forget my true citizenship and help me to be loyal to You always. Amen.**

**No good thing does he withhold from those who walk uprightly. (Psalm 84:11)**

What shall I render to the Lord for all his benefits to me? I will lift up the cup of salvation and call on the name of the Lord (Psalm 116:12–13). "Let the one who is thirsty come; let the one who desires take the water of life without price" (Revelation 22:17). "Come to me, all who labour and are heavy laden, and I will give you rest. Take my yoke upon you, and learn from me, for I am gentle and lowly in heart, and you will find rest for your souls. For my yoke is easy, and my burden is light" (Matthew 11:28–30). Take up the whole armour of God, that you may be able to withstand in the evil day, and having done all, to stand firm . . . and take . . . the sword of the Spirit, which is the word of God (Ephesians 6:13, 17).

*Those who come to Christ are invited to 'take' three things. The cup. In Bible days water was often so precious that it had to be sold, but Christ offers it to us 'without price'. We can imagine how often a cup of water must have brought something like salvation to a weary traveller, and it is in that way He can refresh and satisfy us. The yoke. The Christian is not to be idle. When we are linked to Christ there is work for us to do, but it is work we will enjoy because the yoke doesn't chafe and the burden is light. The sword. Not only is there work to be done for Christ in the world, but there are also battles to fight – against the power of darkness, against the evil all around us, against personal temptation. We need to be well armed if we are to survive, let alone to conquer.*

**Thank You, Lord, that You provide for my deepest needs, employ me in your service, and equip me to fight your battles. Amen.**

## So now faith, hope, and love abide, these three ... (1 Corinthians 13:13)

Blessed be the God and Father of our Lord Jesus Christ! According to his great mercy, he has caused us to be born again to a living *hope* through the resurrection of Jesus Christ from the dead, to an inheritance that is imperishable, undefiled, and unfading, kept in heaven for you, who by God's power are being guarded through faith for a salvation ready to be revealed in the last time. In this you rejoice, though now for a little while, if necessary, you have been grieved by various trials, so that the tested genuineness of your *faith* – more precious than gold that perishes though it is tested by fire – may be found to result in praise and glory and honour at the revelation of Jesus Christ. Though you have not seen him, you *love* him. Though you do not now see him, you believe in him and rejoice with *joy* that is inexpressible and filled with glory, obtaining the outcome of your faith, the salvation of your souls (1 Peter 1:3–9).

*Notice three familiar words which appear in this passage (my italics). Hope. The resurrection of Jesus from the dead has given a new dimension to life because it means that it can be an everlasting reality, and not just a temporary one, for all who are 'born again'. Hope is a very Christian word. You don't find that other religions have much to say about it. Faith. Hope looks forward, but faith looks upward – finding in Christ the strength to live life as it is and to face its problems and trials. Love. Our love for Christ is a reflection of His love for us, just as a mirror reflects the sun. It comes when we are in the right attitude towards Him and in the right relationship: 'sitting in the sun'. Notice one more word – joy. For the Christian this equation is always true: Hope + Faith + Love = Joy.*

**Lord, bring to life my hope, strengthen my faith and deepen my love for You. Amen.**

## "God has made me fruitful in the land of my affliction." (Genesis 41:52)

"The patriarchs, jealous of Joseph, sold him into Egypt; but God was with him" (Acts 7:9). And he became a successful man . . . His master saw that the Lord was with him . . . And . . . his master's wife cast her eyes on Joseph and said, "Lie with me." But he refused and said . . . "How . . . can I do this great wickedness and sin against God?" . . . His master came home, and she told him . . . "The Hebrew servant . . . came in to me to laugh at me." . . . And Joseph's master . . . put him into the prison . . . But the Lord was with Joseph and showed him steadfast love (Genesis 39: 2–3, 7–9, 16–17, 20–21). Then Pharaoh said to Joseph, "Since God has shown you all this, there is none so . . . wise as you are. You shall be . . . over all the land of Egypt" (Genesis 41:39–41). His brothers also came and fell down before him . . . But Joseph said to them, ". . . you meant evil against me, but God meant it for good" (Genesis 50:18–20).

*What a remarkable man Joseph was – an exile, a slave and a prisoner who ended up as prime minister of Egypt!* The prison. *He was the victim of jealousy, cruelty, intrigue and injustice, but he took it calmly and without a trace of bitterness.* The palace. *When the tide turned and he found himself at the top, there was no sign of arrogance or vindictiveness. Like Paul, he had 'learnt in whatever situation he was to be content'. Over the door leading from the centre court to the dressing room at the All England Tennis Club at Wimbledon are Kipling's words, 'If you can meet with triumph and disaster, and treat those two impostors just the same . . .' Joseph learnt to do that. He was not soured by shame; neither was he spoiled by fame. And the secret? It keeps peeping out – 'God was with him' at every stage, sustaining and encouraging. Try tracing the parallels between the lives of Joseph and Jesus.*

**Lord, help me to face failure without resentment, and success without pride. Amen.**

## Christ . . . lives in me. (Galatians 2:20)

For this reason I bow my knees before the Father, from whom every family in heaven and on earth is named, that according to the riches of his glory he may grant you to be strengthened with power through his Spirit in your inner being, so that Christ may dwell in your hearts through faith – that you, being rooted and grounded in love, may have strength to comprehend with all the saints what is the breadth and length and height and depth, and to know the love of Christ that surpasses knowledge, that you may be filled with all the fullness of God. Now to him who is able to do far more abundantly than all that we ask or think, according to the power at work within us, to him be glory in the church and in Christ Jesus throughout all generations, forever and ever. Amen (Ephesians 3:14–21).

Dwelling. *When we become true Christians, Jesus Christ comes to live in our hearts in the person of His Holy Spirit. We cannot see Him, and we do not necessarily feel Him, but we know He is there 'through faith'.* Filling. *As time goes on, He will want to take over every room in the house of our lives, spreading His influence throughout and filling us with His strength and His love. He does not just want to be there as a resident but as president – guiding and controlling all we do. This is a lovely prayer of Paul's, and one we can use for ourselves. We can sum it up in two words: grace and glory. Grace is what He gives to us, and glory is what we give to Him. Grace works downwards, and glory works upwards.*

**Lord Jesus, I ask You to make my heart Your palace and Your royal throne. Amen.**

## Heirs with you of the grace of life. (1 Peter 3:7)

Then the Lord God said, "It is not good that the man should be alone; I will make him a helper fit for him" (Genesis 2:18). Male and female he created them (Genesis 1:27). Therefore a man shall leave his father and his mother and hold fast to his wife, and they shall become one flesh (Genesis 2:24). "So they are no longer two but one flesh. What therefore God has joined together, let not man separate" (Matthew 19:6). "For the man who hates and divorces, says the Lord, the God of Israel, covers his garment with violence, says the Lord of hosts. So guard yourselves in your spirit, and do not be faithless" (Malachi 2:16). Husbands, love your wives, as Christ loved the church . . . and let the wife see that she respects her husband (Ephesians 5:25, 33). Do not be unequally yoked with unbelievers. For what partnership has righteousness with lawlessness? Or what fellowship has light with darkness? . . . Or what portion does a believer share with an unbeliever? (2 Corinthians 6:14–15). "The Lord shall be between me and you . . . forever" (1 Samuel 20:42).

*Marriage is one of God's oldest institutions, but it is threatened today from many directions and the Christian needs to approach it carefully and prayerfully.* It is a leaving and a cleaving. *It is a break with the past life and, in God's eyes, a new and permanent and eternal relationship.* It is a giving and a taking. *Marriage, like an ordinary friendship, won't flourish unless we take the trouble to work at it. It requires humility, patience and thoughtfulness if it is going to succeed.* It is spiritual as well as physical. *A couple must have deeper things in common than just the magnetism of sex. For the Christian it should go without saying that marriage is unthinkable with someone who does not share his or her faith. It is when the Lord is between two people – like the mortar between the bricks or the jam in a sandwich – that their marriage has a firmness and a flavour found nowhere else.*

**Lord, save me from the disaster of a marriage that fails. Amen.**

## Whose names are in the book of life.
## (Philippians 4:3)

Then I saw a new heaven and a new earth, for the first heaven and the first earth had passed away, and the sea was no more. And I saw the holy city, new Jerusalem, coming down out of heaven from God . . . And I heard a loud voice . . . saying, "Behold, the dwelling place of God is with man. He will dwell with them, and they will be his people, and God himself will be with them as their God. He will wipe away every tear . . . and death shall be no more, neither shall there be mourning nor crying nor pain anymore" . . . And the city has no need of sun or moon to shine on it, for the glory of God gives it light, and its lamp is the Lamb. By its light will the nations walk, and the kings of the earth will bring their glory into it . . . But nothing unclean will ever enter it, nor anyone who does what is detestable or false, but only those who are written in the Lamb's book of life (Revelation 21:1–4, 23–24, 27).

*We have here a vivid poetical description of heaven and what it will be like. The language, though symbolical, is full of significance. Notice three things that we shall not find in heaven. No sea. The Jews never felt at home with the sea, and for them it stood for separation and death. This reminds us that heaven is a place 'where partings are no more'. No sun. Again, this is a slightly depressing thought until we realize that the glory of the Lord will illuminate heaven, and we shall need the sun no more than we need electric light on a summer's day. No sin. Everyone is invited to come, but only those whose sins have been blotted out and forgiven, and whose names are in 'the book of life', qualify. Make sure you are registered!*

**Lord, prepare me here and now for that life which I have been invited to live with You for ever. Amen.**

## Precious in the sight of the Lord is the death of his saints. (Psalm 116:15)

And I heard a voice from heaven saying, "Write this: Blessed are the dead who die in the Lord from now on." "Blessed indeed," says the Spirit, "that they may rest from their labours, for their deeds follow them!" (Revelation 14:13) "And those who are wise shall shine like the brightness of the sky above; and those who turn many to righteousness, like the stars forever and ever" (Daniel 12:3). After this I looked, and behold, a great multitude that no one could number, from every nation, from all tribes and peoples and languages, standing before the throne and before the Lamb, clothed in white robes, with palm branches in their hands, and crying out with a loud voice, "Salvation belongs to our God who sits on the throne, and to the Lamb!" . . . "Therefore they are before the throne of God, and serve him day and night in his temple; and he who sits on the throne will shelter them with his presence" (Revelation 7:9–10, 15).

*Today is 'All Saints' Day', on which we specially remember with gratitude to God some of the millions of those who have fought a good fight in the past and now 'rejoice with us, but upon another shore and in a clearer light'. I have always found it challenging and stimulating to read about the lives of great Christians of the past – men like Wesley, Whitefield and Wilberforce – who turned many to righteousness and whose deeds follow them. I am sure we ought to thank God for those who have served Him in days gone by, whose 'bodies are buried in peace, but their name lives for evermore'. But the word 'saint' must not be confined to those who traditionally bear that title (St Paul, St John and so on). It is the Bible's word for all who believe in Christ. A 'saint', as a small boy once put it, thinking of the figure in a stained glass window, is 'someone whom the light shines though'.*

**Lord, I thank You today for those of whom I have read, and those whom I have known, who have loved You and lived for You. Amen.**

## We walk by faith. (2 Corinthians 5:7)

Faith is the assurance of things hoped for . . . By faith we understand that the universe was created by the word of God, so that what is seen was not made out of things that are visible . . . And without faith it is impossible to please him . . . By faith Noah, being warned by God concerning events as yet unseen, in reverent fear constructed an ark . . . By faith Abraham obeyed when he was called to go out to a place that he was to receive as an inheritance. And he went out, not knowing where he was going . . . By faith Moses, when he was grown up, refused to be called the son of Pharaoh's daughter, choosing rather to be mistreated with the people of God than to enjoy the fleeting pleasures of sin . . . By faith he kept the Passover. . . . By faith the people crossed the Red Sea . . . By faith the walls of Jericho fell down (Hebrews 11:1, 3, 6–8, 24–25, 28–30). I live by faith (Galatians 2:20).

*Yesterday we thought about saints, past and present, and today we see that the one thing they all had in common was faith. Let us look at two aspects of faith.* Personal. *Faith is the confidence we put in the character and ability of another – the doctor, the motor engineer, the cook. To withhold that 'vote of confidence' from someone who deserves it is very hurtful, even insulting, and that is why 'without faith it is impossible to please God'. He demands our faith.* Practical. *It was because these people had such complete confidence in God that they were able to do what they did. They risked mockery, danger, opposition and even death because they knew that God would never let them down and that His loving purposes would be fulfilled for them.*

**Lord, give me a faith that will not shrink from taking risks in Your service. Amen.**

## Flee from sexual immorality. (1 Corinthians 6:18)

Do you not know that your body is a temple of the Holy Spirit within you, whom you have from God? You are not your own, for you were bought with a price. So glorify God in your body (1 Corinthians 6:19–20). Each one of you know how to control his own body in holiness and honour, not in the passion of lust like the Gentiles who do not know God (1 Thessalonians 4:4–5). "You shall not commit adultery" (Exodus 20:14). "Abstain from . . . sexual immorality" (Acts 15:20). "Everyone who looks at a woman with lustful intent has already committed adultery with her in his heart" (Matthew 5:28). "I have made a covenant with my eyes" (Job 31:1). "For from within, out of the heart of man, come evil thoughts, sexual immorality . . . adultery" (Mark 7:21). How can a young man keep his way pure? By guarding it according to your word (Psalm 119:9).

*Sexual intercourse outside marriage is presented to young people today as a most attractive and even necessary experience. But is this really so? For the Christian there can only be one answer, for unchastity in every form is expressly forbidden. But there are also some very sound and practical reasons for following this scriptural rule. Quite apart from the risk of producing unwanted babies, there is the lasting emotional disturbance which a casual liaison can cause. It is also a well established fact that chastity before marriage makes faithfulness in marriage more, rather than less, likely. Christians should regard their bodies in this matter as something to be kept sacredly for the person for whom, in God's good time, it is ultimately intended. But the temptations are strong, and to do this we need to guard our thoughts and our looks.*

**Help me, Lord, not to use my body to gratify my own desires but to do Your will. Amen.**

## "Follow me, and I will make you fishers of men." (Matthew 4:19)

"Do you not say, 'There are yet four months, then comes the harvest'? Look, I tell you, lift up your eyes, and see that the fields are white for harvest" (John 4:35). "The harvest is plentiful, but the labourers are few; therefore pray earnestly to the Lord of the harvest to send out labourers into his harvest" (Matthew 9:37–38). "And I have other sheep that are not of this fold. I must bring them also" (John 10:16). "When he saw the crowds, he had compassion for them, because they were harassed and helpless, like sheep without a shepherd" (Matthew 9:36). "Feed my sheep" (John 21:17). And how are they to believe in him of whom they have never heard? And how are they to hear without someone preaching? And how are they to preach unless they are sent? (Romans 10:14–15) And I heard the voice of the Lord saying, "Whom shall I send, and who will go for us?" Then I said, "Here am I! Send me" (Isaiah 6:8). And he said . . . "Go into all the world and proclaim the gospel" (Mark 16:15).

*We think today of the world's great need for the gospel and we see a little of what we can do to meet that need. We can pray that God will raise up men and women and send them out into the world to work for Him. Later we can go, and perhaps become the answers to our own prayers. This does not necessarily mean becoming a clergyman or a missionary, for Christ wants His witnesses in every walk of life. But it does mean that wherever we are – at school or college, in an office, a factory or a regiment – we shall be ready to take the opportunities that come from telling people about Christ and what He can do for them. It is interesting that the very first words Jesus spoke to Peter invited him to be a 'fisherman', and the last words invited him to be a 'shepherd'. That is our task – to win people for Christ and then to care for them. We are to work by 'hook' and by 'crook'.*

**Lord, help me to think of, and to speak to, the individuals You want to win through me. Amen.**

**I am stirring up your sincere mind by way of reminder. (2 Peter 3:1)**

Remember also your Creator in the days of your youth, before the evil days come and the years draw near of which you will say, "I have no pleasure in them" (Ecclesiastes 12:1). I remember the days of old; I meditate on all that you have done; I ponder the work of your hands (Psalm 143:5). I will remember the deeds of the Lord; yes, I will remember your wonders of old (Psalm 77:11). My soul will be satisfied . . . when I remember you upon my bed, and meditate on you in the watches of the night (Psalm 63:5–6). "Remember all the commandments of the Lord, to do them" (Numbers 15:39). Remember Jesus Christ, risen from the dead (2 Timothy 2:8). "Remember the words of the Lord Jesus" (Acts 20:35). "I remember my offences today" (Genesis 41:9).

*'Remember, remember, the fifth of November . . .' It is a very good idea, and a healthy exercise, occasionally to look back over a period of time and remember. Memory can be a great encouragement to us when we are going through a bad patch or a difficult time. As we call to mind all that God has done for us in the past, our faith in Him to look after the future for us will get stronger. Memory can also be a warning to us. We don't want to brood over past failures and faults, but they often have something useful to teach us before we try to put them away for ever, 'forgetting what lies behind'. Memory can act like an accelerator and a brake on our lives: constraining and restraining.*

**Lord, You have done so much for me. Please help me to forget not all Your benefits but to look back upon them with a grateful heart. Amen.**

## A harvest of righteousness. (James 3:18)

"Abide in me, and I in you. As the branch cannot bear fruit by itself, unless it abides in the vine, neither can you, unless you abide in me . . . By this my Father is glorified, that you bear much fruit and so prove to be my *disciples* . . . If you keep my commandments, you will abide in my love, just as I have kept my Father's commandments and abide in his love . . . You are my friends if you do what I command you. No longer do I call you *servants*, for the servant does not know what his master is doing; but I have called you *friends*, for all that I have heard from my Father I have made known to you. You did not choose me, but I chose you and appointed you that you should go and bear fruit and that your fruit should abide" (John 15:4, 8, 10, 14–16).

*The Christian has a threefold relationship with Christ, as we see above (my italics). We start as* disciples, *whose job it is to* learn. *Of course there is a sense in which we never cease to learn, for in the Christian life it is a case of 'the more you know, the more you know you don't know'. Then we become* servants, *whose job it is to* labour *– undertaking fruitful service for our master. Finally, we become* friends. *At this point the relationship has developed into one of love. The test all the way through is fruitfulness ('fruit', 'much fruit', 'fruit that abides') – that is, a life which is pleasing to Christ and which reflect His joy, peace, patience and love. Is your fruit sweet or sour?*

**Lord, I ask that You may not be disappointed in me. Make me an apt learner, a willing servant and a faithful and loving friend. Amen.**

## "Honour your father and your mother."
### (Exodus 20:12)

"Every one of you shall revere his mother and his father" (Leviticus 19:3). Children, obey your parents in everything, for this pleases the Lord (Colossians 3:20). And Jesus went down with them and came to Nazareth and was submissive to them (Luke 2:51). Hear, my son, your father's instruction, and forsake not your mother's teaching, for they are a graceful garland for your head and pendants for your neck (Proverbs 1:8–9). A wise son makes a glad father, but a foolish son is a sorrow to his mother (Proverbs 10:1). Listen to your father who gave you life, and do not despise your mother when she is old . . . The father of the righteous will greatly rejoice . . . Let your father and mother be glad; let her who bore you rejoice (Proverbs 23:22, 24–25).

*What does it mean to 'honour' our parents? When we are still quite young we honour them by obedience. They feed, clothe and shelter us, and it is only right that they should make the rules and expect us to obey them. Even Jesus was obedient to His parents. But there comes a time when we are too old to be ordered about, and no sensible parent tries to do it. It is then that respect takes over from obedience. We must be free to choose our own career, our own husband (or wife), where we live, and so on. But the special relationship we have with our parents, and the fact of their age and experience, will mean that we won't easily or lightly flout their wishes and opinions. We will listen to them with reverent attention. Finally, to honour our parents means to love them and, perhaps especially as they get older, to surround them with sympathetic care.*

**Lord, may I remember Your commandment to honour my parents when I am tempted to be thoughtless, selfish and offhand towards them. Amen.**

## Love is kind. (1 Corinthians 13:4)

"Then the righteous will answer him, saying, 'Lord, when did we see you hungry and feed you, or thirsty and give you drink?' . . . And the King will answer them, 'Truly, I say to you, as you did it to one of the least of these my brothers, you did it to me'" (Matthew 25:37, 40). But if anyone has the world's goods and sees his brother in need, yet closes his heart against him, how does God's love abide in him? . . . Let us not love in word or talk but in deed and in truth (1 John 3:17–18). Julius treated Paul kindly and gave him leave to go to his friends and be cared for (Acts 27:3). The native people showed us unusual kindness, for they kindled a fire and welcomed us all, because it had begun to rain and was cold (Acts 28:2). Epaphroditus my . . . fellow worker . . . and minister to my need (Philippians 2:25). May the Lord grant mercy to the household of Onesiphorus, for he often refreshed me and was not ashamed of my chains, but . . . searched for me earnestly (2 Timothy 1:16–17). Put on . . . kindness (Colossians 3:12). Be kind to one another (Ephesians 4:32). Supplement your faith . . . with brotherly affection (2 Peter 1:5, 7).

*'Kindness' is 'love in action' – in heraldry terms, not 'love couchant', but 'love rampant'. Kindness is the way in which love expresses itself. Love is like the manuscript score of music, but to be appreciated properly it must be reproduced in actual sound. What a lot Paul owed to the kindness of others! He remembers the Roman centurion, the inhabitants of Malta where he was shipwrecked and his visitors in prison because of the practical ways in which they helped him. Soon after he became king, David asked this question: 'Is there any one left of the house of Saul, that I may show him kindness?' It is a good question to ask ourselves from time to time. 'Is there anyone to whom I can show kindness today?' Remember, kindness is the universal language of love. Everyone understands it.*

**Thank You, Lord, for all Your loving kindness to me. Help me in turn to be kind to those who need help, bringing joy where there is sorrow and pleasure where there is pain. Amen.**

## Hard questions. (1 Kings 10:1)

*"Can you find out the deep things of God?"* (Job 11:7) No one has ever seen God; the only God . . . He has made him known (John 1:18). In him the whole fullness of deity dwells (Colossians 2:9). "Whoever has seen me has seen the Father" (John 14:9). The exact imprint of his nature (Hebrews 1:3). *"Who can bring a clean thing out of an unclean?"* (Job 14:4) Sin came into the world through one man, and death through sin (Romans 5:12). Behold, I was brought forth in iniquity, and in sin did my mother conceive me (Psalm 51:5). None is righteous, no, not one . . . All have turned aside; together they have become worthless; no one does good, not even one . . . All have sinned and fall short of the glory of God (Romans 3:10, 12, 23). *"How can a man be in the right before God?"* (Job 9:2) For by works of the law no human being will be justified in his sight . . . They are justified by his grace as a gift, through the redemption that is in Christ Jesus (Romans 3:20, 24).

*Many years ago a book was written called* The Answers of Jesus to the Questions of Job, *and today we have three of his most penetrating questions (my italics) with the New Testament answers. Jesus Christ came into the world to do two things. He came to reveal God to human beings. Until He came, people had a very incomplete idea of what God was like. But Jesus 'translated' God for them so that they could understand Him better. For a series of photographs, He substituted a living portrait. Second, He came to redeem human beings to God. We had fallen into the wrong hands, like some valuable article in a pawnshop, and the death of Jesus was necessary to redeem us and to restore us to our rightful owner.*

**Thank You, Lord – not just for giving the answers, but for being the answer and the solution to all our needs Yourself. Amen.**

## "I am alive." (Revelation 1:18)

Jesus . . . presented himself alive to them [the apostles] after his suffering by many proofs, appearing to them during forty days and speaking about the kingdom of God (Acts 1:1–3). "I am the first and the last, and the living one. I died, and behold I am alive for evermore" (Revelation 1:17–18). "And behold, I am with you always, to the end of the age" (Matthew 28:20). And the Lord said to Paul one night in a vision, "Do not be afraid . . . for I am with you" (Acts 18:9). The following night the Lord stood by Paul and said, "Take courage" (Acts 23:11). At my first defence no one came to stand by me, but all deserted me . . . But the Lord stood by me and strengthened me (2 Timothy 4:16–17). The Lord is at hand (Philippians 4:5). Now may the Lord of peace himself give you peace at all times in every way. The Lord be with you all (2 Thessalonians 3:16). Jesus Christ is the same yesterday and today and forever (Hebrews 13:8).

*We are told that there was a moment in the Battle of Hastings when William of Normandy was in serious danger of defeat and, to make matters worse, a rumour ran round his soldiers that he himself had been slain. When he heard it, he leapt on his horse, threw back his visor, and rode up and down the lines shouting out, 'I am alive!' 'I am alive!' With these words he rallied his troops, restored morale and made one final successful assault on Harold's stockades. And it was those words of Jesus that turned a demoralized group of disciples into an army that turned the world upside down. The difference, of course, is that William the Conqueror died some years later. Jesus the conqueror, on the other hand, is 'alive for evermore', always 'at hand', everywhere at once, and able to strengthen, encourage and help His followers in every circumstance.*

**Lord, I thank You that You are alive – and not only alive, but available; and not only available, but active in the world today. Amen.**

## He himself is our peace. (Ephesians 2:14)

The God of peace (Hebrews 13:20). "As I live, declares the Lord God, I have no pleasure in the death of the wicked, but that the wicked turn from his way and live" (Ezekiel 33:11). The Lord is not . . . wishing that any should perish (2 Peter 3:9). The gospel of peace (Ephesians 6:15). Making peace by the blood of his cross. And you, who once were alienated and hostile in mind, doing evil deeds, he has now reconciled . . . by his death (Colossians 1:20–22). Upon him was the chastisement that brought us peace (Isaiah 53:5). For if while we were enemies we were reconciled to God by the death of his Son, much more, now that we are reconciled, shall we be saved by his life (Romans 5:10). Therefore . . . we have peace with God through our Lord Jesus Christ (Romans 5:1). God was reconciling the world to himself . . . and entrusting to us the message of reconciliation (2 Corinthians 5:19).

*November 11, 1918 was the day on which an armistice was signed between Great Britain and Germany, marking the end of World War I. The first Good Friday was another Armistice Day on which peace was declared between God and human beings. The God of peace. God has always wanted peaceful relations with us, but we have announced our independence, set up an illegal regime and defied God. So a state of war has existed between us. The gospel of peace. God took the initiative to end this state of affairs and, in the person of His Son, cancelled the debt we owed Him by dying upon the cross. He has made an unlimited sacrifice in the interests of peace. But, if we want to enjoy it, we must be prepared for unconditional surrender.*

**Lord, I thank You that a state of war no longer exists between us, and I ask that your work of reconstruction in my life may go ahead unhindered. Amen.**

## "Six days you shall labour." (Exodus 20:9)

"Why do you stand here idle all day?" (Matthew 20:6). We labour, working with our own hands (1 Corinthians 4:12). "You yourselves know that these hands ministered to my necessities and to those who were with me" (Acts 20:34). Nor did we eat anyone's bread without paying for it, but with toil and labour we worked night and day, that we might not be a burden to any of you (2 Thessalonians 3:8). Man goes out to his work and to his labour until the evening (Psalm 104:23). Sweet is the sleep of a labourer (Ecclesiastes 5:12). An excellent wife who can find? She . . . works with willing hands . . . She looks well to the ways of her household and does not eat the bread of idleness (Proverbs 31:10, 13, 27). In all toil there is profit, but mere talk tends only to poverty (Proverbs 14:23). Whatever you do, work heartily, as for the Lord and not for men (Colossians 3:23). Do all to the glory of God (1 Corinthians 10:31).

*The work that many people have to do is pretty soul-destroying, and you can hardly blame them if they only see it as a means to an end. But every job has a measure of 'choredom' about it which we would like to bypass if we could. What can make all the difference, and what must have helped Jesus in the carpenter's shop and Paul at his tent-making, is the feeling that we are doing what we have to do for the Lord and not for ourselves – from the heart, as well as with the hands. 'Nothing can be so mean, which with this tincture – For Thy Sake – will not grow bright and clean.' There are three attitudes towards work of any sort. Will it pay? (That is, 'What can I get out of it?') Will it pass? (That is, 'Can I get away with it?') Will it please? If we can get there, we shall be in top gear.*

**Help me, Lord, to do the difficult things with determination, the easy things with thoroughness, and the dull things with cheerfulness. Amen.**

NOVEMBER 13

## "You shall not covet." (Exodus 20:17)

Achan answered Joshua, "Truly I have sinned against the Lord
. . . when I saw among the spoil a beautiful cloak . . . and 200
shekels of silver, and a bar of gold . . . then I coveted them and
took them" (Joshua 7:20–21). David . . . saw from the roof a
woman bathing; and the woman was very beautiful . . . So
David sent messengers and took her, and she came to him, and
he lay with her (2 Samuel 11:2, 4). Then . . . Judas Iscariot went
to the chief priests and said, "What will you give me if I deliver him over to you?" And they paid him thirty pieces of
silver (Matthew 26:14–15). And Jesus said to them, "Take care,
and be on your guard against all covetousness, for one's life
does not consist in the abundance of his possessions" (Luke
12:15).

*Covetousness is a sin on its own, because it shows discontent with
what God has done for us, and a greedy desire for more. But what
makes it far worse is that so often it leads to other and more serious
sins. You can see in today's reading how it lead Achan into theft,
David into adultery and Judas into murder. Covetousness is like one
of those diseases which, though serious, can be dealt with. If it is
treated in time all may be well, but it can also have terribly serious
complications – and if these set in, then there is real trouble. If you
find the egg of a poisonous snake you don't turn it over and warm it
– you turn it out at once. That is how we must deal with covetousness. It must be strangled at birth.*

**Lord, make me content with what I have and save me from
casting greedy eyes on the possessions of others. Amen.**

## "It is more blessed to give than to receive."
## (Acts 20:35)

They still kept bringing Moses freewill offerings every morning, so that all the craftsmen . . . said to Moses, "The people bring much more than enough for doing the work that the Lord has commanded us to do." . . . So the people were restrained from bringing (Exodus 36:3–6). Then the people rejoiced because they had given willingly, for with a whole heart they had offered freely to the Lord (1 Chronicles 29:9). So the disciples determined, everyone according to his ability, to send relief to the brothers living in Judea (Acts 11:29). For they gave according to their means, as I can testify, and beyond their means, of their own free will (2 Corinthians 8:3). Each one must give as he has made up his mind, not reluctantly or under compulsion, for God loves a cheerful giver (2 Corinthians 9:7).

*'The collections have been so generous in recent weeks that I must ask you to offer rather less in future.' Imagine what a stir an announcement of that sort would cause in the average church today! And yet that is exactly what Moses had to say, so generous and wholehearted was the response to his appeal. Christian work depends largely on the generosity of Christian people, and it is up to us all to see what we can do. Giving should be cheerful, and indeed it will be if we remember what Jesus said – that giving is a happier experience than getting. Giving should be regular, because we are so fickle that unless we have some sort of rule we may 'forget' altogether. Giving should be intelligent, because there are all sorts of ways in which charities can benefit from tax concessions, and we want to make the best possible use of these.*

**Lord, show me what sort of work I ought to support, how much I should give, and how I can do so to the best possible advantage. Amen.**

**Truly God has listened; he has attended to the voice of my prayer. (Psalm 66:19)**

"To the Lord our God belong mercy and forgiveness, for we have rebelled against him and have not obeyed the voice of the Lord our God by walking in his laws, which he set before us . . . We do not present our pleas before you because of our righteousness, but because of your great mercy. O Lord, hear; O Lord, forgive (Daniel 9:9–10, 18–19). David blessed the Lord in the presence of all the assembly. And David said: "Blessed are you, O Lord, the God of Israel . . . forever and ever. Yours, O Lord, is the greatness and the power and the glory . . . And now we thank you, our God, and praise your glorious name" (1 Chronicles 29:10–11, 13). "Have regard to the prayer of your servant and to his plea, O Lord my God, listening to the cry and to the prayer that your servant prays before you, that your eyes may be open day and night toward this house" (2 Chronicles 6:19–20).

*These three great prayers of Daniel, David and Solomon are worth reading in full, but the particular extracts have been chosen because each in turn illustrates a valuable part of a framework for our own prayers.* Sorry. *We should begin prayer by asking God to forgive us. There are nearly always some things that come pretty easily to mind – deeds we wish we had not done, words we would like to have left unsaid, and thoughts which were unkind, untrue or impure.* Thanks. *Next we should give thanks for all that He has done for us – for success in some piece of work or game, for finding what we had lost, for friends, health, nature, art and a thousand other things. Especially, of course, we give thanks for God's gift of Jesus Christ to us.* Please. *Finally, we begin to ask for things – but not just for ourselves, for other people as well, and particularly for those in any kind of need or trouble.*

**Forgive, O Lord, what I have been, cleanse what I am, and order what I shall be. Amen.**

## "Tell me all the great things that Elisha has done." (2 Kings 8:4)

One day Elisha went on to Shunem, where a wealthy woman lived, who urged him to eat some food. So whenever he passed that way, he would turn in there to eat food. And she said to her husband, "Behold now, I know that this is a holy man of God who is continually passing our way. Let us make a small room on the roof . . . so that whenever he comes to us, he can go in there." . . . Then . . . [the woman's son] died . . . When Elisha came into the house, he saw the child lying dead on his bed. So he went in . . . and prayed to the Lord. Then he went up and lay on the child . . . And as he stretched himself upon him, the flesh of the child became warm. Then . . . the child sneezed seven times, and the child opened his eyes . . . And when she came to him, he said, "Pick up your son." She came and fell at his feet, bowing to the ground. Then she picked up her son and went out (2 Kings 4:8–10, 20, 32–37).

*Elijah and his successor Elisha form an interesting contrast. Elijah's ministry was largely in public while Elisha's was in private, with individuals rather than with crowds. Elijah was a man of great power; Elisha was a man of great influence. Elijah was like the sea, majestic in its strength; Elisha was more like a peaceful river 'which to the sleeping wood all night singeth a quiet tune'. He was a* spiritual *man, and the Shunammite woman quickly recognized a true man of God. She welcomed him into her home, and we can believe that much prayer went on in that little 'prophet's chamber'. He was also a* practical *man who took immediate and sensible action – not only on this, but on many other occasions as well. He sets a fine example. Every Christian needs a good 'Aerial' and a good 'Earth'. Make sure you have both.*

Thank You, Lord, for men like Elijah and Elisha, for the hurricane and the breeze, the strong and the gentle. Amen.

**And my God will supply every need of yours according to his riches in glory in Christ Jesus. (Philippians 4:19)**

You know the grace of our Lord Jesus Christ, that though he was rich, yet for your sake he became poor, so that you by his poverty might become rich (2 Corinthians 8:9). As poor, yet making many rich (2 Corinthians 6:10). In him we have redemption through his blood, the forgiveness of our trespasses, according to the riches of his grace, which he lavished upon us (Ephesians 1:7–8). That you may know what is the hope to which he has called you, what are the riches of his glorious inheritance in the saints, and what is the immeasurable greatness of his power toward us who believe, according to the working of his great might that he worked in Christ when he raised him from the dead (Ephesians 1:18–20). To me, though I am the very least of all the saints, this grace was given, to preach . . . the unsearchable riches of Christ (Ephesians 3:8). To make known how great . . . are the riches of the glory of this mystery, which is Christ in you (Colossians 1:27).

*We have here a picture of an immensely wealthy man deliberately and completely impoverishing Himself in order to help those in desperate need. He uses His wealth first to cancel the great debts that have mounted up against them. It is said that the inhabitants of Domremy, where Joan of Arc was born, were for some years after her death excused all their taxes. Bills were returned with the words, 'Cancelled for the sake of the Maid'. In the same way our debts have been forgiven 'for the sake of Christ'. Secondly, His wealth provides an income on which we can prosper spiritually for the rest of our lives. His presence in our hearts and His power available for our use will meet 'every need of ours'.*

**Thank You, Lord, for remembering me in Your will. I am grateful that through Your poverty and Your passion You have made me rich for life. Amen.**

**"If anyone hears my voice and opens the door, I will come in to him and eat with him, and he with me." (Revelation 3:20)**

And Jesus said to them, "O foolish ones, and slow of heart to believe all that the prophets have spoken! Was it not necessary that the Christ should suffer these things and enter into his glory?" And beginning with Moses and all the Prophets, he interpreted to them in all the Scriptures the things concerning himself. So they drew near to the village to which they were going. He acted as if he were going farther, but they urged him strongly, saying, "Stay with us, for it is toward evening and the day is now far spent." So he went in to stay with them. When he was at table with them, he took the bread and blessed and broke it and gave it to them. And their eyes were opened, and they recognized him. And he vanished from their sight. They said to each other, "Did not our hearts burn within us while he talked to us on the road, while he opened to us the Scriptures?" (Luke 24:25–32).

*These two people, perhaps man and wife, were walking back from Jerusalem to Emmaus when Jesus joined them. But they did not know who He was and they told Him the sad story of Good Friday. But what a wonderful evening followed!* The open Scriptures. *This must have been the greatest Bible reading of all time: the architect taking you round the cathedral, the composer conducting his own symphony.* The open house. *How glad they must have been that they persuaded Him to stay! He was not going to force His way in. He waited to be invited.* The open eyes. *They had seen Him physically, of course, but now the eyes of their understanding were opened, as when we say 'I see' when a riddle or puzzle is explained to us. Light suddenly dawns. The Christ of the story had become the Christ of their hearts.*

**'Who like Yourself my guide and stay can be? Through cloud and sunshine, Lord, abide with me.' Amen.**

### Remove far from me falsehood and lying. (Proverbs 30:8)

Who shall dwell on your holy hill? He who walks blamelessly and does what is right and speaks truth in his heart (Psalm 15:1–2). Do not lie to one another, seeing that you have put off the old self with its practices (Colossians 3:9). Therefore, having put away falsehood, let each one of you speak the truth with his neighbour, for we are members one of another (Ephesians 4:25). Hear, for I will speak noble things, and from my lips will come what is right, for my mouth will utter truth; wickedness is an abomination to my lips. All the words of my mouth are righteous; there is nothing twisted or crooked in them (Proverbs 8:6–8). Buy truth, and do not sell it (Proverbs 23:23).

*Most of us probably try to avoid telling deliberate lies, but there are more subtle ways in which we can offend in this. Lies have several 'close relations'. We can suppress the truth, so that someone else's lie (perhaps about another person) is allowed to go unchallenged. This can cause as much damage as if we had told the lie ourselves. We are accessories after the fact. We can twist the truth, for sometimes by a slight change of emphasis we can put ourselves in a more favourable light and cast doubt or blame on another. We can exaggerate the truth so that a shower becomes a storm, a broken leg is amputated, and a sick aunt dead and buried. How careful we have to be! Cultivate a great love for the truth and a hatred of falsehood. Never listen to those who say 'And after all what is a lie? 'Tis but the truth in masquerade.' Rubbish!*

**Lord, teach me to speak the truth with my lips and to hate every false way. Amen.**

## Righteousness exalts a nation. (Proverbs 14:34)

"For a long time Israel was without the true God, and without a teaching priest and without law, but when in their distress they turned to the Lord . . . and sought him, he was found by them. In those times there was no peace to him who went out or to him who came in, for great disturbances afflicted all the inhabitants of the lands" (2 Chronicles 15:3–5). In those days . . . Everyone did what was right in his own eyes (Judges 17:6). "Be appalled, O heavens, at this . . . for my people have committed two evils: they have forsaken me, the fountain of living waters, and hewed out cisterns for themselves, broken cisterns that can hold no water . . . Know and see that it is evil and bitter for you to forsake the Lord your God; the fear of me is not in you, declares the Lord God of hosts" (Jeremiah 2:12–13, 19).

*It is considered rather old-fashioned in these days to suggest that prosperity has anything to do with religion, but the obvious fact remains that godliness does breed those very qualities which make individuals and nations prosperous – namely integrity, industry and thrift. Think, for example, of the millions of pounds stolen every year through shoplifting or misusing the national insurance system. If everyone were honest, prices could be lowered and taxes cut at a stroke. But we must remember, too, that God withdraws His favour from an individual and a nation who turn their backs on Him. So, as well as punishing ourselves, we expose ourselves to His judgment if as a nation we do not exalt Him to His rightful place in our midst.*

**Lord, You have blessed our country in past days and made it great. Bless it now, I pray, by turning it back again to obey Your laws and do Your will. Amen.**

## At night his song is with me. (Psalm 42:8)

As a deer pants for flowing streams, so pants my soul for you,
O God. My soul thirsts for God, for the living God. When shall
I come and appear before God? My tears have been my food
day and night, while they say to me continually, "Where is
your God?" . . . I say to God, my rock: "Why have you forgotten me? Why do I go mourning because of the oppression of
the enemy?" As with a deadly wound in my bones, my adversaries taunt me, while they say to me continually, "Where is
your God?" Why are you cast down, O my soul, and why are
you in turmoil within me? Hope in God; for I shall again
praise him, my salvation and my God (Psalm 42:1–3, 9–11).

*There are times in the life of every Christian when our feelings are
matched by the mood expressed in this psalm. 'Where is your
God?' Why doesn't He intervene and do something to arrest the mad
rush of the world towards disaster? The answer is that He has done
something. He has sent His Son to die for our sins, and if people
would only turn to Him then the world could be put right. The ball
is firmly in our own court. 'Why have you forgotten me?' Of
course He has not forgotten, though at times it seems that we don't
hear from Him. But this is where faith comes in. He wants us to trust
Him and His promises – even when we cannot see the answers, and
even when at times He seems to be silent. The psalmist found that
praise was a very good antidote to doubt. Try it and see.*

**Lord, I thank You that though it may not always seem so,
You are in complete control of events. Help me to remember
that nothing can thwart Your ultimate purpose for the world.
Amen.**

## Blessed is the one who considers the poor! (Psalm 41:1)

If a man wearing . . . fine clothing comes into your assembly, and a poor man in shabby clothing also comes in, and if you pay attention to the one who wears the fine clothing and say, "You sit here in a good place," while you say to the poor man, "You stand over there." . . . have you not then made distinctions among yourselves and become judges with evil thoughts? . . . You have dishonoured the poor (James 2:2–4, 6). The poor is disliked even by his neighbour, but the rich has many friends . . . blessed is he who is generous to the poor . . . Whoever oppresses a poor man insults his Maker, but he who is generous to the needy honours him (Proverbs 14:20–21, 31). If anyone has the world's goods and sees his brother in need, yet closes his heart against him, how does God's love abide in him? (1 John 3:17)

*If we were to ask the very poor what sort of treatment they would like to receive from the Christian church, I think the answer might surprise us. I don't think they would ask for hampers at Christmas time, free food or even, in the first instance, for money. I think they would ask for two things. Respect. After all, they are God's creatures too. They have human dignity, and to discriminate against them is to insult their Maker. Justice. They don't want charity but a fair opportunity in life that will give them the chance to save and to provide for themselves and their children. There is much less real poverty in this country than there was before the last war, largely thanks to the welfare state. It is perhaps to the two-thirds world that we ought now to apply our thinking on this subject.*

**Lord, help me to do what I can to help those in need and give me genuine respect for them. May justice reach them in increasing measure. Amen.**

## "Behold, the Lamb of God, who takes away the sin of the world!" (John 1:29)

God tested Abraham and said to him . . . "Take your son, your only son Isaac, whom you love, and go to the land of Moriah, and offer him there as a burnt offering . . ." So Abraham . . . arose and went to the place of which God had told him . . . And Isaac said to his father . . . "Behold, the fire and the wood, but where is the lamb for a burnt offering?" Abraham said, "God will provide for himself the lamb . . ." So they went both of them together. When they came to the place . . . Abraham built the altar there and laid the wood in order and bound Isaac . . . and laid him on the altar . . . Then Abraham . . . took the knife to slaughter his son. But the angel of the Lord called to him . . . "Do not lay your hand on the boy . . . for now I know that you fear God, seeing you have not withheld your son, your only son, from me." And Abraham . . . looked, and behold, behind him was a ram, caught in a thicket . . . And Abraham . . . offered it up . . . instead of his son (Genesis 22:1–3, 7–13).

*This story is important for two reasons. First, it gives us a picture of the cross. Just as the ram was substituted for Isaac and died instead of him, so Jesus Christ the Lamb of God took our place upon the cross so that we could be ransomed and forgiven. It is also a lesson in obedience. Imagine Abraham's thoughts as they walked towards Moriah. God seemed to be taking back the very thing He had given. What a contradiction! Yet Abraham obeyed without delay and without discussion. Sometimes God treats us like that. He points to a very special treasure – a possession, a hobby, an ambition, a boy (or a girl) friend – and He says, 'Would you be willing to do without that if I felt it was best for you that you should?' Let us be careful not to say, 'Lord, anything but that: Jacob and Esau, Lord, but please not Isaac'.*

**Not my will, O Lord, but Yours be done. Amen.**

## Let the favour of the Lord our God be upon us. (Psalm 90:17)

The Lord is my light and my salvation; whom shall I fear? The Lord is the stronghold of my life; of whom shall I be afraid? . . . One thing have I asked of the Lord, that will I seek after: that I may dwell in the house of the Lord all the days of my life, to gaze upon the beauty of the Lord and to inquire in his temple. For he will hide me in his shelter in the day of trouble; he will conceal me under the cover of his tent; he will lift me high upon a rock . . . Hear, O Lord, when I cry aloud; be gracious to me and answer me! You have said, "Seek my face." My heart says to you, "Your face, Lord, do I seek." . . . I believe that I shall look upon the goodness of the Lord in the land of the living! Wait for the Lord; be strong, and let your heart take courage; wait for the Lord! (Psalm 27:1, 4–5, 7–8, 13–14)

*Notice the 'one thing' which David made his ambition – 'to gaze upon the beauty of the Lord.' An artist once used to keep a number of highly coloured stones on a shelf in his studio. There was a ruby, an emerald, a sapphire and others. When asked why he did it, he said that after working all day long at his canvas with mixed colours he lost his sense of colour. So he would restore it by feasting his eyes upon the perfect standard set by the stones. We, too, are at work on the canvas of our lives, and it does us good to think of Jesus from time to time and consider His humility, kindness, courage, patience and peace. In this way we grow like Him. To us all He says, 'Seek my face'. Give yourself time to do this. 'Wait for the Lord!'*

**Help me, Lord, to seek Your face and to learn Your will for my life in what You reveal. Amen.**

## He satisfies the longing soul. (Psalm 107:9)

"Why do you spend your money for that which is not bread, and your labour for that which does not satisfy? Listen diligently to me, and eat what is good" (Isaiah 55:2). Jesus said to them, "I am the bread of life; whoever comes to me shall not hunger, and whoever believes in me shall never thirst" (John 6:35). Jesus said to them, "My food is to do the will of him who sent me and to accomplish his work" (John 4:34). How sweet are your words to my taste, sweeter than honey to my mouth! (Psalm 119:103) "And the Lord will guide you continually and satisfy your desire in scorched places and make your bones strong; and you shall be like a watered garden, like a spring of water, whose waters do not fail" (Isaiah 58:11). "My people shall be satisfied with my goodness, declares the Lord" (Jeremiah 31:14).

*The Christian's motto in life must never be 'satisfied', but rather 'He satisfies'. How can we be 'satisfied' 'with so much unattained, so many peaks unconquered yet, and heights we have not gained?' There ought to be a sort of restlessness about each of us as Christians, as we strive forward to what we have not yet reached. But the fact that 'He satisfies' is a wonderful truth. To know Christ is to have an unending spiritual supply of bread and water, meat and honey. So many people today are looking for satisfaction in things that can never give it, however much they may tickle our fancy for a time. 'Solid joys and lasting pleasures none but Zion's children know'. To 'feed on Christ in our hearts by faith' is the one sure source of permanent joy and peace.*

**Thank You, Lord, that those who seek You shall not lack any good thing. Amen.**

## "What do you think about the Christ?" (Matthew 22:42)

Jesus asked them, "Who do the crowds say that I am?" (Luke 9:18). Andrew first found his own brother Simon and said to him, "We have found the Messiah" (which means Christ) (John 1:41). The woman . . . went away into town and said to the people, "Come, see a man who told me all that I ever did. Can this be the Christ?" (John 4:28–29) When the centurion and those who were with him, keeping watch over Jesus, saw the earthquake and what took place, they were filled with awe and said, "Truly this was the Son of God!" (Matthew 27:54) Thomas answered him, "My Lord and my God!" (John 20:28) Simon Peter replied, "You are the Christ, the Son of the living God" (Matthew 16:16). Now Jesus did many other signs in the presence of the disciples, which are not written in this book; but these are written so that you may believe that Jesus is the Christ, the Son of God, and that by believing you may have life in his name (John 20:30–31).

*Gradually it began to dawn upon those who met Jesus that He was not just an ordinary man, not even some kind of superhuman being, but the Son of God Himself. The claims He made to be equal with God, the miracles He performed, His sinless life and the authority of His teaching – all these things combined to bring out the sort of answers we have just read to His tremendous question. Like so many other great truths in our religion, this is not one we shall ever fully understand with our minds. But, just as a person's reach exceeds his grasp, so we can touch by faith what we cannot always grip with our intellect. It is a case of 'Credo ut intellegam' – 'I believe so that I may understand'.*

**Lord, I do believe, and I ask that as I do so You will give me a clearer understanding of these great things. Amen.**

## Multitudes, multitudes, in the valley of decision! (Joel 3:14)

"Then what shall I do with Jesus who is called Christ?" (Matthew 27:22) Now when they heard of the resurrection of the dead, some mocked. But others said, "We will hear you again about this." . . . But some men joined him and believed (Acts 17:32, 34). And as Paul reasoned about righteousness and self-control and the coming judgment, Felix was alarmed and said, "Go away for the present. When I get an opportunity I will summon you" (Acts 24:25). Jesus said to him, ". . . Go, sell what you possess and come, follow me." When the young man heard this he went away sorrowful, for he had great possessions (Matthew 19:21–22). Jesus . . . saw a tax collector named Levi, sitting at the tax booth. And he said to him, "Follow me." And leaving everything, he rose and followed him (Luke 5:27–28). "How long will you go limping between two different opinions? If the Lord is God, follow him" (1 Kings 18:21). "I have set before you life and death . . . Therefore choose life" (Deuteronomy 30:19).

*Yesterday we considered an intellectual question, today we ask a very practical one. In any important decision there are three stages in arriving at a result. First,* the alternatives. *What can we do? We can reject Him or receive Him. There is no tenable middle ground, no position of friendly neutrality. Not to ask Him into our lives is to leave Him outside. Second, there are* the arguments. *What should we do? Our own great need and His great love surely outweigh any argument on the other side about the difficulties and the cost. Finally, there is* the answer. *What will we do? He waits for us to lift the latch, turn the handle and open the door. He will not force His way in. It is up to us to invite Him, if we really want Him.*

'Dear Saviour, I have nought to plead, in earth below or heaven above, but only my exceeding need and Your exceeding love.' Amen.

## The hope laid up for you in heaven.
### (Colossians 1:5)

Blessed be the God and Father of our Lord Jesus Christ! According to his great mercy, he has caused us to be born again to a living hope through the resurrection of Jesus Christ from the dead, to an inheritance that is imperishable, undefiled, and unfading, kept in heaven for you (1 Peter 1:3–4). We have this as a sure and steadfast anchor of the soul, a hope that enters into the inner place behind the curtain (Hebrews 6:19). Now hope that is seen is not hope. For who hopes for what he sees? But if we hope for what we do not see, we wait for it with patience (Romans 8:24–25). May the God of hope fill you with all joy and peace in believing, so that by the power of the Holy Spirit you may abound in hope (Romans 15:13). Christ in you, the hope of glory (Colossians 1:27).

*The word 'hope', as it is used in the New Testament, is not a kind of vague optimism about the future, as when we say, 'I hope it will be fine tomorrow'. It is something much more positive (almost 'material') than that. It is a confidence about the future outcome which is based upon the promises of God and the presence of Christ in our hearts – 'Christ in you, the hope of glory'. We might compare it to the deposit which is paid when you are trying to sell a house. You know that the purchaser would only have parted with that ten percent of the full price if he or she had every intention of paying in full when the time came. Or again, changing the metaphor, it is like the anchor which attaches us firmly to a future life. Hope is a twin sister to faith.*

I thank You, Lord, that I can look forward with such complete confidence and hope, because I know whom I have believed. Amen.

**"My master is delayed in coming." (Luke 12:45)**

Knowing this first of all, that scoffers will come in the last days
. . . They will say, "Where is the promise of his coming? For
. . . all things are continuing as they were from the beginning
of creation." . . . But do not overlook this one fact, beloved, that
with the Lord one day is as a thousand years, and a thousand
years as one day. The Lord is not slow to fulfil his promise as
some count slowness . . . But the day of the Lord will come like
a thief . . . and the earth and the works that are done on it will
be exposed. Since all these things are thus to be dissolved,
what sort of people ought you to be in lives of holiness and
godliness, waiting for and hastening the coming of the day of
God (2 Peter 3:3–4, 8–12).

*Imagine a mediaeval castle whose wealthy owner has gone away for
a long time. Quickly his servants fall into two groups. The foolish.
'There's no sign of his return,' they say. 'Perhaps he doesn't intend
to come back at all. Let's forget about him and take over the castle for
ourselves.' You can imagine their dismay when one day the lord does
return, and they meet face-to-face the man they have wronged so
badly. The faithful. 'But he said he would return, and he has never
broken his word before. In any case, he probably looks at time differently from us. Let us get on with what he has asked us to do.' How
gladly and unashamedly they will greet their master when he finally
returns! We ought to ask ourselves which group we belong to – the
shirkers or the workers?*

**I thank You, Lord, that You have said, 'I will come again.' I
ask that I may be ready to greet You without fear or shame
on Your return. Amen.**

## While walking . . . Jesus saw . . . Andrew.
## (Matthew 4:18)

Andrew . . . first found his own brother Simon and said to him, "We have found the Messiah" . . . He brought him to Jesus (John 1:40–42). "Follow me, and I will make you fishers of men" (Matthew 4:19). One of his disciples, Andrew . . . said to him, "There is a boy here who has five barley loaves and two fish, but what are they for so many?" Jesus said, "Have the people sit down." . . . Jesus then took the loaves, and . . . distributed them . . . So also the fish (John 6:8–11). And they all ate and were satisfied (Matthew 14:20). "With man this is impossible, but with God all things are possible" (Matthew 19:26). Some Greeks . . . came to Philip . . . and asked him, "Sir, we wish to see Jesus." Philip went and told Andrew; Andrew and Philip went and told Jesus (John 12:20–22). Servants through whom you believed . . . For we are God's fellow workers (1 Corinthians 3:5, 9).

*Andrew was never quite in the front rank of disciples. He was always a little overshadowed by his lively and impetuous elder brother, Simon Peter, whom he brought to Jesus in the first place and to whom he was always happy to play second fiddle. And that is the first thing I like about Andrew. He didn't push himself forward. He was quite content to be what he was. And what a useful person he was! Three times he formed vital links between Jesus and someone else – with Peter; with the boy with the packed lunch; and with the Greek visitors. Each time it was Andrew who made the introduction. He may not have been a great public speaker, like Peter, but he knew how to work in private. No doubt there were many who thanked God that they had met Andrew. Perhaps God is calling you to be a link.* Don't be a missing link!

**Lord, show me if there are others who may be waiting for me to introduce them to You. Give me the wisdom and courage I need. Amen.**

**For his invisible attributes, namely, his eternal power and divine nature, have been clearly perceived, ever since the creation of the world, in the things that have been made. (Romans 1:20)**

The heavens declare the glory of God, and the sky above proclaims his handiwork. Day to day pours out speech, and night to night reveals knowledge. There is no speech, nor are there words, whose voice is not heard. Their measuring line goes out through all the earth, and their words to the end of the world . . . The law of the Lord is perfect, reviving the soul; the testimony of the Lord is sure, making wise the simple; the precepts of the Lord are right, rejoicing the heart; the commandment of the Lord is pure, enlightening the eyes; the fear of the Lord is clean, enduring forever; the rules of the Lord are true, and righteous altogether. More to be desired are they than gold, even much fine gold; sweeter also than honey and drippings of the honeycomb. Moreover, by them is your servant warned; in keeping them there is great reward (Psalm 19:1–4, 7–11).

*In this psalm it is rather as though God were taking us round His studio and His library, showing us first His works and then His words. The studio. Wherever we look in nature we see God's handiwork. The mountains are His sculpture, the sunset His painting, the sea and the wind His poetry, and the song of the birds His music. How we should praise Him for such a magnificent exhibition! The library. We learn much from what a person has made – about their wisdom, power and sense of beauty – but we learn even more from what they have written. And as we read God's Word (variously described as the law, the testimony and so on), we see His holiness and His love. When the psalmist wants a metaphor for the Word of God he thinks of the finest metal and the sweetest food. Gold endures for ever, and honey delights the taste buds.*

**Thank You, Lord, for all I can learn from You in nature and in the Bible. May my study of Your works and words revive my soul and enlighten my eyes. Amen.**

## "The Son of Man." (Luke 19:10)

Jesus . . . was made lower than the angels . . . so that by the grace of God he might taste death for everyone . . . Since therefore the children share in flesh and blood, he himself likewise partook of the same things . . . For surely it is not angels that he helps, but he helps the offspring of Abraham. Therefore he had to be made like his brothers in every respect (Hebrews 2:9, 14, 16–17). For we do not have a high priest who is unable to sympathize with our weaknesses, but one who in every respect has been tempted as we are, yet without sin (Hebrews 4:15). Although he was a son, he learned obedience through what he suffered (Hebrews 5:8). And after fasting forty days and forty nights, he was hungry (Matthew 4:2). And a great windstorm arose . . . But Jesus was in the stern, asleep on the cushion (Mark 4:37–38). Jesus wept (John 11:35). And when he drew near and saw the city, he wept over it (Luke 19:41). After this, Jesus, knowing that all was now finished, said . . . "I thirst." . . . And he bowed his head and gave up his spirit (John 19:28, 30).

*The price required to set us free from sin had to be paid by a fellow human being, but it could only be paid by God. Therefore God became man in the person of Jesus Christ. Jesus was not just God disguised as man or masquerading as man – He really did take upon Himself our human nature. Physically, He knew what it was to be tired, hungry and thirsty. And He knew what it was to die. Emotionally, He was able to sympathize with our weaknesses. He was moved with compassion and indignation, He rejoiced and He wept. Morally, too, He faced temptation but lived a life of discipline and obedience to His Father.*

**O Lord Jesus, You know what it is to be human, and You have experienced all that we experience. Thank You that You know all about us and still love us. Amen.**

### The whole world lies in the power of the evil one. (1 John 5:19)

If our gospel is veiled, it is veiled only to those who are perishing. In their case the god of this world has blinded the minds of the unbelievers, to keep them from seeing the light of the gospel of the glory of Christ (2 Corinthians 4:3–4). Separated from Christ . . . having no hope and without God in the world (Ephesians 2:12). Alienated and hostile in mind (Colossians 1:21). Enemies of the cross of Christ (Philippians 3:18). Far off (Ephesians 2:13). Dead in the trespasses and sins (Ephesians 2:1). "Whoever does not believe is condemned already, because he has not believed in the name of the only Son of God. And this is the judgment: the light has come into the world, and people loved the darkness rather than the light because their deeds were evil" (John 3:18–19).

*When we divide people up in our minds we are apt to do so horizontally – by floors, as it were. On the top floor we put the very good people we call 'saints'. Those are the ones who are trying as hard as they can to qualify for halos. On the next floor down we put the ordinary, decent citizens and on the ground floor the people whose existence we accept without very much enthusiasm. In the basement we place the drop-outs and misfits of society. But God divides people vertically – by doors. With Him there are really only two types of people – the lost and the found, the enemies and the friends, the condemned and the pardoned. His question is not 'Which floor are you living on?' but 'Which side of the door are you?'*

**Lord, show me the deadly nature of sin and remind me of the great need people have if they do not know You. Amen.**

## The word of the Lord remains forever.
## (1 Peter 1:25)

The word of God is living and active (Hebrews 4:12). "For as the rain and the snow come down from heaven and do not return there but water the earth, making it bring forth and sprout, giving seed to the sower and bread to the eater, so shall my word be that goes out from my mouth; it shall not return to me empty, but it shall accomplish that which I purpose, and shall succeed in the thing for which I sent it" (Isaiah 55:10–11). You have been born again, not of perishable seed but of imperishable, through the living and abiding word of God (1 Peter 1:23). The words of the Lord are pure words, like silver refined in a furnace on the ground, purified seven times (Psalm 12:6). How can a young man keep his way pure? By guarding it according to your word (Psalm 119:9). I have stored up your word in my heart, that I might not sin against you (Psalm 119:11).

*Stanley Baldwin, a former prime minister, once compared the Bible to high explosive because wherever it goes in the world it 'startles' people into a new faith and a new life. You can measure the power of high explosive, but you cannot measure the power of this book. Through its influence countless people owe more than they can ever say to its effect on their hearts and minds. But it does more than that, because those who read it find that it helps them to live a life which is pleasing to God. It has been said that 'Sin keeps people from the Bible or the Bible keeps people from sin'. Have you become a daily reader of the Bible yet? Let it be your 'Daily Mail', when God speaks to you about Himself and shows you His love and wisdom. Let it also be your 'Daily Mirror', when He speaks to you about yourself, warning and guiding you aright.*

**Lord, may the Bible become increasingly precious to me, and may its power and its purity influence me day by day. Amen.**

## "Can a man be profitable to God?" (Job 22:2)

Every way of a man is right in his own eyes, but the Lord weighs the heart (Proverbs 21:2). There are those who are clean in their own eyes but are not washed of their filth (Proverbs 30:12). Jesus also told this parable to some who trusted in themselves that they were righteous, and treated others with contempt: "Two men went up into the temple to pray, one a Pharisee and the other a tax collector. The Pharisee, standing by himself, prayed thus: 'God, I thank you that I am not like other men . . . or even like this tax collector" (Luke 18:9–11). Jesus said to them, "You are those who justify yourselves before men, but God knows your hearts" (Luke 16:15). "You say, I am rich, I have prospered, and I need nothing, not realizing that you are wretched, pitiable, poor, blind, and naked" (Revelation 3:17). All our righteous deeds are like a polluted garment (Isaiah 64:6). That I may . . . be found in Christ, not having a righteousness of my own . . . but . . . the righteousness from God that depends on faith (Philippians 3:8–9).

*I remember once seeing from my study window a chimney sweep standing in the road below in thick snow. He looked wretched, pitiable and poor. But later that day I was walking down the same street and I drew out of my pocket a clean handkerchief. Against the dazzling whiteness of the snow it too looked like a wretched, pitiable object. We are so apt to compare ourselves with each other. Just because we appear more respectable and righteous than some we suppose that God is more pleased with us than He is with them. But this is not so. He looks at the heart, and He sees that all have fallen short of his perfect standard. A 'fault' at tennis only has to be an inch over the line. To miss by a mile is no worse in the eyes of the umpire. God cannot accept us in our own 'clothes', but only in the 'uniform' of His righteousness.*

**Lord, save me from thinking that I am better than others and any less in need than they are of Your forgiveness and righteousness. Amen.**

## We were eyewitnesses of his majesty.
## (2 Peter 1:16)

Jesus took with him Peter and John and James and went up on the mountain to pray. And as he was praying, the appearance of his face was altered, and his clothing became dazzling white. And behold, two men were talking with him, Moses and Elijah, who appeared in glory and spoke of his departure, which he was about to accomplish at Jerusalem . . . A cloud came and overshadowed them, and they were afraid as they entered the cloud. And a voice came out of the cloud, saying, "This is my Son, my Chosen One; listen to him!" And when the voice had spoken, Jesus was found alone. And they kept silent and told no one in those days anything of what they had seen (Luke 9:28–31, 34–36).

*Peter, James and John were like three people who suddenly discovered that their friend was the son of a king and the heir to vast estates – a person to whom even the most famous people paid homage.* The vision. *Perhaps they were allowed this glimpse of His majesty, even if they did not understand it all, so that their faith would be strengthened for the dark days ahead. Now and then God does give us these 'mountain-top' experiences – sometimes it is a conference or perhaps a meeting. Make the most of them, but don't rely too heavily upon them.* The visitors. *Moses stood for the Law and Elijah for the Prophets, and they had come to talk to Jesus not about His teaching or miracles, but about His death. The word really means 'exodus' – for His departure was to be a triumph, not a tragedy.* The voice. *Was it all just 'a waking dream'? God Himself spoke to confirm it all, reminding them of the sovereignty of Jesus.*

**Grant, O Lord, that what I learn on the mountain may prepare me for what I have to do in the valley. Amen.**

## Zealous for good works. (Titus 2:14)

We are his workmanship, created in Christ Jesus for good works, which God prepared beforehand, that we should walk in them (Ephesians 2:10). Faith by itself, if it does not have works, is dead. But someone will say, "You have faith and I have works." Show me your faith apart from your works, and I will show you my faith by my works . . . Faith apart from works is useless (James 2:17–18, 20). Keep your conduct among the Gentiles honourable, so that . . . they may see your good deeds and glorify God (1 Peter 2:12). "Let your light shine before others, so that they may see your good works and give glory to your Father who is in heaven" (Matthew 5:16). Show yourself in all respects to be a model of good works (Titus 2:7). Equipped for every good work (2 Timothy 3:17). Bearing fruit in every good work (Colossians 1:10).

*Good deeds can never earn our forgiveness, but they can and they should express our gratitude to God. If we have really put our faith in Jesus Christ as our Saviour, then there should be plenty of evidence of the fact in the kind of life we live. If I say to you, 'I trust in Jesus Christ but I still swear, cheat, lie, bully and grumble' it is about as silly as saying, 'I have a marvellous apple tree in my garden, but it never produces any apples.' Good works – that is, lives which are pleasing to God and kind and helpful to others – are the only evidence which will really convince other people that we are true followers of Jesus Christ. But notice that we ourselves do not really produce the good works. They are the fruit of God's presence in our lives. We bear 'fruit in every good work', 'for it is God who works in you both to will and work for his good pleasure' (Philippians 2:13).*

**Lord, You went about doing good. Help me to follow Your example and show by my good deeds that I am Your true disciple. Amen.**

## Making peace by the blood of his cross.
## (Colossians 1:20)

Therefore, since we have been justified by faith, we have peace with God through our Lord Jesus Christ. Through him we have also obtained access by faith into this grace in which we stand, and we rejoice in hope of the glory of God. More than that, we rejoice in our sufferings, knowing that suffering produces endurance, and endurance produces character, and character produces hope, and hope does not put us to shame, because God's love has been poured into our hearts through the Holy Spirit who has been given to us. For while we were still weak, at the right time Christ died for the ungodly. For one will scarcely die for a righteous person – though perhaps for a good person one would dare even to die – but God shows his love for us in that while we were still sinners, Christ died for us (Romans 5:1–8).

*I wonder whether from previous readings and comments you now know the meaning of some of the technical words used today – 'justified', 'grace', 'peace', 'glory'. Why not test yourself out by seeing if you can write down a clear, one-sentence definition of each? Notice three other familiar words – faith, hope and love. Think of a gift someone purchased for you at a store and left for you to collect. Love is what bought that gift, perhaps at very great cost. Faith is what claims that gift, when you go and ask in person for what has been paid for and put aside for you. Hope is what enjoys that gift, as you carry it home and look forward to the time – perhaps still some way in the future – when you can put it to the fullest possible use.*

**Thank You, Lord, for the salvation You have made possible for me. Stir up in my heart an answering love for all Your goodness to me. Amen.**

### Making the best use of the time.
### (Ephesians 5:16)

For everything there is a season, and a time for every matter under heaven: a time to be born, and a time to die; a time to plant, and a time to pluck up what is planted . . . a time to weep, and a time to laugh . . . a time to tear, and a time to sew; a time to keep silence, and a time to speak; a time to love, and a time to hate; a time for war, and a time for peace (Ecclesiastes 3:1–2, 4, 7–8). It is in vain that you rise up early and go late to rest, eating the bread of anxious toil; for he gives to his beloved sleep (Psalm 127:2). So teach us to number our days that we may get a heart of wisdom (Psalm 90:12). Look carefully then how you walk, not as unwise but as wise, making the best use of the time, because the days are evil (Ephesians 5:15–16). My times are in your hand (Psalm 31:15). "As your days, so shall your strength be" (Deuteronomy 33:25). Commit your work to the Lord, and your plans will be established (Proverbs 16:3).

*In their use of time, Christians have to try to keep a sensible balance. On the one hand we must not be slack and lose the opportunities God gives us of doing good. But on the other hand we must not be so feverishly occupied that our family life is threatened, our health is undermined or we become a bore to our friends. Jesus got this balance perfectly. He always seemed at leisure for people who wanted to see Him, yet He was always busy. He loved being amongst people but He also knew the value of solitude. Paul, too, had the same balance. He lived each day as if it were his last, ready at any time to meet his Master. But he worked as if he had a reasonable expectation of life as he planned ahead and looked forward.*

O Lord, please take control of my life today so that I only do and say what You want me to. Amen.

"Remember the Sabbath day, to keep it holy . . .
On it you shall not do any work."
(Exodus 20:8, 10)

One Sabbath . . . Jesus' disciples began to pluck heads of grain.
And the Pharisees were saying to him, "Look, why are they
doing what is not lawful on the Sabbath?" . . . And he said to
them, "The Sabbath was made for man, not man for the Sabbath.
So the Son of Man is lord even of the Sabbath" (Mark 2:23–24,
27–28). Again he entered the synagogue, and a man was there
with a withered hand. And they watched Jesus, to see whether
he would heal him on the Sabbath . . . And he said to them, "Is it
lawful on the Sabbath to do good or to do harm, to save life or to
kill?" But they were silent (Mark 3:1–2, 4). "If you turn back your
foot from the Sabbath, from doing your pleasure on my holy day
. . . then you shall take delight in the Lord" (Isaiah 58:13–14). As
was his custom, Jesus went to the synagogue on the Sabbath day
(Luke 4:16). Not neglecting to meet together, as is the habit of
some (Hebrews 10:25). On the Sabbath they rested according to
the commandment (Luke 23:56).

*How should Christians, who are free to plan their own time, try to
spend Sunday? Three things seem to emerge from these verses.*
Church. *We ought to try to get to church at least once. Not only do we
need the help a really lively service can give, but our presence there will
also be an encouragement to others.* Rest. *It is sad if Sunday has to be
spent tackling work which we have brought back from the office or from
school – nor will it pay us in the long run, because we shall return to
our desks on Monday stale and tired.* Service. *These Pharisees tried to
insinuate that any sort of work was wrong, but of course some things
have to be done – and Sundays also provide an opportunity for us to do
something to help others. What about that letter or visit or invitation
which might be a great help to someone we know?*

**Help me, O Lord, to use my Sundays wisely and well. Amen.**

### "I have no pleasure in you, says the Lord."
### (Malachi 1:10)

For you are not a God who delights in wickedness; evil may not dwell with you (Psalm 5:4). Those who are in the flesh cannot please God (Romans 8:8). But my righteous one shall live by faith, and if he shrinks back, my soul has no pleasure in him (Hebrews 10:38). And without faith it is impossible to please him, for whoever would draw near to God must believe that he exists and that he rewards those who seek him (Hebrews 11:6). And so, from the day we heard, we have not ceased to pray for you, asking that you may be filled with the knowledge of his will in all spiritual wisdom and understanding, so as to walk in a manner worthy of the Lord, fully pleasing to him, bearing fruit in every good work and increasing in the knowledge of God (Colossians 1:9–10).

*If you have a friend to stay with you, you are careful to prepare the sort of activities and menu that you know will appeal to him or her. You take note, for example, of the fact that they like coffee for breakfast, that they normally take a bath in the morning and that they are bored by cricket. In this way you hope to make their stay really pleasurable. God also has His likes and dislikes. To practice sin, to make the 'flesh' (our old nature) our standard of conduct, to draw back from our original commitment, and to show lack of faith in His love and power – all these things make Him sad. On the other hand, He will take great pleasure in a life which has deep spiritual roots and the fruits of good living in practice.*

**Lord, help me to please You throughout every day, in all that I do and in all that I say. Amen.**

## Christ, our Passover lamb, has been sacrificed. (1 Corinthians 5:7)

Then Moses called all the elders of Israel and said to them, "Go and select lambs for yourselves according to your clans, and kill the Passover lamb. Take a bunch of hyssop and dip it in the blood that is in the basin, and touch the lintel and the two doorposts with the blood that is in the basin. None of you shall go out of the door of his house until the morning. For the Lord will pass through to strike the Egyptians, and when he sees the blood on the lintel and on the two doorposts, the Lord will pass over the door and will not allow the destroyer to enter your houses to strike you" . . . Then the people of Israel went and did so; as the Lord had commanded Moses and Aaron, so they did (Exodus 12:21–23, 28).

*In this story we have another Old Testament picture of the gospel, Just as there was safety for all those sheltering behind doors marked with the blood of the lamb, so no judgment will fall upon those who have put their trust in Jesus Christ, the Lamb of God who takes away the sin of the world. But it was not enough for them to have a living lamb in their house or garden. The lamb had to be slain. So it is not the example of Jesus or even His teaching which rescues us from sin, but His death. And it was not enough for the lamb to be slain – the blood had to be applied to the door. So it is only when we personally trust in Christ, and apply to our own lives what He has done for us on the cross, that we are saved from the consequences of our sin.*

I thank You, O Lord, for the safety and peace You give to those who trust in Your death for them. Amen.

## To me to live is Christ. (Philippians 1:21)

Whatever gain I had, I counted as loss for the sake of Christ. Indeed, I count everything as loss because of the surpassing worth of knowing Christ Jesus my Lord. For his sake I have suffered the loss of all things and count them as rubbish, in order that I may gain Christ and be found in him . . . Not that I have already obtained this or am already perfect, but I press on to make it my own, because Christ Jesus has made me his own. Brothers . . . one thing I do: forgetting what lies behind and straining forward to what lies ahead, I press on toward the goal for the prize of the upward call of God in Christ Jesus (Philippians 3:7–9, 12–14).

*'All things'. Paul had enjoyed many very great privileges. His birth, his education and his Roman citizenship gave him a tremendous advantage in life. He was a much favoured person and was no doubt envied by many. But when he put all these things on the scales and weighed them against his friendship with Christ, they counted for nothing – mere dust. He was prepared to sacrifice them all if it would help him to know Christ better. 'One thing'. Paul had only one ambition left in life, and that was to follow Christ wherever He might lead and whatever it might cost. Resolutely he put the past behind him, with its successes as well as its failures, and pressed on like a runner who sees the tape stretched out some distance ahead.*

**Lord, give me something of Paul's single-minded determination to run with patience and endurance. Amen.**

## "Let not your hearts be troubled."
## (John 14:1)

"You will hear of wars and rumours of wars . . . For nation will rise against nation, and kingdom against kingdom, and there will be famines and earthquakes in various places" (Matthew 24:6–7). "And there will be . . . distress of nations . . . people fainting with fear and with foreboding of what is coming on the world" (Luke 21:25–26). "In those times there was no peace to him who went out or to him who came in, for great disturbances afflicted all the inhabitants of the lands" (2 Chronicles 15:5). How long will the land mourn? . . . "The whole land is made desolate, but no man lays it to heart" (Jeremiah 12:4, 11). The whole creation has been groaning together in the pains of childbirth until now (Romans 8:22). The righteous will never be moved . . . He is not afraid of bad news; his heart is firm, trusting in the Lord. His heart is steady; he will not be afraid (Psalm 112:6–8). "In me you may have peace. In the world you will have tribulation. But take heart; I have overcome the world" (John 16:33).

*The idea that the world would go on getting better and better until one day it became the kingdom of God on earth was very popular at one time. But two world wars and an almost endless catalogue of trouble ever since have pretty well destroyed that myth, and it can have few supporters today. The Bible has always taken the opposite view – that things will go on deteriorating until we reach a point at which Christ will intervene in power and justice. As Christians, therefore, we ought not to be dismayed by what we read in the newspapers. The peace of God can guard our minds, and we are buoyed up by the sure and certain hope that God has not lost control. He will choose His own perfect moment to deal with the chaos we have made of His world.*

I thank You, Lord, that because You are never surprised by events I need never be dismayed by them. Amen.

## Watching daily at my gates. (Proverbs 8:34)

Blessed be the Lord, who daily bears us up; God is our salvation. Our God is a God of salvation, and to God, the Lord, belong deliverances from death (Psalm 68:19–20). So will I ever sing praises to your name, as I perform my vows (Psalm 61:8). Every day I call upon you, O Lord; I spread out my hands to you (Psalm 88:9). Now these Jews were more noble than those in Thessalonica; they received the word with all eagerness, examining the Scriptures daily to see if these things were so (Acts 17:11). And Jesus said to all, "If anyone would come after me, let him deny himself and take up his cross daily and follow me" (Luke 9:23). I protest, brothers, by my pride in you, which I have in Christ Jesus our Lord, I die every day! (1 Corinthians 15:31)

*A favourite question people ask when they are talking about cars is, 'How thirsty is it?' And one merit of a car these days is low petrol consumption. Sooner or later most Christians find that, if they are to be successful and victorious, they need to be refuelled daily. Every single day we need: times of prayer and Bible reading; to resolve to put Christ first; to determine to take up His cross and be known as one of His disciples. We must resist the temptation to become weekly Christians, depending solely on a Sunday service or meeting and slipping into a trough for the rest of the week. We are not 'eight-day clocks'. We need to be wound up each day.*

**Lord, each new day I give myself to You again, so that I may live today in the way You want me to. Amen.**

## One Lord, one faith. (Ephesians 4:5)

So then you are . . . built on the foundation of the apostles and prophets, Christ Jesus himself being the cornerstone, in whom the whole structure, being joined together, grows into a holy temple in the Lord. In him you also are being built together into a dwelling place for God by the Spirit (Ephesians 2:19–22). There is one body and one Spirit (Ephesians 4:4). We are to grow up in every way into him who is the head, into Christ, from whom the whole body, joined and held together by every joint with which it is equipped, when each part is working properly, makes the body grow so that it builds itself up in love (Ephesians 4:15–16). Husbands, love your wives, as Christ loved the church and gave himself up for her . . . that he might present the church to himself in splendour, without spot or wrinkle or any such thing, that she might be holy and without blemish (Ephesians 5:25, 27).

*In these verses Paul gives us three pictures of the Christian church. It is like a building, whose cornerstone is Christ and in which the Holy Spirit lives. Wherever Christians meet together, Christ Himself promises to be among them (Matthew 18:20). Where they are He is. Second, the church is like a body, because all of its members have different functions – some prominent and some less so. When the whole body is working properly, then it becomes the instrument by which God is able to work in the world to do His will. Third, we see that the church is like a bride, because it is a society of people joined together with Christ in an indissoluble union of love. We might sum it up by saying that the Christian church exists where there is any group of people, great or small, in which Christ lives, through which He works, and by which He is loved and honoured.*

**Lord, help me to be a really worthy member of my church – to make my contribution, to offer my help and to pull my weight. Amen.**

## The Spirit helps us in our weakness.
## (Romans 8:26)

"The Helper, the Holy Spirit, whom the Father will send in my name, he will teach you all things and bring to your remembrance all that I have said to you" (John 14:26). "I still have many things to say to you, but you cannot bear them now. When the Spirit of truth comes, he will guide you into all the truth, for he will not speak on his own authority, but whatever he hears he will speak, and he will declare to you the things that are to come" (John 16:12–13). And the Spirit said to Philip, "Go over and join this chariot." So Philip ran to him and heard him reading Isaiah the prophet and asked, "Do you understand what you are reading?" (Acts 8:29–30). And they went through the region of Phrygia and Galatia, having been forbidden by the Holy Spirit to speak the word in Asia (Acts 16:6). Agabus took Paul's belt and bound his own feet and hands and said, "Thus says the Holy Spirit, 'This is how the Jews at Jerusalem will bind the man who owns this belt'" (Acts 21:11). For all who are led by the Spirit of God are sons of God (Romans 8:14).

*There are two areas in life where we specially need the guidance of the Holy Spirit – in knowing what to believe and deciding how to behave. As we read the Bible thoughtfully and prayerfully, the Holy Spirit will bring to our notice truths which He wants us to understand and believe. It will be rather like having a light switched on inside a city clock – the Spirit and the Word combine to give us the answer. It is more difficult when it comes to knowing what to do. There can be no doubt at all that the Spirit prompts our conscience, our emotions and our will. But young Christians will be wise to check such inner guidance with the advice of older friends and against the way in which God is ordering our circumstances.*

**Lord, make me the sort of person You can guide. May I respond sensitively to Your word. Amen.**

## God with us. (Matthew 1:23)

"But will God indeed dwell on the earth? Behold, heaven and the highest heaven cannot contain you; how much less this house that I have built!" (1 Kings 8:27) Thus says the Lord: "Heaven is my throne, and the earth is my footstool; what is the house that you would build for me, and what is the place of my rest?" (Isaiah 66:1) "Do I not fill heaven and earth? declares the Lord" (Jeremiah 23:24). For thus says the One who is high and lifted up, who inhabits eternity, whose name is Holy: "I dwell in the high and holy place, and also with him who is of a contrite and lowly spirit" (Isaiah 57:15). "Behold, the dwelling place of God is with man. He will dwell with them, and they will be his people" (Revelation 21:3). And the Word became flesh and dwelt among us . . . full of grace and truth (John 1:14). A dwelling place for God by the Spirit (Ephesians 2:22). That Christ may dwell in your hearts through faith (Ephesians 3:17).

*God has, so to speak, three 'residences'. First, he 'inhabits eternity'. This lovely expression conveys the idea of someone of infinite power and wisdom – no building can possibly contain Him and He exceeds all thought and imagination. Second, He 'dwelt among us'. For about thirty-three years this eternal God was seen and known by people on this earth. He limited Himself deliberately in human flesh for the great purpose of redemption. Third, He promises to live by His Spirit 'in the hearts' of His followers everywhere. As the hymn puts it, 'For Thou within no walls confined, inhabitest the humble mind!' God the Father inhabits eternity, God the Son dwelt among us, and God the Holy Spirit lives in our hearts by faith.*

**Lord, I thank You for Your majesty and humility and that You, who inhabit eternity, can dwell also with me. Amen.**

### "My judgment is just." (John 5:30)

"The kingdom of heaven may be compared to a man who sowed good seed in his field, but while his men were sleeping, his enemy came and sowed weeds among the wheat and went away. So when the plants came up and bore grain, then the weeds appeared also. And the servants of the master of the house came and said to him, 'Master, did you not sow good seed in your field? How then does it have weeds?' He said to them, 'An enemy has done this.' So the servants said to him, 'Then do you want us to go and gather them?' But he said, 'No, lest in gathering the weeds you root up the wheat along with them. Let both grow together until the harvest, and at harvest time I will tell the reapers, Gather the weeds first and bind them in bundles to be burned, but gather the wheat into my barn'" (Matthew 13:24–30).

*Sowing seeds in your neighbour's field was a common way of show-ing spite – a modern equivalent might be putting sugar in his petrol tank. Moreover there was a weed called a 'tare' which was a degen-erate form of wheat indistinguishable in the early stages of growth from the real thing. From this parable, which was one of the few that Jesus Himself interpreted, we learn about Satan's malicious desire to spoil God's world by sowing seeds of sin. How hard it is to tell those who conform outwardly to Christian standards from genuine believ-ers. We must be very careful that we 'do not judge by appearances' (John 7:24) and 'do not pronounce judgment before the time' (1 Corinthians 4:5). The unravelling of Satan's work requires more expert hands than ours and must await God's final verdict. But despite their superficial likeness to the wheat, the weeds are funda-mentally different. They belong to a different family; they bear a dif-ferent fruit; and they face a different future.*

**Lord, save me from making hasty judgments about others. Help me instead to make sure of my own relationship with You. Amen.**

## Little children, keep yourselves from idols.
## (1 John 5:21)

Our God is in the heavens; he does all that he pleases. Their idols are silver and gold, the work of human hands. They have mouths, but do not speak; eyes, but do not see. They have ears, but do not hear; noses, but do not smell . . . Those who make them become like them; so do all who trust in them (Psalm 115:3–6, 8). Claiming to be wise, they became fools, and exchanged the glory of the immortal God for images resembling mortal man and birds and animals and reptiles (Romans 1:22–23). What agreement has the temple of God with idols? For we are the temple of the living God . . . "Therefore go out from their midst and be separate" (2 Corinthians 6:16–17). Your faith in God has gone forth everywhere . . . and how you turned to God from idols to serve the living and true God (1 Thessalonians 1:8–9). Delight yourself in the Lord, and he will give you the desires of your heart (Psalm 37:4).

*The idea of carving an image of a bird or beast and falling down to worship it may seem very primitive to our sophisticated western minds (though perhaps it still lingers on in the modern and superstitious use of mascots and talismans). An idol is anything which, as the dictionary puts it, demands 'excessive devotion'. It is any thing or person which usurps the place that God ought to occupy in our hearts and lives and for which, in the last resort, we would be prepared to sacrifice our Christian faith. Many Christians, alas, have 'retired early' because 'at all costs' they have felt they must make money, fulfil an ambition, cling to some interest, marry a certain girl, own a particular house or car. They have 'idolized' these things and Christ has had to take second place. How can we avoid this danger? David has the answer: we need to delight ourselves in the Lord.*

**Lord, give me such love for You and such a strength of purpose that I may guard against the entwining influence of would-be idols. Amen.**

### "O you of little faith, why did you doubt?" (Matthew 14:31)

Now Thomas . . . was not with them when Jesus came. So the other disciples told him, "We have seen the Lord." But he said to them, "Unless I see in his hands the mark of the nails, and place my finger into the mark of the nails, and place my hand into his side, I will never believe." Eight days later, his disciples were inside again, and Thomas was with them. Although the doors were locked, Jesus came and stood among them and said, "Peace be with you." Then he said to Thomas, "Put your finger here, and see my hands; and put out your hand, and place it in my side. Do not disbelieve, but believe." Thomas answered him, "My Lord and my God!" Jesus said to him, "Have you believed because you have seen me? Blessed are those who have not seen and yet have believed" (John 20:24–29).

*Thomas is often presented to us as a fair example of the sceptic – the man who genuinely cannot believe. We may feel some sympathy for him. But you will notice that he did not say 'I cannot believe', but 'I will not believe'. Fundamentally, faith is a matter of the heart and not the head, the will and not the mind. That is not to say that faith is unreasonable – it is not trying to believe what is not true. But it does mean that God can only impart His truth to those who are willing to receive it. He cannot reveal Himself to the stubborn and disobedient heart. Thomas's hardness quickly melted in the presence of Christ, whose reply brought a gentle rebuke to Thomas himself but a wonderful reward to those millions of Christians ever since who have had to learn to walk by faith and not by sight.*

**Lord, give me that faith that Thomas lacked, the faith that rests upon Your promises rather than upon Your physical presence. Amen.**

## The fruit of the Spirit is . . . self-control.
## (Galatians 5:22–23)

I do not run aimlessly; I do not box as one beating the air. But I discipline my body and keep it under control (1 Corinthians 9:26–27). "If your right eye causes you to sin, tear it out and throw it away . . . If your right hand causes you to sin, cut it off . . . It is better that you lose one of your members than that your whole body go into hell" (Matthew 5:29–30). If you have found honey, eat only enough for you, lest you have your fill of it and vomit it (Proverbs 25:16). Be not among drunkards or among gluttonous eaters of meat, for the drunkard and the glutton will come to poverty, and slumber will clothe them with rags (Proverbs 23:20–21). If anyone does not stumble in what he says, he is a perfect man, able also to bridle his whole body (James 3:2). Your cords hang loose; they cannot hold the mast firm in its place or keep the sail spread out (Isaiah 33:23). Walk by the Spirit, and you will not gratify the desires of the flesh (Galatians 5:16). Stopping the indulgence of the flesh (Colossians 2:23).

*Isn't it interesting how human beings, who have learnt to control almost every disease, most animals and many of the forces of nature, have never managed to control themselves? All the cruelty and injustice in the world are really due to the fact that human desires and appetites, passions and lusts, have never been mastered. Think how easily the eye looks where it should not, or the stomach demands more than is good for it! Self-control is the most difficult of all human arts, and perhaps the secret lies in realizing that it can't be 'self-control' at all. It may appear to others that we are 'the king of the castle', but like some weak, mediaeval monarchs we need a 'power behind the throne' – namely Jesus Christ Himself.*

**Lord, I cannot control my desires and appetites unless You in turn control my will. Amen.**

## "I have the keys." (Revelation 1:18)

The people who walked in darkness have seen a great light; those who dwelt in a land of deep darkness, on them has light shined. You have multiplied the nation; you have increased its joy . . . For to us a child is born, to us a son is given; and the government shall be upon his shoulder, and his name shall be called Wonderful Counsellor, Mighty God, Everlasting Father, Prince of Peace. Of the increase of his government and of peace there will be no end, on the throne of David and over his kingdom, to establish it and to uphold it with justice and with righteousness from this time forth and for evermore. The zeal of the Lord of hosts will do this (Isaiah 9:2–3, 6–7).

*How disillusioned we become with political parties at the time of a general election! Their manifestos sound marvellous, but all too often hopes are unfulfilled, promises forgotten and ideals abandoned. Today we read about the Lord's 'election manifesto' for all who will put the 'government on his shoulder' and give Him control of their lives. He promises light for darkness, joy for sorrow, peace, justice and righteousness. You will find those things in the world today just in proportion to the extent to which people and countries accept His sovereignty. The word translated 'government' really means 'key', for the keys of a city were the symbol of authority and control. It is a stimulating thought to remember that if Christ is King, then He has the key to every problem – personal and global.*

**'You hold the key of all unknown, and I am glad: if other hands should hold the key, or if You trusted it to me, I might be sad.' Amen.**

## When the fullness of time had come, God sent forth his Son. (Galatians 4:4)

Now the birth of Jesus Christ took place in this way. When his mother Mary had been betrothed to Joseph, before they came together she was found to be with child from the Holy Spirit. And her husband Joseph, being a just man and unwilling to put her to shame, resolved to divorce her quietly. But as he considered these things . . . an angel of the Lord appeared to him . . . saying, ". . . Do not fear to take Mary as your wife, for that which is conceived in her is from the Holy Spirit. She will bear a son, and you shall call his name Jesus, for he will save his people from their sins." All this took place to fulfil what the Lord had spoken by the prophet: "Behold, the virgin shall conceive and bear a son, and they shall call his name Immanuel" (which means, God with us) . . . Joseph . . . did as the angel of the Lord commanded him: he took his wife, but knew her not until she had given birth to a son. And he called his name Jesus (Matthew 1:18–25).

*Two natures, Jesus was 'Son of Man' and 'Son of God' – human and divine. Because He was 'born of the virgin Mary' He inherited all the usual attributes of human nature. Because He was 'conceived by the Holy Spirit' we know that He inherited a divine nature as well. He was God and man: God manifest in the flesh. Two names. The name 'Jesus' means 'Saviour' (in the Old Testament it was 'Joshua'), and it reminds us of the great purpose of redemption which brought Him into the world. 'Emmanuel' introduced the note of friendship and answered the age-old question, 'Will God indeed dwell with us on the earth?' It was not only to die for us that Jesus came, but also to live with us. His very last words remind us of the precious and permanent nature of that friendship – 'Lo, I am with you always, even to the end of the world.'*

**Lord Jesus, I thank You today for who You are and for what You came to do. Amen.**

## Who made himself nothing. (Philippians 2:7)

And Mary gave birth to her firstborn son and wrapped him in swaddling cloths and laid him in a manger, because there was no place for them in the inn. And . . . there were shepherds out in the field, keeping watch over their flock by night. And an angel of the Lord appeared to them, and the glory of the Lord shone around them, and they were filled with fear. And the angel said to them, "Fear not, for behold, I bring you good news of a great joy . . . For unto you is born this day in the city of David a Saviour, who is Christ the Lord. And this will be a sign for you: you will find a baby wrapped in swaddling cloths and lying in a manger." And suddenly there was with the angel a multitude of the heavenly host praising God and saying, "Glory to God in the highest and on earth peace among those with whom he is pleased!" (Luke 2:7–14).

'When the Lord of glory came unto His own,
There were few to greet Him at His manger throne;
There was no one present Christmas bells to ring;
What a lonely welcome for so great a King!'

*And that loneliness and rejection were to follow Jesus all through His life, for even over the cradle there lay the shadow of a cross. There is a nativity play in which the child Jesus is made to stand in the middle of the stage and an angel approaches him on each side. One offers Him a glorious bouquet of roses and the other a crown of thorns. For a moment the child hesitates. He fingers the petals of the roses, enjoys their fragrance and then, with an almost imperceptible sigh, He takes the crown of thorns. In all our rejoicing today, on the birthday of Jesus, let us never forget the supreme purpose for which He came into this world.*

**Lord, I thank You today for the love that took You all the way from the manger to the cross for me. Amen.**

## A Carol
## for Christmas Day

In a distant country, many years ago
Jesus left His glory for this world below,
Left His Father's presence, left His home of joy,
Came and dwelt amongst us, as a little boy.

When the Lord of glory came unto His own,
There were few to greet Him at His manger throne.
There was no one present Christmas bells to ring;
What a lonely welcome for so great a King!

Sheltered in a stable, cradled in the hay,
Peacefully He slumbered, silently He lay;
Beasts were His companions, cattle sought their rest,
Where His gentle mother held Him to her breast.

Shepherds on the hillside heard the angels sing,
Left their flocks and hastened simple gifts to bring;
Wise men from a distance costly presents brought
From their richest treasures for the King they sought.

I am not a shepherd, nor am I a king,
Yet I want to join them in their offering.
I have no gold or silver, worthy though Thou art;
Take my greatest treasure, Saviour take my heart.

## "Men of good repute, full of the Spirit and of wisdom." (Acts 6:3)

They chose Stephen, a man full of faith and of the Holy Spirit . . . And Stephen, full of grace and power, was doing great wonders and signs among the people (Acts 6:5, 8). And gazing at him, all who sat in the council saw that his face was like the face of an angel (Acts 6:15). They were enraged, and they ground their teeth at him . . . And he said, "Behold, I see the heavens opened, and the Son of Man standing at the right hand of God." . . . Then they cast him out of the city and stoned him. And the witnesses laid down their garments at the feet of a young man named Saul. And as they were stoning Stephen, he called out, "Lord Jesus, receive my spirit." And falling to his knees he cried out with a loud voice, "Lord, do not hold this sin against them." And when he had said this, he fell asleep (Acts 7:54, 56, 58–60).

*Stephen was chosen to be a deacon, to look after the business affairs of the church. It is worth noting what very high spiritual qualities were required for this role. It must never be thought that those who are called to manage the practical side of church life need be less spiritually minded than those chosen for its pastoral work. And it is interesting, too, that the longest sermon in the New Testament was preached by a deacon. Two things about Stephen's life are especially important. His inspiration. The power of his sermon and the calmness with which he faced death sprang from the inspiration of that deep inner faith he had in God. His influence. His enemies 'could not withstand the wisdom and the Spirit with which he was speaking'. And there is no doubt that the intelligent and sensitive young man who was watching was deeply moved in his conscience and brought at last to the point of final surrender by the memory of Stephen's death.*

**Lord, give me what Stephen had – the abiding eloquence of a Christian life. Amen.**

## The disciple whom Jesus loved. (John 19:26)

Jesus saw two . . . brothers, James . . . and John . . . and he called them. Immediately they left the boat and their father and followed him (Matthew 4:21–22). James . . . and John . . . (whom he gave the name Boanerges, that is, Sons of Thunder) (Mark 3:17). The people did not receive him . . . And when his disciples James and John saw it, they said, "Lord, do you want us to tell fire to come down from heaven and consume them?" But he turned and rebuked them (Luke 9:53–55). When Jesus saw his mother and the disciple whom he loved standing nearby, he said to his mother, "Woman, behold, your son!" Then he said to the disciple, "Behold, your mother!" And from that hour the disciple took her to his own home (John 19:26–27). I, John, your brother and partner in the tribulation . . . was on the island called Patmos on account of the word of God and the testimony of Jesus (Revelation 1:9).

*I have a copy of Augustus John's* The Disciple *which I always take to depict St John. It shows a beautiful, sensitive, refined face, and yet I cannot believe that John (at first anyway) was like that. He was ambitious and vindictive, and Jesus gave the nickname 'Sons of Thunder' – or, as we might say, 'Thunderbolts' – to John and his brother James. And yet this was the man to whom Jesus entrusted His mother, and who later suffered exile for His sake – the disciple always referred to as the one Jesus loved. What is the explanation? Perhaps John yielded himself more completely than the others to Jesus' influence and so saw further into His heart and mind. 'How do you know when the gold is refined?' an old Indian gold-refiner was asked. 'When I can see my face in it', was his reply. Maybe Jesus saw more of Himself in John than He did in the others.*

**Lord, I ask that the beauty of Jesus, His grace, wisdom and love, may be seen in me. Amen.**

## The Father has sent his Son to be the Saviour of the world. (1 John 4:14)

In the beginning was the Word, and the Word was with God, and the Word was God. He was in the beginning with God. All things were made through him, and without him was not any thing made that was made. In him was life, and the life was the light of men. The light shines in the darkness, and the darkness has not overcome it . . . He came to his own, and his own people did not receive him. But to all who did receive him, who believed in his name, he gave the right to become children of God, who were born, not of blood nor of the will of the flesh nor of the will of man, but of God. And the Word became flesh and dwelt among us, and we have seen his glory, glory as of the only Son from the Father, full of grace and truth (John 1:1–5, 11–14).

*Someone has said that 'Jesus became what we are in order that we might become what He is'. Can you see how the truth of that is borne out in today's reading?* The Word became flesh. *Suppose you were an all-powerful 'god' who had created a race of beings called 'Nomans' who rebelled against you, defied your laws and killed your agents. What would you do? Leave them to drift into eternal misery? Reduce them to a cinder? Or would you, as a last desperate measure, come among them, assume their 'Nomanity' and try even at the cost of infinite sacrifice to restore them to yourself? That is what our God did for us 'Humans'.* To become children of God. *Those who respond to the claims of Christ and who receive Him as their Saviour are brought into a relationship with God which can be brought about in no other way. It does not come through inheritance or any effort on our own or anyone else's part. It is a relationship which is spiritual (not physical), personal and eternal.*

**Thank You, Lord, for becoming the Son of man so that we might become the sons and daughters of God. Amen.**

## The gifts . . . of God are irrevocable.
## (Romans 11:29)

Do not be deceived, my beloved brothers. Every good gift and every perfect gift is from above, coming down from the Father of lights with whom there is no variation or shadow due to change (James 1:16–17). That everyone should eat and drink and take pleasure in all his toil – this is God's gift to man (Ecclesiastes 3:13). Jesus answered her, "If you knew the gift of God, and who it is that is saying to you, 'Give me a drink,' you would have asked him, and he would have given you living water" (John 4:10). For by grace you have been saved through faith. And this is not your own doing; it is the gift of God (Ephesians 2:8). For the wages of sin is death, but the free gift of God is eternal life in Christ Jesus our Lord (Romans 6:23). Thanks be to God for his inexpressible gift! (2 Corinthians 9:15)

*This is the time of year when as a child I was expected to write 'thank you' letters for the gifts I had received at Christmas time. It was important to keep some sort of a list, so that the right person could be thanked for the right thing in the right way. It is a very healthy exercise to pause from time to time to think of everything we owe to God and to say 'thank you' to Him. The lists are pretty formidable. There are the physical gifts of life, health, food, shelter, nature and so on; social gifts which include family, friends, work and leisure; and the spiritual gifts of salvation and eternal life in Jesus Christ. But how do we say 'thank you' to God? As the famous prayer puts it, we do so 'not only with our lips, but in our lives; by giving up ourselves to His service, and by walking before Him in holiness and righteousness all our days'.*

**Lord, make my life a thank offering for all that You have done for me. Amen.**

### "Pay careful attention to yourselves." (Acts 20:28)

You are . . . God's building . . . Let each one take care how he builds upon it (1 Corinthians 3:9–10). Let anyone who thinks that he stands take heed lest he fall (1 Corinthians 10:12). Take care, brothers, lest there be in any of you an evil, unbelieving heart, leading you to fall away from the living God (Hebrews 3:12). And Jesus said, "See that you are not led astray. For many will come in my name, saying, 'I am he!' and, 'the time is at hand!' Do not go after them" (Luke 21:8). Keep a close watch on yourself and on the teaching. Persist in this, for by so doing you will save both yourself and your hearers (1 Timothy 4:16). "Take care lest your heart be deceived, and you turn aside and serve other gods and worship them" (Deuteronomy 11:16). How can a young man keep his way pure? By guarding it according to your word (Psalm 119:9).

*Every six months or so cars need to go to the garage to be serviced, and when they come back we know that they're fit for another 6,000 miles. The brakes have been tested, the steering checked, the oil changed and so on. If I do not 'take heed' to my car in this way, I will run into trouble. But do I take as much care about my Christian life? I ought to! Am I making the sort of progress I should? Am I in danger of slipping into unbelief or idolatry? Is my message as clear and sound as it was? December 30 is not a bad day for a little bit of spiritual stock-taking of this sort. Check yourself by the 'Handbook', by your own past experience ('that rattle used not to be there') and by the performance of others ('he gets much better petrol consumption than I seem to do'). Can you spare the time for that today?*

**Lord, I ask You today to point out the weaknesses in my life and to put right the faults. Amen.**

## "Till now the Lord has helped us."
## (1 Samuel 7:12)

"You shall remember the whole way that the Lord your God has led you . . . that he might humble you, testing you to know what was in your heart, whether you would keep his commandments or not" (Deuteronomy 8:2). "And you know in your hearts and souls, all of you, that not one word has failed of all the good things that the Lord your God promised concerning you. All have come to pass for you; not one of them has failed" (Joshua 23:14). "For the Lord your God has blessed you in all the work of your hands . . . the Lord your God has been with you. You have lacked nothing" (Deuteronomy 2:7). The Lord said ". . . there remains yet very much land to possess. This is the land that yet remains . . ." (Joshua 13:1–2). That I may know him and the power of his resurrection (Philippians 3:10). That we may . . . grow up in every way into him (Ephesians 4:14–15). That you may proclaim the excellencies of him who called you out of darkness into his marvellous light (1 Peter 2:9).

*Try to take a little time today, or tonight as you lie in bed, to pick out some of the many 'good things' which God has done for you during the past year. Has there been some difficulty or challenge for which He has given you the strength? Some unexpected joy or blessing? Some important lesson learnt? Some bad habit conquered or a good one formed? Some sorrow or disappointment for which He has more than compensated you with His peace and love? And, having done that, turn the binoculars of your mind on to the future and the coming year and 'view the landscape o'er'. Let us determine unitedly to possess the land ahead of us – to come to know Him a little better, to grow a little more like Him than we are at present, and to show forth His virtues a little more faithfully.*

**Thank You, Lord, for doing so much for me this year. Please strengthen my resolve to do all I can for You next year. Amen.**

ND - #0150 - 270225 - C0 - 216/138/26 - PB - 9781850788195 - Gloss Lamination